T0356717

TAKE
TO THE
TREES

ALSO BY MARGUERITE HOLLOWAY

The Measure of Manhattan

TAKE
TO THE
TREES

A STORY OF HOPE, SCIENCE,
AND SELF-DISCOVERY IN
AMERICA'S IMPERILED FORESTS

Marguerite Holloway

Drawings by Ellen Wiener

W. W. NORTON & COMPANY
Independent Publishers Since 1923

For information about permission to reproduce selections
from this book, write to Permissions, W. W. Norton &
Company, Inc., 500 Fifth Avenue, New York, NY 10110

For information about special discounts for bulk purchases, please contact
W. W. Norton Special Sales at specialsales@wwnorton.com or 800-233-4830

Manufacturing by Lake Book Manufacturing
Book design by Beth Steidle
Production manager: Lauren Abbate

ISBN: 978-1-324-03644-9

W. W. Norton & Company, Inc.
500 Fifth Avenue, New York, NY 10110
www.wwnorton.com

W. W. Norton & Company Ltd.
15 Carlisle Street, London W1D 3BS

1 0 9 8 7 6 5 4 3 2 1

For Eric and Weezee

And all the lives we ever lived
and all the lives to be are full
of trees and changing leaves.

Virginia Woolf
To the Lighthouse

Contents

TAKE
TO THE
TREES

Prologue

Three hemlocks stand close in the small grove. They have grown up together, about twenty feet apart, their branches touching in places, their life histories intertwined. They have been through the same storms, felt the same winds, the same heat, and the same winters. They have shared creatures. Squirrels, chipmunks, warblers, flycatchers, thrushes, spiders, and dozens of other animals have moved between them. Deer, skunk, turkey, porcupine, bobcat, fisher, hare, bear, and perhaps a moose or few have moved beneath them. Hemlocks are among the longest-lived trees on the East Coast and in the right conditions—in cool damp, absent certain pests—these conifers can live at least five hundred years and reach over one hundred feet.

These three are about seventy years old and eighty feet tall. Even young hemlocks have gravitas. They are stunning dark trees, their bark deeply creviced and thick. Some hemlocks have bottom branches that droop toward the ground at the tips, creating around the trunk a circular open-air room with a low roof. These three have no lower branches that are easy to grab hold of. Their green-needled limbs start fifteen feet up.

Fifteen feet can be fifteen feet too high when you are learning to climb trees, as I set out to do one May weekend at Camp Hi-Rock in Mount Washington, Massachusetts. The sign for the YMCA camp is tucked back from a main road and although I had spotted a fox loping through underbrush, I missed the turnoff. A hiker who had been looking for birds and butterflies on the nearby Alander Mountain Trail—"lots of warblers, including a black-throated green . . . not many fritillaries, but a lot of swallowtails at lower elevations"—gave directions and said that the road to the camp was long and I might think it was never going to end. Somewhere along that pitted dusty road, cell service fell away. The cluster of cabins that finally appeared felt remote and the woods a bit wild.

Two dozen women and I had come to participate in the Women's Tree Climbing Workshop, an organization founded by identical twin sister arborists Bear LeVangie and Melissa LeVangie Ingersoll. The workshop has trained over two thousand women, mostly those who care for trees professionally, but also lichenologists, ornithologists, primatologists, other ologists, circus performers, dancers, artists, photographers, writers, and the generally arboreally curious. That weekend, some of the women were office-based or ground-crew arborists who wanted to learn to climb. Some were arborists who wanted to improve their skills or get back in trees after a hiatus or injury. Some wanted to have an adventure and to escape pandemic isolation. Some wanted just to spend time in trees.

I was there to be in trees and to better understand them. Trees and forests are facing existential threats because of climate change, but it can be a struggle to grasp the extent of the danger or to make sense of the complex and deadly interactions playing out between heat, drought, fire, water, disease, and pests. I hoped that being in trees would allow me to better see them through the eyes of people, like the LeVangies, who care for trees and who perceive so much more about trees and forests than many of us do.

I also wanted to overcome, if possible, a terror of heights that had developed after I became a mother. If either of my kids or anyone I was with moved toward the edge of something, my shins felt squeamish and fuzzy, coursed by waves of electric buzzing. The fear traveled from my legs and sometimes from the back of my hands to my core, becoming a gut-lurching sense of being on a precipice that I am going to fall off and yet can't step back from. Dizzying and destabilizing, it is a feeling not unlike the one I have when thinking about climate change.

That spring weekend at Hi-Rock turned out to be the start of an ascent in ways I did not anticipate. As I came to understand more fully what climate change is doing to trees and forests, I began to climb regularly, returning to the workshop several times as a participant and traveling around the country to observe others. I met women of all ages—from those in their twenties to those in their seventies—and of all backgrounds. Over and over, I heard stories of sexism, many set in the predominantly male arboriculture industry. But the stories could be set most anywhere. They are experiences familiar to many women, to many people: stories of disregard, indifference, othering, dehumanization, hierarchy, and subjugation. They are the origin stories of the climate crisis: centuries of exploitation of people and the nonhuman natural world.

Over and over, I observed and spoke with people transformed by the Women's Tree Climbing Workshop. The LeVangies and the other instructors—many of them tree-climbing champions who excel in a dangerous, difficult profession and who are working to transform it—create community that is respectful and, frequently, hilarious. They express confidence in everyone's ability to do seemingly impossible new things. Participants learn technical skills while routinely discovering physical, mental, and emotional strength they didn't know they had, or that they had lost touch with. Climbing made them feel more confident, more powerful, more hopeful, and part of an ever-expanding community—"a mycelial network," the LeVangies say. Many have gone on to change their work culture or to change their jobs, their lives, their relationships. For many, climbing also rekindled a connection to the natural world. "It reconnected me with nature in a way that I haven't really felt since I was a kid," says Sian Bareket, who took the workshop when she was a college sophomore. "They really highlighted that you're not just climbing a tree, you are entering an ecosystem and you are being held up by a living organism."

Climbing in the way that the LeVangies and team teach it—engendering a culture of consideration, attention, and care—can change people in surprising ways. You think you are learning one set of things, but discover you are learning a whole different set. As I learned to climb, I did things I never thought I could do. I overcame physical weakness and phobias. I came to rely on other people and trust myself in new ways. I came to terms with tragedy and loss in my family. I found a new way to confront climate anxiety. And I came to know trees more deeply. I began to look closely, to see and to understand our profound connection to them.

Everything that flows from trees and forests—clean air, biodiversity, cooler temperatures, clean water, human health, carbon kept solid and out of atmospheric currency, rain, regional weather patterns, culture, history—is unraveling. If trees are to continue to sustain us and to help us address our apocalyptic mess, we need to pay them more attention, give them more care. We need to take to the trees.

PART I

Groundie

In the early afternoon on Saturday, the first full day of the Women's Tree Climbing Workshop, I stood at the base of one of the great hemlocks, my neck strained from looking up at the branches I wanted to reach.

Earlier, Melissa had talked about tree health. Do you see mushrooms around the base of the trunk that might indicate rot? Perhaps don't climb. Is the canopy looking thick or sparse? Are the ends of some branches bare, absent leaves or buds—what is called tip die-back? Perhaps don't climb. Are there wounds at the bottom of the tree? Is there a root girdling the base, cutting into the tree's circulatory system? Is the soil compacted? Perhaps don't climb. Is that discoloration an indication of decay? If you tap the tree with a mallet, does it sound hollow, does it sound solid? "When in doubt, stay out" is a workshop mantra. As is "know what you know and know what you don't know."

Melissa, Bear, and the four other instructors had also gone over the basics of climbing safety and of essential gear: harness, helmet, protective glasses, gloves—"so your hands don't become hamburger meat"—ropes, and carabiners. The participants had been asked to learn twelve knots before arriving, including several termination knots (an anchor, a buntline, and a double fisherman's), some friction hitches (a Knut, a Michoacán, and a Blake's), a slip knot, a figure eight, and four hitch knots. I had gone to a hardware store and bought what turned out to be too-flimsy, easily unraveled rope. Even with homemade flash cards, online videos, and an animation app, learning knots felt like learning a new language. My hands were awkward and in each other's way. They had no fluency. Top and bottom, front and back, over and under lost definition.

My hemlock was the largest of the trio, and there was no way to get my arms around it. I was wearing a harness that buckles around the hips and has wide leg-pads for the back of the upper thighs, so that when you hang from a rope it can feel like sitting in a small foldable chair. I observed several women new to climbing move like squirrels up nearby trunks, having quickly grasped the basic climbing technique we were learning: a moving rope system that doesn't require lots of fancy gear.

The instructors had already installed in all the climbing trees ropes that hung down on either side of a tie-in point selected because it looked strong and healthy. The green branches of the hemlock prevented me from seeing if my line ran through a union between branch and trunk or through a fork in the trunk. "Never shall I have a tie-in point far away from the trunk," Bear and Melissa often caution. Arborists are governed by "shoulds" and "shalls"; most of what we first learn at the workshop are the "shalls," the absolute musts. At the tie-in point, the rope passes through a length of tubing or leather, or two rings attached to a strap. This friction saver protects the tree, allowing the rope to move freely without rubbing the bark and destroying the cambium. Such damage can girdle a branch and kill it.

The cambium is where the tree grows. This living layer of tissue just below the bark is part of the tree's meristem system: stem cells that give rise to all parts of the tree. In the spring, buds formed late the previous summer sense the lengthening, warming days and start making hormones that radiate from the buds and travel around the tree, bringing that year's cambium to life.

In the trunk and branches, the cambium makes anew each year the circulatory system needed to carry life-sustaining compounds around the tree. The outer part becomes the phloem, interconnected cells that move sugars from canopy to root. The inner part becomes the xylem, or sapwood, cells that carry water and nutrients, such as stored sugars, from root to canopy; maple syrup is ascending sap siphoned from the xylem in early spring. The cambium is also how the tree heals. It creates woundwood that can, over time, close a cut or gash, a scab become a scar. I can see many small round scars on the lower trunk of the hemlocks, memories of lost branches.

On this May day, the cambium is still at its most busy. Most of us learned—usually when we were young—about the fundamental, foundational reciprocity of plants and animals. Plants take in what we exhale; we inhale what they breathe out. The great photosynthetic intake of carbon dioxide that marks the Northern Hemisphere summer and that can be detected by satellites as deciduous forests leaf out is getting underway in the Hi-Rock trees as we climb them.

Even in conifers like hemlock, the majority of which keep their tiny, pointed leaves year-round, springtime in the cambium is exuberant. But the thin, precious skin, just a few cells thick, is invisible to the naked eye: we cannot see the pulse of a hemlock as we can see the rhythmic rise and fall of an artery beneath skin. And so I imagine the ebb and flow happening beneath the bark beneath my fingers, quiet, secret, vast.

That morning I had practiced with Bear and two other participants in a young red oak. The tree's diameter was such that I could get my arms around it; its thin branches complex and invit-ing, its spring-red leaves unfurling from their buds. Bear had talked us through tying the harness with an anchor knot to one side of the rope and with a hitch knot to the other, making the climber part of a rope circle. Then she showed us how to do a hip thrust. The climber puts her feet on the

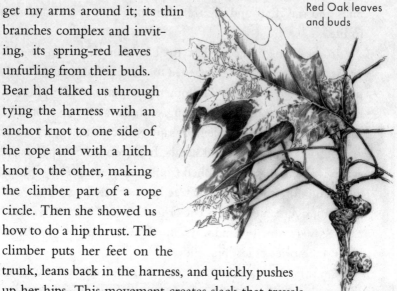

Red Oak leaves and buds

trunk, leans back in the harness, and quickly pushes up her hips. This movement creates slack that travels up one side of the rope and down the other, softening the hitch knot's hold so the climber can push it up a few inches. The circle of rope gets smaller as the climber ascends.

This can be a lot to remember when you are new to it all. The climber needs to know how to tie the right anchor knot, the right hitch knot, and a figure-eight knot that serves as a safety catch, as well as knowing how long the rope should be between the anchor knot and hitch knot. Getting that length right is an art. But all that was not even as challenging for me as pushing up my hips while leaning back in the harness, trying to keep my hiking boots planted on the little red oak's trunk while I spun awkwardly, like a drunken spider. Unlike the women I was practicing with, I could not find the right rhythm or angle. I could not move with any grace; my short climb in the red oak had been staccato, messy, uncomfortable. Now the same thing was happening to me on this much more substantial hemlock.

On another hemlock, June Moulis was struggling too. Moulis is an arborist and horticulturalist based in Connecticut, and she was recovering from an autoimmune disorder that Lyme disease had exacerbated. "It was kind of like an episode of *House* where no one could give me a solid diagnosis and I was kind of in and out with doctors," she says. "For seven years, I was just too sick to do much of anything." During those years, she had given up studying horticulture at the University of Connecticut and the scholarship she had won; she had given up a beloved internship at an arboretum; she had given up working; she gave up generally for a while, she says, "and I had to learn to forgive myself for that." Moulis spent the years caring for her grandmother, who had developed dementia, fostering cats, and reading through the library she had inherited from her high school plant science teacher: "staying up all night reading books, normally about plants, but also a lot of literature."

When Moulis became pregnant with her first daughter, the pregnancy pushed her illness into remission. She got a job in a bookstore. She had her second daughter. She took a job at an appliance store. "I was pretty miserable working retail." Moulis remembers watching arborists working on trees in the Home Depot parking lot next door. "I could smell the fertilizer, which, to me, is just like the sign of spring. It's like happy memories." Soon she found herself complaining to her boss about what a terrible job the arborists were doing pruning. "I was just laying into him," she says. "And he looked at me and he was like, 'What are you doing here?'" Within six months she had completed an arboriculture course and the state certification test—"I kind of did everything backward: got my arborist's license before I actually practiced as an arborist!"—and joined a tree-care company.

Moulis was at the workshop that May because she wanted to be in the trees she loves, not only in the office or on ground crew. "I want to keep working toward being able to help the trees," she says. "They're my friends." She had tried to climb with another arborist a few weeks earlier. "I almost passed out, the exertion was just so much, and I realized, hey, I've made a lot of strides with my health, but maybe this is too much." Daunted and on the cusp of withdrawing from the workshop, Moulis rallied. She wanted to show her two young daughters "that when you have something that is like an all-consuming passion, which plants and trees have been to me for such a long time, you've got to find a way."

Over what seemed like several hours, Moulis and I struggled up our respective hemlocks. I tried to lug myself up using muscle instead of strategy or helpful physics. With each haul, I felt more fear; I was sure the knots I had tied would fail. When I was not slamming into the hemlock's rough bark, I was hugging it. I was scared to move away from the trunk and rely on the rope, scared to move farther away from the earth, scared to be up in the tree I so wanted to be in.

My groundie—everyone has a workshop buddy watching from below—reminded me to tie a slip knot on the falling side of the rope under me. If tied in the right orientation, the slip knot would catch me if the hitch knot were to fail or I were to squeeze it in panic: squeezing the hitch is how a climber descends, hopefully only when they intend to. Successfully making the slip knot gave me a moment of confidence. Now I wouldn't fall on the hemlock's great roots and the gray mica-flecked rocks and boulders they wove between. I was two feet off the ground.

Most of us are groundies. We see a tree's flares, the widening bark-covered buttress-like structures that are the uppermost part of the roots. We see the lower trunk, or bole, and touch the patterns of bark. We see leaves and branches from below or from afar. But there is so much we often don't see. The life of the canopy, for instance, or the life of the roots. We don't see the entire world living in trees, the insects, the lichens, the amphibians, reptiles, birds, small mammals, the other plants; trees can be entire ecosystems unto themselves. We don't see the beneficial pharmacopeia trees provide. Mostly we don't even see the forest or the trees, a well-known phenomenon called plant blindness. Despite the fact that people are utterly dependent on plants and trees—we wouldn't be here if they weren't—plants and trees are taken for granted.

A great dying is underway in forests the world over. There are, by one recent reckoning, 3 trillion trees, half as many as there were at the end of the last ice age. Some 15 billion are lost every year. More than 17,500 of the estimated 58,000 tree species are threatened and heading toward extinction. In North America, between 97 and 141 of the 881 native trees are threatened and at risk of disappearing; 6 may already be extinct. These species are not all rare or obscure—some pines and ashes are among them. Most of the global loss is driven by deforestation for agriculture, logging, and development. But pests, diseases, and climate change are increasingly having profound and cumulative effects. The scale of death and disease is unimaginable in extent and speed.

Some trees are heat-stressed, drought-stressed, burnt by fires too hot and too frequent for them to survive or come back after. In Yellowstone National Park, lodgepole pine, a species that evolved with regular low-intensity wildfires, began regrowing after the massive fire of 1988. But new fires have swept through before many trees could regrow. Resilience and regeneration in a large part of the park appears jeopardized. Lack of regeneration has been observed in forests everywhere, even in those not repeatedly incinerated. This is concerning for many reasons, including the fact that it can take trees decades before they can reproduce, and because invasive plants often flourish in their stead.

Trees are declining and dying as seasons change and as the vicissitudes of weather prove too erratic and rapid for many of these highly adaptive organisms to adapt to. Trees are being downed by winds stronger than they were raised in and at times coming from directions they didn't build themselves to withstand. Roots are rotting in too much rain that comes too fast. This abundance of water is often followed by drought and deadly heat. Trees are being stripped of protective bark because there is less snow to deter herbivores. Trees flowering in the ever-earlier spring lose their flowers and leaves in snap frosts.

Because trees are stressed and struggling, many are weakened. Climate change is impairing their ability to fend off or survive infestations of insects or pathogens that they were more readily able to combat in the past. Bark beetles that typically didn't venture into cooler areas, or that were culled during long subfreezing winters, have killed pines across millions of acres. High-elevation bristlecone pine, which can live over four thousand years, were thought to be beyond the beetles' reach, but no more. "The bristlecone are giving up the ghost because of climate change and beetles. That just blew me out of the water," says Diana Six, an ecologist at the University of Montana. Bristlecone "have been through utter hell, through everything the planet has thrown at them. Except for what humanity has thrown at them. Nothing can withstand humanity, including humanity."

The bark beetles, and many other insects and diseases supercharged by climate change, are familiar species. They have been engaged with their host trees for millennia, up in some eras, down in others. Trees also face an expanding number of pests and pathogens they did not co-evolve with and many are simultaneously combatting surges of foes they know and foes they don't. Some newly arrived organisms have the capacity to eliminate entire species. Emerald ash borer. Sudden oak death. Rapid 'ohi'a death. Butternut canker. Laurel wilt disease. Beech leaf disease. Forests are increasingly unrecognizable to those who know them well. "I've gone back to places in the Adirondacks . . . in western and southeastern Pennsylvania that I was in twenty or thirty years ago and those forests are different," says Neil Pederson, a forest ecologist at Harvard University. "In my lifetime now I'm going to see beech gone, hemlock gone, ash gone. Like we all heard the stories of chestnut."

The magnitude and pace of what is happening can be hard to take in, even by those studying it. Even for those who do not suffer from plant blindness. "I'm used to the bad news," says Valerie Trouet, a dendrochronologist at the University of Arizona. In the early 2020s, she gave a talk in Yosemite, a place she hadn't visited for a while. "I was really in shock. I was crying to see how little there is left in just the past fifteen years of those majestic trees . . . and this in one national park. You hear about it. You know it. But then to see it is a different thing."

It is late afternoon on Saturday. The trees at Hi-Rock are alive with voices and laughter. Climbers are in maples and hemlocks; some have reached two high hammocks, others are sitting together on the trillium, a triangular flat green platform of tent-like fabric suspended thirty feet up between the three hemlocks. My shoulders and arms burn and ache. I feel crazy self-consciously inept and like a failure despite all the positive exhortations—"you've got this!" (no, I truly do not!)—and expressions of support. I give up on the hip thrust, which is, according to the *Tree Climbers' Guide*, "an effective but tiring way to ascend." Alex Julius, coauthor of this arborists' sacred text, is teaching climbers in a nearby tree. It is time to try the lanyard.

Melissa shows me how to unhook a rope that has been daisy-chained to the side of my harness. There are so many things hanging from my harness. I have no idea what they are for, but the weight of them and their wonderful metallic click and clink make me feel—when I am on the ground—extremely professional. Now I am supposed to clip this lanyard rope to a D-ring on one side of my harness, swing the carabiner at the other end of the lanyard around the trunk of the hemlock, without hitting myself or nearby climbers in the face or tooth or eye, and attach it to a second D-ring.

With a lot of encouragement and many tries, I manage this. The workshop, I am already coming to understand, is generally not about other people doing things for you as a shortcut. "It's not about sharing your knowledge when you want to share it," Bear says of the instructors' approach. "Don't assume when you see someone struggling that they want your help because they might not."

Now I am dangling in my harness, hugging the hemlock with my lanyard. Lanyards are sometimes called an arborist's third hand. They allow arborists to tie themselves in when they need to move to a different climbing rope or get around an obstacle. This one was going to help me do the lanyard crawl. "Although the technique is slow, it is an effective approach for a climber with limited upper body strength," says the *Tree Climbers' Guide*.

The technique leverages two rope systems. The climber flips the lanyard up the far side of the trunk and leans back to make it go taut. Then she places her feet on the trunk and walks up until she is horizontal. Because the lanyard holds her weight, there is no tension on the climbing rope, making it easy to push up the hitch knot and to anchor herself slightly higher than before. When she squats back in, the lanyard relaxes and can be flipped up again. Back and forth, using one rope and then the other, she ascends without the hip thrust.

On another hemlock, I can see Moulis doing the lanyard crawl too. Moulis first heard about the workshop at a conference. "This guy comes up to me and he's like, 'You're an arborist. Do you know about the women climbers? You need to know about this group,'" Moulis says. "And me, I'm an overweight woman. I'm the only woman in the room. Most people look at me and think I can't climb." Moulis has seen this guy again twice at other meetings, but he always slips away before she can get his name, ask him how he knew she dreamed of climbing, and thank him for changing her life.

We both lean out and away from the trunk, lying back into the air, looking up into the dark canopy. I walk a few steps up the trunk, push up the hitch, lean back in, slap into the trunk, flail around as I try to flip the lanyard up, lean out, walk up a few more steps, push up the knot, smash awkwardly back into the trunk. I apologize to the hemlock. There are fleeting moments of rhythm, of accomplishment. Then my lanyard gets stuck on a sign: a rough carved board pointing the way to "waterskiing." I pant and sweat with effort to unhook the rope. I cannot move it. I feel scared and like an awkward failure. I am seven feet up.

A breeze comes off the lake, the ninety-acre Plantain Pond next to which the camp was built in the 1940s. A great blue heron chuffs in the shallows down the slope from the hemlock. It is cool in the little grove. The hemlock's bark is black and dark yellow and red-brown with whorls and rivulets of blue-gray lichen and pale-yellow lichen and vivid almost iridescent green lichen. The bark seems to flow down the trunk, a world of deep rivers and long narrow islands. Or a world of mountain ranges, canyons in shadow between them. An enormous black ant is traveling the rivers and ravines of the hemlock's bark. Everything feels still and quiet. There is just the hemlock and its beautiful rough bark and the ant, ascending.

Forests are always shifting; they change form and location, they are in constant motion. The hemlock I am climbing is a descendant of trees that made their way here after glaciers started to recede some twenty thousand years ago. Eastern hemlock, *Tsuga canadensis,* likely traveled up from various sites in what is now Georgia or North Carolina and started settling in New England about ten thousand years ago. Pollen from lake sediments show that white pine had by then replaced the spruce and jack pine that had become abundant in the area soon after the ice left. Hemlock arrived as the climate kept warming and rainfall increased as ice melted, refilling ocean basins. Beech, birch, and oak arrived too. By roughly eight thousand years ago, the forests of the region had many of the tree species common today.

Hemlock, slow-growing and shade-loving, gave rise to forests that were dark and cool, that held onto the moisture key to their survival. The hemlock grew in clusters among other trees and in vast uninterrupted stands. Hemlock forests lined creeks, streams, and rivers, keeping temperatures low and holding soil in place with their roots. In their shade, salamanders, frogs, and brook trout flourished. In their branches, ants, arboreal spiders, and dozens of birds found homes.

The hemlocks' journey north is one of many arboreal migration stories that have helped scientists understand the climate and ecology of the postglacial period we live in. Hemlock have also helped unlock a fine-grained weather and climate record that tells us what trees have been through in the last several thousand years, what they have adapted to and survived, and how perilous and divergent their current experience is proving to be.

In the early 1970s, Edward Cook, now a researcher at Columbia University's Lamont-Doherty Earth Observatory, enlisted in the Army and was stationed at West Point, New York. He spent his free time driving around looking for rock-climbing sites and old trees. He had finished college at the University of Arizona, where he had been captivated by dendrochronology—the science of reconstructing past climate by examining tree rings—and now everywhere he went, he looked closely at trees. In the Shawangunks, which form a northern ridge of the Appalachian Mountains, he saw some ancient-looking gnarled pitch pines. From a dendrochronologist's perspective, the older the tree, the better.

When the cambium comes to life each spring, it needs to get photosynthesis going fast. To do that, the leaves need a lot of water, which is elemental to breaking down carbon dioxide to make sugars. To get water quickly from roots to canopy, the cambium initially creates big xylem cells that stack vertically, forming long pipes running up the tree. These gallon-bucket cells form the early wood. As the growing season wanes, the tree starts to pack things up after the picnic and produces compact, thick-walled xylem cells that make up the late wood. The next spring, the process begins again, and the cambium comes to life between last year's late wood and the bark. The old dead or dying wood becomes the internal foundation on which the new live wood lies.

Cook wasn't sure how many rings—each one marking a year of early wood and late wood—he would see in the pitch pines. He used an increment borer to take his first samples. These devices only pierce a tiny bit of cambium, allowing dendrochronologists to see a tree's growth without causing it significant harm. They are elegant tools: two metal tubes, one nested inside the other. The tubes are assembled into a T, with the outer tube serving as a perpendicular handle. The extremely sharp end of the smaller tube is cranked until it reaches the heartwood or pith, the innermost and oldest part of the tree. Once the dendrochronologist has reached the heartwood, they often make a half reverse twist, which breaks adhesion between the metal tube and surrounding wood. Then they carefully pull out a tray that runs inside the boring tube, on which lies a delicate dowel-like core.

In a lab, the core is sanded and burnished to bring out the details of the bands of dark and light that to the expert eye can tell of rain or drought or fire or fallout. Although the annual cycle of early wood, late wood, and dormancy is generally similar in temperate trees, every species has its own fingerprint: a maple and a spruce growing a few feet apart may tell the same story in different colors and textures. Pitch pines, like other conifers, have regular xylem cells, called tracheids. As Valerie Trouet writes in *Tree Story: A History of the World Written in Rings*, "In conifers, individual wood cells queue up in straight lines like Roman soldiers."

From the tidy light–dark bands of the Shawangunk pitch pines, Cook could see that they were what is called sensitive. That is, their rings varied in thickness, reflecting changing environmental conditions. Trees that are not as responsive and have consistently sized rings are termed complacent. He also learned that one of the trees was four hundred years old, two hundred years older than his textbook said pitch pines could be. That was the first surprise. On the Mohonk Preserve, also in the Shawangunk Mountains, Cook found another. There, on a rocky slope with virtually no soil, Cook caught sight of some hemlocks.

Modern dendrochronology had emerged in the early twentieth century in the Southwest, in part because the desert simplified the yearly story trees told about the weather. There was plenty of sun. Plenty of warmth. But there was not plenty of rain. The trees of the region put on a lot of growth when the year was wet: they made bigger cells in those years. Wet and dry years were visible in the thick versus thin rings of ponderosa pine and giant sequoia that came to anchor the young field. The pine told of rainfall in northern Arizona going back five hundred years, the sequoia of rainfall in the Sierra Nevada going back three thousand years.

With a few exceptions, the field in the United States had remained largely fixed in semiarid landscapes. "There was this belief that dendrochronology couldn't reliably be done in the Northeast," Cook says. The concern was that the region had too many variables—rain, snow, seasonal extremes of temperature. It was too complex a place to provide a clear picture about any one aspect of climate. But when Cook saw the hemlocks growing on sere exposed rock, he realized that they might tell a story about rain. He learned that the Smiley family who owned Mohonk Preserve had been recording rainfall and temperature since 1896. Depending on the age of the hemlock, he might be able to fact-check the annual rings against the Smileys' data.

The hemlock turned out to be more than three hundred years old and for the period they overlapped with the family's weather records, they matched. Eastern hemlock showed that decipherable information about rainfall, or not much rainfall, could be found outside semiarid landscapes. They were one of the few regional tree species able to do this. "I knew that hemlock was potentially the single most important species because it was likely to be the most common old-growth community in existence, left in existence, in the forests in the Northeast," Cook says. Some hemlock had survived waves of colonial deforestation because the tree's soft, light, easily decomposed wood made poor lumber or firewood.

In the 1800s, though, hemlock's thick bark was almost its undoing. In most trees, a corky outer layer of phloem becomes bark. In a beech or other smooth-boled tree, this cork cambium puts on little girth each year and the bark that it replaces flecks away. In rough-barked trees, the corky layer grows wildly and the trees package the growth in creases and convolutions. That is why hemlock bark is a mesmerizing world of tectonic folds, of rivulets and ravines that visitors—an ant, a climber—can travel. In the case of hemlock, that profuse growth contains a high concentration of tannins, chemicals produced to stave off herbivores, but that can also render animal skins more water resistant. In the nineteenth century, the American tanning industry expanded and tanneries arose throughout the hemlock's range. In the Catskill Mountains and on the ridges of the Shawangunks alone, an estimated seventy million hemlock were cut, their bark ripped off, their bare trunks left to decay.

Even so, pockets of inaccessible old growth persisted. Cook kept seeking out those stands and, in time, found hemlocks older than those at Mohonk. He read an article describing five-hundred-year-old trees in the Tionesta area of Pennsylvania, so he set out with a friend to find them. The two found plenty of middle-aged hemlocks. They found a forest littered with pipelines from an era of oil exploration. They got lost. Then they happened into a hemlock grove that felt old. Old trees should not be stereotyped: they are not all massively tall, thick, moss draped. They can be small, their age revealed in bent posture and scars, in roots that run close to the surface, like the veins that rise on the backs of our hands as our skin thins with time.

They took cores from several Tionesta hemlocks, one of which, it turned out, had started growing in 1426. The records kept by the Tionesta hemlock joined those kept by the Mohonk hemlock—and Mohonk pitch pine, white pine, and chestnut oak. Those records were, in turn, joined by those of hemlock from Nova Scotia down to the Carolinas and as far west as Michigan. Hemlock became the backbone, as Cook describes it, of the North American Drought Atlas. The atlas, first published in 2004 and expanded and deepened since, is a database of tens of thousands of tree-ring records that reveal patterns of drought in hundreds of locations and as far back, in some regions, as two millennia. Cook's invention became a reference work for understanding historical drought and it allowed novel interdisciplinary work. Fire ecologists, anthropologists, historians, archaeologists, and modelers, among many others, have used the drought atlas to understand environmental history and cultural shifts as well as to fact-check climate models. Similar atlases have since been made for Europe, for South America, for Australia, for Mexico, for Asia.

Tree ring records cover a human-history timescale. The oldest living tree ring record is from a 4,800-year-old bristlecone pine called Methuselah—a sapling during the world of Gilgamesh, of the Minoans and the Mayans, of the last mammoths. (The oldest fossil tree ring record goes back nearly 14,000 years.) Because trees are sessile for their lifetime, the information they hold is specific to a site. That specificity helps researchers know what has been true for a particular place and, when records can be combined across nearby areas, a particular region. Tree rings show that the Northeast, generally now a rain-rich place, underwent severe droughts in the 1500s and 1600s. In places where water is not in short supply but temperature changes, as in a wetland, tree rings can tell the story of temperature. They can also reveal global temperature patterns: tree rings document the "year without a summer" triggered by the explosion of Mount Tambora in Indonesia in 1815, which spewed ash and ejected sulfur particles into the stratosphere, where they reflected the sun's warmth back to space until some washed down as acid rain.

Increasingly, tree rings are adding detail about how we are changing the climate, making clear that we are in a new era. Valerie Trouet and her colleagues can see in European tree rings that the North Atlantic jet stream—the westerly wind that determines so much about formerly familiar weather patterns, season length, and temperature across the Northern Hemisphere—has become more erratic since the 1960s. Tree rings are helping scientists document precipitously declining snowpack in the Rockies and other mountain ranges. Tree rings are ground-truthing satellite observations of changes in forest extent and productivity. Tree rings reveal that the new character of wildfires—their intensity, their frequency—has no precedent in the last two thousand years. And drought, the tree rings show, is going rogue with its coconspirator heat.

Dendrochronological drought atlases emerged in the Northeast, extended across the country and then across the world, in some small part because several wind-pummeled strong-rooted hemlocks on a talus in the Shawangunk Mountains shared their memories of the rain that came, or did not, for every one of their more than three hundred years. And because amateur naturalists kept records down through generations and shared them with a young scientist who happened to show up one day. Mohonk Preserve and its trees remain deeply special to Cook. "Hemlock always has a very soft spot in my heart because it turned out to be such a pivotal species," he says.

As far as I know, the three Hi-Rock hemlocks have never been cored. I don't know their exact age. The hemlocks must feel the seasons changing length, the winters becoming less cold, the summers longer and drier and hotter. They may feel a pull to migrate as their ancestors did and as some of their contemporaries have: in the last three decades, hemlock seeds carried by wind have been able to germinate and survive farther north; hemlocks have shifted range by about eight miles over that time. It is entrancing to be in a huge hemlock and to feel its solidity and rootedness and to think about it as a traveler.

Mohonk Preserve is a deeply special place to me too, for different reasons than it is for Cook. My parents split in the mid-seventies, and my younger brother Eric and I lived with our mother, Louise. At some point, she decided to create a few new traditions to celebrate our little trio. We lived in New York City, but because my mother loved being outdoors, she made one of those traditions visiting Mohonk Preserve and staying at the famous Mountain House run by the Smileys. Our own giving-thanks holiday. Our chronology overlaps with that of Cook, who cored hemlocks and other Mohonk trees in the same era that we were walking paths circling the glacial lake, hiking the carriage trails that lace the woods, climbing up and down the rocks of the Shawangunks, feeling agile and safe in the comfort of so many footholds and handholds; we had no fear of heights.

There is one Mohonk photo, taken by my mother, that I have kept on my desk for the last several years. In it I can see a scrappy oak sprouting from a rock crevice, beginning to change color for the fall. I am wearing an olive-green sweatshirt and have my left arm on Eric's right shoulder, and he has his left arm on a shelf of gray-white rock. He is smiling and handsome in a bright red flannel shirt. He looks as I thought he would always be: impish, strong, solid. My brilliant, charismatic, warm, lovely brother. Over my right shoulder I can make out some conifers in the background. I am sure they must be hemlocks.

On Saturday evening, after the first full day of climbing, the workshop participants and instructors gather in a circle around a fire next to Plantain Pond and, as the night sets in, share something about what they have experienced so far. This is a ritual at every workshop, I come to learn. Kristina Bezanson, a lecturer in arboriculture and urban forestry at the University of Massachusetts Amherst, notes that this gathering is the first time many of us have been in a group since the pandemic began a year-and-a-half earlier and that this is a "re-en-tree." Her phrase catches on and becomes this workshop's motto, printed on the purple (color chosen by majority vote) sweatshirts that arrive in the mail once we are home. Intimacy emerges in the falling dark, in the moving shadows, the soft bursts of sparks. I am not sure what I will say, but discover that what comes out is seeing the ant in the hemlock and the joy of getting lost in its world for a while.

The following morning, I forget the ant. I have no joy. I am miserable and sore. Looking at the ropes and the lanyard, having forgotten all the knots, fills me with a sense of defeat and dread. I decide this tree-climbing endeavor is absolutely not for me. I think about how it is the last day of the workshop and I can go home soon. Perhaps I might even leave early. Then Melissa gives me a foot ascender.

The device comes in several varieties, and today I have an orange right-foot one. Its straps slip around my boot, meeting at a toothed mechanism called a cam. It is tiny but mighty. Melissa shows me how to release the cam's locking mechanism—not intuitive!—and thread the rope through it. She helps me set up a different climbing system, with a pulley, a friction cord, Knut knot, and various carabiners. This is a variation of the moving-rope system, but with more sophisticated gear. When I pull my right foot up along the falling side of line, the rope flows through the cam. When I step down, the cam's teeth grab the line and hold it tight. Suddenly, I am rope walking. I am standing up, using the strength of my quad muscles, so much stronger than my arms. I begin to move up the smallest hemlock in the trio.

Melissa had generously moved me to an ascender, but the other participants are not using them yet. Gear can fail and is expensive, so knowing how to be minimalist is important for climbers. The workshop starts with the most basic system and equipment so arborists can be self-reliant if they need to be. All you need is "a rope, your harness, your personal protective equipment," Melissa says, "and then you can climb trees." A foot ascender can be improvised by doing a foot lock: pulling your legs up under you, wrapping the rope around one boot, placing the other boot on top of the rope, and stepping. Many participants were successfully doing the foot lock, but as it requires great upper body strength and agility, it was clear—to me and very much to my instructors, although they did not say so— that I best not do a thing requiring great upper body strength and agility.

Every few steps, I freeze. My mind shrieks: Why are you doing this! Melissa had shown me how to set up the pulley system used with the ascender, but I hadn't grasped the how-it-works details. I try to look only at the hemlock's trunk, but sometimes glance down and feel a whirl of emptiness in my stomach and that electric weirdness in my shins.

When I don't look at the ground, there are moments in which I forget I am afraid. Soon I develop a slow steady step-pause-step-make-a-slip-knot rhythm. I reach first branch, fifteen feet or so up, at the point where this hemlock stretches toward the other two across the small grove. Fortunately, I had absorbed what Melissa said about the importance of removing the rope from the ascender before free climbing or descending. If you don't, it is possible to end up in painful tangle with leg akimbo, your boot near your face. I release the rope from the ascender and sit on the branch, snuggling close to the trunk.

Moulis is working on her lanyard crawl, making steady progress. She is feeling excited. "The fact that I got like more than ten feet off the ground was an achievement," she says. "They found a way. They found a way for me to be able to climb." Other participants are hanging out on the trillium, swinging in hammocks, and plucking neon pink ribbons off the ends of branches or tie-in points. The instructors and Bear and Melissa put the ribbons in during setup, a few days before the workshop started. Some climbers tie the ribbons to their harnesses; some are seriously festooned.

I am simply amazed to be sitting on a branch. It is a precarious, tentative amazement. My sense of stability is laced with a terror of the harness or knots giving way. In this superposition of security and fear, I catch a glimpse of bright pink at the end of my branch, my new home, the place I might never leave. It is far out, where the branch radiates into twigs.

In the hemlock closest to mine, the smallest one—smallest likely because it is closest to the compacted soil of the road, not a comfortable place to stretch out one's roots—Bezanson is climbing with Alex Julius, aforementioned coauthor of the *Tree Climbers' Guide*. Alex works with Davey Tree, one of the nation's largest tree care and research companies. She has been with the Women's Tree Climbing Workshop since it began, the first year as a participant and the second year as an instructor. She started as a rock climber in college, then became a work-study campus arborist while getting her degree in architecture. "When I learned that I could get paid to climb trees, I was like, wait a minute!" she says. "I think unless you've grown up with a family business or somehow had a tie to a tree company, there's not very much knowledge of it as a career path. So I find that a lot of my peers come into it quite by accident." Alex met Melissa and Bear at a tree climbing competition. "I am just very competitive. So the second I knew that there was an opportunity to compete, I was in it," she says. "I have resigned myself to lose pretty much all of the time . . . I generally don't like to enter into a competition that I don't think I can win, but tree climbing is the exception. My first event was against Bear and Melissa. Like, I am not going to win that!"

Melissa and Bear started the Women's Tree Climbing Workshop in 2009, the same year they began climbing as part of an effort to eradicate the Asian longhorned beetle. The beetle is thought to have arrived on wooden packing material, one of the main ways wood-boring insects travel internationally, and was first spotted in Brooklyn, New York, in the mid-1990s. Once here, the beetles began to travel nationally, reaching Worcester, Massachusetts, about a decade into a federal program to contain them. The beetles are generalists. They feed on dozens of tree species, but they particularly like maples, and the Department of Agriculture was worried about the maple industries: syrup, timber, and tourism. "I thought it was going to be the Dutch elm disease of my generation, that's how I really viewed it at the time," Melissa recalls. (Dutch elm disease—caused by a fungus original to Asia, but named for the nationality of the scientists who identified it—arrived in Europe in the 1910s and in the United States in the 1930s, killing more than seventy-seven million elm thus far.) So Melissa sought a job with the department's Animal and Plant Health Inspection Service, and Bear did too.

For six years, the sisters climbed between two and forty trees for eight to ten hours a day, six days a week, in and around Worcester, looking for thumbtack-size holes. There were many mysteries then about the beetle's life cycle and behaviors. Over time, the sisters say they began to think like the beetle. They could tell which trees it would go for, where to find it on that tree, and at what time of year. It generally deposited its eggs in depressions it had chewed out on the underside of branches, in places protected from birds. It liked to bore under the cover of vines. "Poison ivy," says Melissa. An annoyance followed in abundance by mosquitoes. "And ticks. Poison ivy and poison oak and poison ivy and ticks. Ticks. And poison ivy." The sisters tested a series of poison-ivy products. Bear did a multiyear anecdotal study on tick preferences: men versus women, upper body versus lower body, light clothes versus dark clothes, citronella versus DEET, on the ground versus in the trees. Finding: bloodsucking tick don't care.

Climbing so many types of trees and trees in so many settings and of various ages, as well as having to climb out along and under limbs, far from the trunk, transformed Melissa and Bear's arborist skills. They learned to triangulate, and they made geometry into games. "We would pick the hardest trees to climb, healthy trees, but the hardest," Melissa says, and set challenges: "Bet you can't get out there!" To get into trees in and near swamps without getting their ropes and gear wet, they would often traverse tree to tree, dozens a day, without touching the ground. They came to appreciate, and rely on, the physics of connection between roots and canopy. In wetlands when they would take a big swing, they could see how the roots felt the sway of branches and trunk but never gave way: the ground and everything on it—ferns, hummocks, grasses—would rise and fall, as if the ground were breathing. "The movement of you up there, you can see it transmitted all through the roots," Bear says.

They climbed elm. They climbed birch. They climbed cottonwoods. They climbed katsura. They climbed willows. "Willows! I could care less if I ever climb another willow in my life. They are unpredictable. They are fragile. They are very weak-wooded trees," Melissa says. They climbed many, many maples. Norway maples are "like jungle gyms when they are young. But they decay very quickly." Silver maples are vocal: "They are always chattering . . . but brittle brittle brittle brittle!" Melissa especially loved climbing sugar maples. "There are so many birds and insects and amphibians in there. You'll hear a little tree frog and oriole and a little pack of goldfinch will come in. And then a phoebe and a titmouse. Sugar maple are very playful."

Melissa had learned basic techniques in an outdoor climbing lab in the late nineties while getting her degree in arboriculture at the University of Massachusetts Amherst—where the male instructors, perhaps oblivious, talked about humping trees and sexualized that basic climbing move, the hip thrust. She remembers an early climb in which her waist-length hair got caught in a hitch knot. "I am stuck and I am in pain . . . it's a total shit show. We would never let that happen in a workshop situation, because we follow people around with hairbands. 'Put your hair in a bun! Put up your hair! This is not ok!' I mean, it is a safety thing."

Both sisters, "madly in love with trees," had initially studied forestry but disliked the view of trees as crops that came with the industry jobs they had found. Bear worked as a timber cruiser in Montana for a while. "I had a really hard time measuring trees for a company just to take them down," she says. "The whole thing would be clearcut, stripped off, and the soil would erode away . . . the forest comes back, yes, but it's different—and often times invasive plants come in." Melissa had started a forestry degree at UMass when a friend mentioned arboriculture. "I felt hit by a lead balloon," Melissa recalls. "I wish I had found this earlier. This is awesome!" Both sisters love the interaction between trees and people that arboriculture offers. "Our primary focus is the trees that people interface with every day," Melissa says. They also loved the athleticism—both had gone to college on athletic scholarships, Bear for track and field with a specialization in javelin, Melissa for softball.

Although she was an excellent climber, Melissa had been unable to get an arborist job after she graduated, for reasons known only to the potential employers but that suggest sexism. (Many years later, she saw one of the arborists who hadn't hired her. "He said, 'I really regret not hiring you,'" says Melissa. "I said, 'Good, you should because I would have made you a lot of money. And you did me wrong.' And he said, 'I did. And I apologize.'") She started her own tree-care business and, in 2004, asked Bear to be her occasional groundie. A groundie in the field is more than a buddy; they're a critical part of an arborist crew, someone who assesses dangers, drags brush and branches, rigs lines to lower cut limbs, sends up and retrieves equipment like chainsaws, and basically does everything to support and ensure the safety of the climbers. "She's like, 'Yeah, teach me what I need to do.' And you know we can communicate without talking, so working with her is always fun," Melissa says. "I asked her to run some ropes for me . . . and I could see it in her eyes: I Need To Do That."

In addition to learning at the lab and on the job, Melissa had been climbing competitively. The International Society of Arboriculture had started in the 1970s what were called jamborees. Over time, those events, designed to educate the public about what arborists do—"we are industrial athletes," as Bear says— became more formalized. There were few women competitors, however. Wenda Li, the first woman municipal tree climber for Toronto, Ontario, remembers often being the only woman and given fewer challenges. Women were first allowed to compete in all five events in Seattle in 2002: aerial rescue, belayed speed climb (climbing the tree, but tied in for safety), ascent event (climbing the rope not the tree), throwline (target practice with a throwbag), and work climb (visit a series of challenges throughout the tree). Wenda and Melissa remember that competition vividly. Throwline in giant tulip poplars. A climb in a redwood so tall that "they had an air horn at the top because you couldn't hear a bell," says Wenda, who was the women's international champion that year.

More women began to climb at the events, including Bear. At one competition, Melissa almost lost Bear. The full-body harness for the ascent event was too big for Bear; the back part pushed her head forward and a strap in the front pushed against her neck. She couldn't get enough air. She became too exhausted to move and to release the knot that would allow people on the ground to lower her. She says she finally heard Melissa's voice break through the thickening fog, stern and commanding, telling her to, in precise language, "take a lock now"—to use a foot lock to step up. She did, which opened her airway and allowed her to undo the knot, which allowed the crew to lower her. "That moment changed me," Melissa says. "There's a time to have fun. There is a time to stop. And there's a time to get everyone's attention without yelling, to make sure you can be heard." Bear says the moment changed her too. "It drove me to be a better climber. I was like, 'That will never happen to me again. Ever. Ever.'"

Competitions have a fair-like feel. Cheers ring out when people finish a particularly beautiful or efficient climb. Arborists can look like ballet dancers in their gracefulness, economy, and power. It is a world few see: full green trees full of people completely at ease, arboreal residents chatting and skipping through branches. It is a world the Women's Tree Climbing Workshop team encourages participants to join so they can up their game. Olivia Davis had completed one workshop before they entered the 2022 New England chapter competition. The most nerve-wracking event for them was aerial rescue. Climbers are timed on setting up their system, ascending, and lowering a dummy, and are awarded points for each aspect of safe rescue: calling emergency services, checking for hazards, coming up with a plan, performing first aid, and narrating the whole time to reassure their injured colleague. "I was very nervous," Davis says. "You have to be talking . . . and I can say it's not my favorite thing to do." Their boss had recommended that they come up with a name for the dummy. "I just went with my younger brother's name, and pretended I was talking to him in the tree, which was honestly super helpful."

The women's division often has fewer participants: only about 7 percent of arborists are women, and only an estimated 1 to 3 percent of climbing arborists are women. But "the men that compete now recognize that the women are badass," says Bear. The atmosphere is more pervasively collegial as well. "I think it's partly an element of the fact that our life is on the line every day with tree work," Alex says. Melissa agrees it is an unusual culture. "I've met my brothers, my tight brothers, my tree-climbing brothers," she says. "I've never been any part of a competition where your competitors are teaching you how to beat them."

In the early years, though, most women at the competitions were in the audience, there to support a husband, a brother, or a father, the twins say. In the New England chapter, women kept coming up to Bear and Melissa, asking them how they had learned to climb, why there was no training specific to women. Can you teach me? Some women had clearly tried climbing but wouldn't talk about the experience when asked. "You can feel a wet blanket go over their body," Bear says. "What happened? They were terrorized, or not taught properly, or treated disrespectfully."

With arborist friends Jen Kettell and Marcy Carpenter, the sisters taught a one-day workshop at Harvard's Arnold Arboretum. Some thirty women attended. "Men and women climb so incredibly differently," Bear notes. "We're just built differently and our mindsets are different." Over time, the workshop grew into a two-and-a-half-day event, folding in yoga and morning meditation. Accommodations shifted from tents brought by participants to sites, like Hi-Rock, with beds. Demand has not waned and registration often fills up immediately. "I think it's important to still have that safe space for people. I won't say specifically for women, but for marginalized groups, that it's important to have that safe space for them to learn and grow and have that sense of belonging," Alex says. "A lot of people, and not even just in tree care, but in life, they feel they don't belong and are trying to find that sense of self. I think the workshop is good for that."

The forces that gave rise to the workshop can be seen in its ethos. The love of and attention to trees. Thoughtfulness about how to teach in ways that empower and support. Vigilance about safety and the right gear and the right gear fit. Technical language that ensures precision and empowers participants with authority. "We speak vocabulary from day one," Melissa says. The roster of instructors: a roster of competitors and champions. Many of the challenges set for the participants, like reaching for a ribbon at the far end of a branch, are the ones posed to Melissa and Bear by the Asian longhorned beetle.

Through the intertwined hemlock branches, Alex sees me and sees me see the pink ribbon. I stand up on the branch—as close to the trunk as is possible without grafting to it—and get rid of the slack on the climbing line. I am nicely tightly tied into the tree. But as I look up, I see that one side of the rope is caught on the far side of a snag. Is the rope going to fray and disintegrate as it rubs on the snag? Alex suggests that I could change the rope's position. How to do that? Will I be able to get back down if I change the fall of the line, as the route up is the route down? Perhaps I won't be able to descend. Alex waits as long as I need to run through every line of panic.

I create slack by squeezing on the hitch knot and pulling up on the falling side of the line, so the climbing side is loose. After several tries, I flip it over the snag. Alex guides me as I step away from the trunk, releasing rope by squeezing on the hitch, little by little so that it allows me to walk slowly forward while holding almost all my weight in the harness. My feet only lightly touch the branch—I am not hurting it. The climbing side of the rope is now creating the lengthening side of a triangle. The branch is at a right angle to the trunk, and the rope is the hypotenuse. I am an angle.

Farther out I go, closer and closer to the ribbon. But the rope, attached to the bridge in front of me, is beginning to feel cumbersome, tugging to the side, pulling awkwardly at my harness. I reach for the ribbon. The rope angles are all wrong. I now have embodied knowledge of what it means to be "out on a limb." I will never use that phrase cavalierly again. Alex sees no problem. "Try to turn around," she suggests. I turn around, slowly. I am facing the trunk. The rope is running clear from my bridge up into the canopy and from the pulley down to the ground. All feels right again. I am ready to walk back to hug the trunk. "Try to lean back," Alex says.

That is completely impossible, undoable, inconceivable. I release some rope. I begin to lean back into air. I release a little more rope. I lean back farther. Little by little, gently releasing the knot, extending the climbing line. Stopping. Breathing until I am calm again. Until I am lying back in the air, high above the ground, relying on my harness, my feet still lightly brushing the branch. I am looking at the sky through the green web of branches of this tall, beautiful hemlock I am coming to know. I am part of the life of its canopy for the moment. I see and feel its strength and its complexity; that it is supporting me from above and from below. There is coolness in the branches, little sunlight filters down. I am floating but I am anchored. There is plenty of time.

I extend my arm over my head. I catch hold of the ribbon.

Linda Coates remembers getting her first ribbon. Her daughter, Emma, was working toward her arborist degree and was facing hurdles as one of two female students. Emma says no one taught her how to climb relying on her legs or using her different center of gravity instead of her arms. There was little workwear designed for women then, no steel-toed boots. "So I had to wear men's clothes. None of it fit, which is really dangerous when you're doing tree work," she says. "There was a lot of pressure for me to be perfect and always be right, because if I gave a wrong answer, it was like, 'Oh, it's a woman who doesn't belong here.'"

Linda had the impression that some students wanted Emma to fail and started looking for ways to support her daughter. "I didn't want someone to take it from her," Linda says, "her courage and her strength. I didn't want them to steal it." She discovered the Women's Tree Climbing Workshop online and the two attended one together. Linda hadn't been up in a tree since she was a kid, when she climbed often and would escape into trees to find refuge when she was upset. "It was absolutely terrifying because at some point in my life, I developed a horrific fear of heights. So it was, it was a real struggle within myself," she says. "I had to face a lot of fear." Emma coached her mother through getting the ribbon, telling her it was just a few more steps, just over there, just a little more. "She made me go after it and I was like, 'I know what you're doing,' because I used to do it with her!" Linda says her whole body was shaking and she was drenched in sweat. She reached the ribbon.

"I thought I was at least fifty feet up. What was that, like, ten?"

"Maybe ten," Emma laughs.

"We were there for tree climbing and that was the focus of it. It was so much more than that . . . tree climbing was the vehicle. You have to trust yourself. You have to know yourself," Linda says. "It's ultimately about your own power."

They are telling me this over Zoom, Emma from her office in Wellesley, Massachusetts, where she was then the town's senior planner, using her arborist degree to inform decisions about tree planting and conservation during construction and development, and Linda from the living room in the house where she runs her business as a physical therapist. "It was just awesome to share that experience with her. I feel like it's not a traditional mother–daughter experience to go and climb some trees with a bunch of women in the woods," says Emma. "It was really powerful and it definitely brought us closer together."

Linda recalls a young woman at the workshop telling her how good it was to see a mother and daughter enjoying each other so much. "I think it probably allowed people to see all sorts of possibilities in terms of relationships that could take another form or could evolve in a different way," she says. "I think also within the setting of two sisters who have this wonderful relationship."

When I was pregnant with my first child, my mother and I started going to therapy together. We were fighting often and over small things like changes in plans. My hope was that we could talk through our worries about our new roles, as she had at times been more child to me than mother, I more mother than child. She had seen therapists before, working through a childhood trauma and staying sober, which she ultimately did for thirty-five years. I had attended many twelve-step meetings with her to support her and to better understand some of the patterns that families can get stuck in; we had talked through a lot of pain. But these fights had a quality to them that neither of us could navigate. I hoped to convince her to see the therapist on her own after some joint sessions, which she did.

My mother, a delightful and delighted grandmother, took care of my daughter Auden for several hours a few days every week. Their bond was profound; both of them intense and observant, both always able to really see other people, both filled with empathy and mischievous joy. But our fights only worsened. A call to say that Auden was still asleep, so could my mother come in the afternoon instead of late morning, or would Wednesday work as well as Thursday, often led her to become furious and to hurl abuse. There was no talking it through or accepting an apology for my fuzzy sleep-deprived brain.

There is no talking cure for dementia. I came to understand later that every change in plan exploded my mother's rehearsed routines, pushed her out of the grooves she spent most of her energy trying to feel her way along, pulled her into whirl and vertigo. In those early years of her dementia, she seemed herself at times and I clung to that normalcy, believing things would go back to being familiar, recognizable. She raked leaves, she read children's books aloud, she took Auden to the park.

By the time my son Julian was born, it was clear that my mother could not care for him as she had for Auden, just three years before. Habits central to her character faded. She no longer cared how she dressed, she no longer worried about hygiene—my mother who had always loved baths, who loved perfume and fragranced powder, who had always worried aloud that she might have body odor. She draped her cherry red bathroom towels over the furniture around her apartment. She wrapped her belongings in white paper towels and elastic bands or inside her socks, most of them patterned with birds—socks with flamingoes, puffins, kiwis, albatross. She draped placemats over the faucets in her bathroom. She forgot to wipe food stains from her face. She forgot to wash her clothes.

Then came the years of more radical extremes. The era of occasional violence toward aides, ultimatums, paranoid terrors, and delusions. In which she knew that things were terribly wrong, in which she told a neighbor not to be offended if she didn't recognize her, that she had dementia. She stopped cushioning things with towels and paper towels, and began wrapping belongings in bubble wrap, protecting them further from some unknown coming turbulence. Her apartment took on a ghostly cast, colors faint under plastic.

Then came the longest years in which her fury and energy and fight ebbed and the bright colors of her language and thought grayed like the items she had wrapped and arrayed around herself. My mother called me Emma and Barbara, her sisters' names. She stopped asking about her grandchildren, whom she had loved so explicitly and fiercely. She stopped talking. She withered from her plump just-under-five-foot self to a well-under-five-foot waif.

Over sixteen years, I went from fighting with her or trying to be logical with her—trying to convince her that no one was stealing water by redirecting her pipes or peeling back the ceiling of her apartment at night to peer at her—to taking over her finances and her medications and her doctors' visits and organizing the transition from elder daycare to full-time home-care with a series of remarkable women who loved her and who knew her loving core, even though they had not known her before. I was organized and efficient, an excellent administrator of practical things. I developed an arrhythmia and an ulcer. I ground my teeth and enamel popped out and a tiny hole had to be filled. My face went numb on one side. I cried after every visit. I felt hollow.

When I cleaned out my mother's apartment after she died, I found only one surprise. As she had become increasingly disoriented, she had asked me to get rid of documents and possessions—if the clutter around her subsided, perhaps the clutter in her mind would recede as well. I came to know every item, every paper, every note she wrote to herself to try to keep herself herself. But I had never seen her tree journal, perhaps because this gift was camouflaged as something ordinary: a white three-ring plastic binder.

For a decade starting in 1953, my mother kept a record of trees she met. It is a gorgeous record with faded tape and faded leaves, pencil sketches of nuts and flowers, descriptions of the occasion of the meeting and of the species' natural history. The first few pages focus on East Coast trees: leaves she collects near her childhood home in upstate New York, a ginkgo leaf from New York City, where she is training to become a nurse. She writes about the challenges facing street trees: pollution, poor and scant soil.

Then West Coast trees. She moves to California, where my father is studying at Berkeley. She meets redwoods. Live oaks. She describes madrone, camphor, magnolia, elm, tulip, buckeye, many species of eucalyptus, bigleaf maple, cherry, karo, plum. She is in love with trees. "Entering a dusky sequoia grove, you do not see the trees with the reality of trunk, branches, and leaves; you see broad shadowy columns . . . at the base, sinews of wood and cordage of bark are tortured and taut, forming elbows and knees, bent but firm. . . . This compression is the only apparent concession which sequoia makes to the law of gravity. All the rest is an uprush of wood." She includes photographs taken by my father of the trees they most enjoyed or were most captivated by. The blackwood acacia "is especially beautiful in early morning and early evening, when the sun touches the upper parts of it and shade envelopes the lower branches." She describes thirty or forty hummingbirds "darting to and fro from one cluster to another of the flowers" on a eucalyptus, "sprays of scarlet flowers all over, against the deep green of the leaves and the dark bark and a clear blue sky."

The last entries are from 1964, the year after my birth, the year before my brother Eric's. At the back of her journal are a dozen leaves layered in the same acetate sleeve. No notes, no stories, no locations or dates. I don't know if they were each to have their own page or if she simply found them enchanting as an assemblage. They are all sizes, two inches to a full page long, and all shapes, lobed and willowy, round, pinnate, oblong, fanlike. There is nothing of her move back among East Coast trees, of trees met during years lived in other countries, of trees in the abandoned pastures and second-growth forest behind my grandmother's trailer home in upstate New York that we often visited. Perhaps because my mother was no longer teaching herself the trees but teaching them to me and Eric. And perhaps because she was losing her bearings bit by bit.

In the front pocket of her tree journal, I found an envelope containing a thin catkin-like flower, five inches long, gently wrapped in white tissue. After recording the year (spring 1994) and the place (Sebring, Florida, where she was visiting a relative), my mother had written another note to herself: "I haven't been able to find the tree yet."

The workshop ends in the late afternoon on Sunday. Everyone brings their gear back to the main lodge and checks to make sure the two-dozen big black gear bags have all the items they are supposed to. Each bag is numbered and all the gear in that bag carries the same number. Because people have tried different harnesses to see which design feels best and different helmets and have had to borrow this and that from other bags, there is a frenetic treasure hunt. Lots of peering at carabiners to find tiny numbers written in fine sharpie. Lots of "has anyone seen helmet-harness-lanyard number . . . ?"

After all is put away and the completed bags arranged in numerical order, participants gather near the back porch, near the remains of last night's fire, to talk about their experience. Then each person selects an item from the giveaway table. Melissa and Bear put everything they have won at climbing competitions on that table; many of the individuals as well as the arborist, gear, and rope companies that sponsor the workshop also donate equipment. Arborist equipment is expensive. Before the workshop, Moulis had used a recent raise to buy $2,000 worth of essential climbing gear. A good harness can be more than $500. A helmet with ear protection $300. Chainsaw protection pants $350. One rope $400—and arborists need many. Serious carabiners, $25 apiece. A foot ascender $100. A knee ascender $140. Pulley $70. It is all costly and wears out fast. Some participants take a needed helmet, safety glasses, a lanyard, a hat, some workshop swag, or clothes by Arborwear, one of the first companies to make arborist clothing for women.

There is a sense of reluctance and sadness about leaving this re-en-tree—some about returning to unenlightened workplaces, some about leaving community after having found it again post-ish pandemic, some about no longer being in trees, some about leaving what has come to feel like an enchantment created by the trees and the team and the twins.

At some point as the workshop evolved, the sisters incorporated a practice suggested by one of their friends: gratitude bags. Over the course of the three days, participants, when moved to do so, write short notes to each other about a moment they shared or a nice thought or insight and place it in a bag, usually brown paper, each marked with a participant's name. After the workshop, if the feeling of fellowship or of being in the trees fades, you can read the notes and remember. I read those notes—from Moulis, Alex, Bear, Melissa, my groundie, and many others—again and again, and feel transported. A simple sentence conjures Hi-Rock, the sun, the wind, the lake, being in the hemlocks.

Shortly after the workshop, I decide to find my mother's tree for her.

PART II

Understories

Bear and Melissa grew up in Halifax, a small town in Massachusetts, about an hour south of Boston. When they were four, their parents divorced and they moved with their mother and older brother to the outskirts, along a road with few other houses. Their mother worked long hours as a waitress, and the twins found their own games and adventures in the surrounding forests and fields. When they look back, they think their mother encouraged them to be outside as much as possible—telling them not to come home until daylight faded—because their stepfather could be abusive. "Crazy smart, a chef, incredibly well read," Melissa says, "but he couldn't stop drinking."

The cartography and adventures of their childhood remain vivid, often in the present tense. The sisters describe stepping from their lawn into the forest behind the house and feeling a great sigh, a feeling of being immediately at home. "We found solace and comfort being in the woods . . . it is a very safe and comforting place once you understand it. It is not scary, it is magical," says Bear. "We learned a lot about ourselves, and how to mitigate our own disasters . . . you can get into a lot of mischief." There was a creek, vernal pool, and a pond to play in and around, and there were varied forests to explore. Some was mostly white pine, some mostly red maple, some mixed oak, white pine, and maple, some shrubby bayberry and scrub pine. They brought seedlings from the forest and planted them around the edges of the lawn, out of the way of their mom's mower. "She's the sun goddess. She loves being outside in a bikini, mowing lawns," Melissa says. "I think it's because she worked her ass off all the time inside." A small forest of white pine saplings began to grow along the lawn; with sun, space, and decades, they became grand trees.

The twins—athletes from an early age—built tree houses, obstacle courses, and running trails. They climbed Norway maples and pines, often picnicking high in trees. They loved the smell of rain, the smell of snow, the keen ozone of a storm. They felt that the trees knew them as well as they knew the trees. "The tree knows we are here," Melissa says. "They react differently when you are in them."

One cherished tree was nicknamed Wolf Pine, a huge Eastern white pine that had not been logged when the land was cleared for farming or timber because it was a property marker. In surveyors' field notes and in old property deeds such trees, often carved with a symbol, would be marked "witness tree." Another of the twins' favorites was a chaotic willow: half was broken, but on its other side, the branches that touched the ground had sprouted up again. "It is marvelous, because it has been there for a long time and it shouldn't even be growing," Melissa says. "It is constantly reinventing itself." Beyond the willow, past Wolf Pine and the red maple woods, was the epicenter of adventure: the Great Cedar Swamp, which they trekked through for miles, sometimes into another town. "We'd pop out on the road and then walk home sopping wet." The sisters still remember the fragrance of the cedar trees.

The Great Cedar Swamp was where Bear hid the surveying stakes that appeared on the adjacent land when the sisters were about ten. "I remember feeling so upset that someone was going to build on the property, and therefore, it's going to be ruined.

I remember thinking about the turtles and the snakes and our fort, and just knowing that it was all going to get destroyed," she says. "So I remember, it was moonlight, and I went out and took all the sticks and I brought them out to the swamp. I put them all in one spot and I just pushed them down so no one would see them." The twins' mother was soon onto the activist, who had to retrieve and replace the stakes.

The outskirts of Halifax have more houses now, fewer forests. The white pines around the lawn were largely felled by the next family to inhabit the house. The willow stopped reinventing itself, and Wolf Pine toppled. Old age took many trees not taken by development. Bear and Melissa have seen all these changes on infrequent drives past their childhood home. Fifty years renders many, if not most, familiar landscapes unfamiliar. "It is weird to see your past in a very different way," Melissa says. "To see it edited." It is also to be expected: part of the tension of memory, the contrast between the intimate childhood knowledge of a place and the view decades later. What has been unexpected and profoundly disturbing to the twins is what they see in the trees and woods they did not grow up in.

Bear now lives in Vermont and Melissa still lives in Massachusetts, in the westernmost, and most forested, part of the state. Both have worked as tree wardens: Bear in Manchester, Vermont, and Melissa in Petersham, Massachusetts (where Bear occasionally filled in for her because "no one could tell the difference"). Tree wardens are required in every New England town with a population of ten thousand or more. The first law mandating tree wardens was passed in Massachusetts in 1899, and in other nearby states soon after. Wardens are responsible for maintaining a town's trees by, among other things, planting, pruning, and checking for unsafe trees.

Both sisters still work as arborists. For several years, Bear was a utility arborist, checking for tree health and for hazard trees along rights-of-way and near people's homes in thirty-five towns in Connecticut. She still works as a contract arborist, often for the company run by Melissa's husband, Tom Ingersoll. They see trees around people's homes, in towns and cities; they live in and near forests and visit many others. They are watching the trees and woodlands of New England decline, dramatically and fast. "They are suffering greatly," Bear says.

Melissa and Bear showed me some of that suffering when I first met them in August 2020 to follow them around Petersham Common, part of reporting an article on climate change in New England's forests. Melissa was still the town's tree warden, a position she had held for six years and continued to fill although she had moved a two-hour drive away. "The town has no replacement for me at the moment," she said. "Most people who live in town don't even know there is a tree warden position until they have a problem with a tree." Tree wardens, trained arborists of all kinds, and urban foresters are in low supply and high demand in many regions.

The sisters arrived on their motorcycles, both Suzuki V-Stroms. Bear was wearing a brown Women's Tree Climbing Workshop shirt: "Climb Like a Girl" printed in a lichen green arc above the circular logo of a tree. Melissa was wearing a brown shirt from Shelter Tree, the family-owned arborist supply company she worked for. The sisters love to travel by moto and are skilled mechanics, fixing and customizing their bikes. That love was a secret they kept from their mother between their late teens and her death in 2015: "Mom said, 'You will never own a motorcycle under my roof.'" Several times a year they attend gatherings and ride with others, reveling in the unspoken synchronicity that arises in small flocks of like-minded riders, the feeling of a road's curves and the physics of angles and centrifugal force, of being close to the landscape and the weather.

Bear later disclosed to me that they had planned to spend a half an hour or so leading me and my colleague—who was taking photographs for the article we were working on—through a quick tour of the common. Instead, they delayed their weekend moto ride and special sister time, and the generosity they are known for became evident. They spent two hours with us talking about almost every tree's challenges. "Oh my goodness, it is so good to see you! You have done so much for Petersham," exclaimed a passerby. "These people," she said to me, "they have so much honor for all life forms."

Most of the Petersham Common trees were experiencing the stresses that arborists see everywhere in urban and suburban areas. Compacted soil that prevents roots from expanding or thriving, soil that water runs off rather than into. As we visited with some strikingly big trees, one maple in particular, the twins suggested that my colleague and I visit the Sunderland buttonball, a gigantic American sycamore that dates to at least 1787 and is a legacy tree—on Massachusetts's register because of its dimensions. Many states have such champion tree lists, and the nonprofit American Forests maintains a national one. "As soon as you start walking toward it, you start moving slower and slower and get goosebumps. The energy just flows from it," said Bear of the buttonball. But she is of two minds about visiting it or any other champion tree: "We are killing the tree with love. Everyone who is visiting it is compacting its soil." (Compaction confession: my colleague and I did visit it. We stood awed for a while, staying on the road and sidewalk running within feet of the stunning sycamore, built, as is typical, without consideration for trees. Even champions do not necessarily get the soil or space they need.)

Melissa and Bear showed us trees on the common with wounds from mowers and weed whackers. They showed us how lawn grass guzzles much of the available water. They showed us trees in need of mulch. Melissa confided that she had snuck out under cover of midnight to remove grass from around the base of some trees, including a London plane, and to lay fortifying, nutritious mulch in a doughnut ring around, but not touching, the lower trunk—the root flares need contact with the air to stay healthy. If covered by mulch, they can rot and die. "We can all plant a tree, but it is about making sure it stays alive," Bear said.

They pointed to lone trees—increasingly, the twins explained, research suggests that trees in similar settings prefer a community. "These individuals are struggling more than they ever have, and it has to do with climate change," Melissa said. "In forests they have one another, they can support one another with water and nutrients." Trees live in symbiosis with various of the estimated fifty thousand species of fungi that associate with plants. These mycorrhizal associations between roots and fungi bring nutrients and water from the soil into the tree and provide fungi with carbohydrate food. Mycorrhizal fungi can form local mycelial networks, connecting different kinds of trees. Melissa and Bear explain that these networks can move water, carbon, nitrogen, and chemicals between trees—the wood wide web, as it has been called.

They showed us trees in wrong places: sugar maples, which don't like salt, right next to the road. New England is road-salt central. The deicing practice started in New Hampshire in the late 1930s and expanded nationally: the country now uses between 15 and 32 million tons of road salt a year, with New York leading the way. Salt is toxic to many organisms; it can poison freshwater ecosystems (and contaminate drinking water) and alter soil chemistry. Salt can wither buds, dehydrate roots, and render trees unable to withstand frost. Maples are among the most vulnerable species. "One by one they are dying, and I can't stop it." Nor could the sisters help a shade-loving spruce planted in full sun. At one point, they fell silent and watched a trailer loaded with saplings drive by.

"Flying trees," said Melissa.

"Those aren't going to make it," Bear said.

Many of the Petersham trees were infested with insects, and some were being chemically treated. But it was the oaks that seemed to be faring the worst. The red oaks were showing signs of drought from the parched summer: their leaves changing color and shriveling.

The drought afflicting the Petersham Common oaks was what is termed a "flash drought," a sudden onset drought. Four inches less rain than historically typical fell that summer: groundwater levels across New England plummeted, streams and rivers shrank. By October, the Department of Agriculture had designated several "crop disaster areas" and over two hundred fifty communities had instituted water restrictions. That intense drought had been preceded by similar ones in 2016 and 2000 and was succeeded by ones in 2022 and 2024, becoming data points in what seems an emergent pattern.

Climate change often brings paradox: a region can get more rainfall and experience more drought. More radical extremes. This is what has been happening in the Northeast. Inundation has been followed by bouts of drought. Drought is anticipated to become more severe and more frequent over the next decades, affecting summer water supply, crops, and many trees.

Northern red oaks, *Quercus rubra*, the most common oak species in the region, are generally considered drought tolerant. They are a tree of choice for city streets and they have been projected to expand in range, thriving in areas that were previously too cold for them. But recent research suggests that the dependable, unwavering oaks—red oaks and some other species—are not faring so well. "While oaks are well adapted to moderate drought, they are highly susceptible to extreme drought," one study found. A tree-ring study in Vermont, in the northernmost part of red oak's range, looked at trees born ninety years ago and saw the same: oaks didn't grow well in hot years with little rain. "The oaks' ability to survive drought may become increasingly difficult in a drier future," another study concluded. Rain patterns are also shifting. Red oak appear to prefer summer rain. Fall rains, which are increasingly frequent in the Northeast, arrive too late, because shortening days and cloud cover limit photosynthesis. And when fall rain arrives as a fierce deluge, it knocks off leaves still green because autumn has been delayed.

People who study and tend to trees and forests in various settings and at various scales—arborists, foresters, silviculturists, modelers, keepers of traditional science and knowledge, biologists, forest ramblers—all have stories to tell about what is changing in the trees and forests they know intimately. A close look at any tree in any landscape can illuminate parts of the whole. Once those changes are pointed out to you—dying leaves, fall colors in spring and summer, branches and twigs like skeletal fingers protruding from the green flesh of intact canopy—you begin to see them everywhere you go. You see them in woods, along highways, around homes, in street trees, in city parks. You look for them in movies and television programs, and you see them there too.

"It's devastating for us because when we move through life, we see the lens of the landscape first and humanity second, and our landscape is our trees," Bear says. "This is what gives us life . . . and we're destroying them as if they're just trash on the side of the road. It's just heart wrenching."

Aspen

Suzanne Marchetti and I are hiking along Beaver Ponds Trail in the West Elk Mountains, about a half an hour from Gunnison, Colorado. It is early fall and the leaves of the quaking aspen have turned brilliant yellow. The forest on either side of the path is abundantly aspen, their pale trunks luminous against the tangle of yellow-green ferns below them and the dark green-to-black subalpine fir that appear like shadows among them. Over the next decades, the slow-growing conifers will likely come to dominate this forest and the aspen will diminish until there is an upheaval—pest, fire, wind—that takes out fir and then aspen will rise again. "The aspen are first up," Marchetti tells me, "but they don't stay long."

Marchetti, an ecologist who works for the Forest Service out of the Gunnison office, stops to point out a fungus, called artist's conk, at the base of one tree. It has a smooth flat side that is pearl-colored, the size of two hands, and shaped like a painter's palette. *Ganoderma applanatum* is a common decay fungus. Marchetti points out aspen that look chimeric. Above three feet, they have the tree's smooth light bark with what look like kohl-lined eyes, black strokes around knobs left by former branches; closer to the ground, the papery outer layer has been stripped by gophers, leaving rough dark underbark. Marchetti points out aspen with galls. Aspen with cankers. Aspen speckled with a black mold feeding on aphid frass. On one tree, she uses a fingernail to scrape away a tiny patch of bark to reveal the fresh green of chlorophyll beneath. This is a healthy forest—birth, growth, and decay.

Quaking aspen are one of my favorite trees. I can sit for hours enthralled by their particular dance. *Populus tremuloides*, the tremulous, trembling aspen. In aspen and all poplars, the petiole, or stem, that connects leaves to branches is long and flat instead of round as in most other deciduous trees. Not only is it flat, but it connects to the leaf on a perpendicular. Leaf latitude meets petiole longitude and adventure follows. When wind catches the petioles and leaves, it seems as if it is arriving from all directions at once. Green or gold, an aspen canopy flashes and shimmers in even a sigh of breeze. Watching aspen makes me feel that I am breathing underwater, that I am living in a sea of wind. Watching aspen is like watching truths made visible: everything is somehow connected; tiny movements have huge impacts; thousands of leaves can each dance their own riff and be part of one tree.

Marchetti and I follow the trail until it opens onto a large pond with a grass-topped beaver lodge near the center. Green conifers, gray mountains, wisps of blue in a moonstone sky, and the astonishing flickering blazing yellow of the aspen. A short drive away, along roads dense with foliage tourists, there is little flickering blazing yellow, except in patches. The landscape looks dull, its color partly washed out. It is a shocking landscape. Miles of dead trees in Kebler Pass, the largest aspen stand in the state.

In 2004, a silviculturist working in the San Juan National Forest, about one hundred fifty miles southwest of Gunnison, noticed swaths of dying aspen. Aspen can reproduce sexually, but they are mostly clonal: the individual trees in a stand generally sprout from one root network. The most renowned clonal forest is Pando, which has some forty thousand trees, covers one hundred acres in Utah, has lived an estimated twelve thousand years, and may be the largest organism in the world. Aspen shoots often emerge after disturbance and arise from the root system in tandem, and because stands are often the same age, it is not unusual for them to senesce and die at the same time. But the silviculturist "said that he was seeing an unusual type of damage . . . and could we come down and look at it," says Jim Worrall, a forest pathologist, now retired from the Forest Service. "What was different about what we saw down in the San Juan was that it was really on a landscape scale, not a stand scale."

Marchetti, who had done her master's on sugar maple decline in Maine, moved to Gunnison in 2008 and heard a lot about dying aspen. She took a job as a ski lift ticket collector, polished her thesis, and dreamed of studying the aspen: "They are my favorite tree in this area. I love deciduous trees, and they are few and far between here." On a whim, she stopped by the Forest Service office to see if any job relating to aspen was available: "somehow, fate or karma or luck would have it that a seasonal position was open." By the time Marchetti started working with Worrall, millions of dying aspen had been reported not only in Colorado, but in Utah, Wyoming, Arizona, Minnesota, and three Canadian provinces. Between 2000 and 2010, about eight million acres of aspen had died or were dying—an area about the size of Maryland—and that tally is likely an underestimate.

The loss of aspen in some regions was not new. An overall waning had been occurring in the West since the 1960s, Worrall says, likely because of federal fire suppression policies put in place a century ago—"whenever aspen burns, it usually comes back like gangbusters"—and the grazing of young trees by cattle, sheep, deer, and elk. That ongoing chronic loss had been referred to as aspen decline. But this mortality was faster and more extensive. Worrall and his colleagues named it sudden aspen decline. Giving a name to what was happening to the much loved aspen seemed to draw more attention to the widespread death. "I do think giving a name to it really helped," Worrall says. "It made it more of a public entity."

Many things play roles in a forest's health: among them, location, soil, slope, moisture, the cardinal orientation of stands, the density and age of the trees, the presence of pests and pathogens, and extreme weather events. Marchetti recalls seeing many patterns in the aspen forests. In some places, healthy aspen stood next to huge stretches of dead ones. In some spots, young sprouts were mostly absent; in others, there was regeneration. In some dying stands, no pests; in others beetle infestations and diseases were killing the trees, although those insects and pathogens do not usually wipe out aspen on their own.

Drought explained the variability. Pests and pathogens could kill weakened and stressed trees. Many of the dying stands were also on low-elevation south-facing slopes, places that tended to be drier, places with less water. A few years after the call from the silviculturist in the San Juan, Worrall and his colleagues were sure that drought was the trigger.

Since about 2000, the West and Southwest had been experiencing a megadrought. The North American Drought Atlas that Cook and his colleagues devised, with founding help from the hemlocks, and other research had revealed that droughts are regular features of the Southwest and West. They are linked to periodic weather fluctuations, known as El Niño and La Niña, which originate in the Pacific Ocean. Megadroughts are unusually severe and long lasting. Tree rings show that megadroughts have periodically occurred in the Southwest, megadroughts that may have played a role in the abandonment of Chaco Canyon and Mesa Verde. The megadrought killing the aspen was to become the worst in the region since the ninth century and there was little natural about it: a substantial part of it, 42 percent, has been attributed to human-caused climate change.

Sudden aspen decline, for many observers, marked an inflection point. "I think that both the scientists studying forests and the broader public in the West hadn't realized that our forests were so close to the edge and so vulnerable," says William Anderegg, a biologist at the University of Utah. "Unfortunately, it really was the canary in the coal mine and we've started to see more and more tree species dying in the West."

Anderegg grew up in southwestern Colorado fishing, camping, hiking, and hunting. In 2008, after living in other parts of the country, he returned to the region. "I remember being simply stunned that these forests, these once vibrant and lush aspen canopies, now looked a lot more like moonscape. There were these skeletal aspen trees just jutting up into the parched Colorado sky," he says. "It was this really visible and visceral change within my lifetime that struck me, and also prompted a whole set of questions." Among the questions Anderegg wanted to answer was a forensic one: How did the aspen die? With other researchers, Anderegg looked for what are considered two principal physiological mechanisms by which drought does its damage.

Carbon is the armature for life on earth, and particularly so for plants, which are autotrophs: they make, consume, and store their own sugars. Virtually all life owes its existence to photosynthesis, the conversion of atmospheric carbon into the carbohydrates that form the hub of the earth's food web—plant makes planet. Plants are largely built of carbon: structural carbohydrates such as cellulose and lignin make up their stems, leaves, and wood. They stand in carbon: their roots give carbon to the soil and its galaxy of organisms, and there can be twice as much carbon in the ground around trees than in them. They speak in carbon: the element is at the core of the chemicals they produce for defense and communication. Whereas about 12 percent of a human body is carbon, for a tree it is about 50 percent.

To take in carbon dioxide, trees open pores, called stomata, on their leaves, allowing the gas to reach a profusion of chloroplasts in the broadleaves, needles, or spines. In the chloroplasts—ancient cyanobacteria that came to live symbiotically within other organisms—carbon dioxide from the air meets water from the soil and a reaction, driven by the sun, results in carbohydrates for the tree and oxygen for the atmosphere. The number of chloroplasts varies hugely; aspen fall in the middle of the chloroplast-density range with perhaps a 1.2 billion chloroplasts per leaf. The number and placement of stomata on leaves is also highly variable, but all serve as portals between air and leaf.

And in the way of all portals, an entrance can also be an exit. As carbon dioxide comes in, oxygen and water go out; they pass each other like neighbors in a revolving door. Generally, a tree uses about 10 percent of the water delivered to the leaves by the xylem; 90 percent is lost to the air. That evapotranspiration, the movement of water from the ground to the air through trees and forests, is a critical part of the world's hydrological cycle, driving rainfall and weather. Amazon rainforest trees, for instance, are thought to release as much as twenty billion tons of water a day.

During a drought, trees need to balance taking in carbon dioxide with losing scarce water. Leaving stomata open can lead to what is called hydraulic failure. Water moves up the tree, against gravity, for a confluence of reasons. The low air pressure outside the leaves beckons to water under higher pressure in the rigid, narrow cells of the xylem. And because water molecules are unevenly charged—one side more negative, one side more positive—they tug on each other, like someone accepting a hand from a climber above them and offering a hand to a climber below. But if the atmospheric pull on the water column exceeds the supply from the soil, air bubbles—like those that enter a cracked straw—can permeate the xylem. These embolisms block, damage, or break the water transport system, leading to what is called xylem cavitation.

Closing stomata to conserve water, however, can lead to carbon starvation. Without carbon dioxide coming in, photosynthesis ultimately ceases. The tree cannot produce sugars and enters a kind of fasting state. Once its reserves are depleted, it has nothing left with which to make cambium, buds, flowers or cones, pollen, or hormones. The tree can't regulate xylem pressure. It can't produce defensive chemicals that would help it ward off an infection or an insect attack. It becomes a shadow of itself.

Carbon starvation and xylem cavitation are not mutually exclusive, but that trees vary in their responses is well documented. The piñon–juniper forests found across some one billion acres in the western United States are no strangers to drought. Both trees are rugged and protean, growing low and shrubby in dry savannah grassland or tall and shady in cooler moister habitats. When the megadrought began to unfold in the early aughts, these iconic forests began to look like a patchwork: live green juniper among dead brown piñon. The two trees, researchers discovered, had different drought strategies. Juniper left its stomata largely open, opting for some xylem cavitation and more photosynthesis; sometimes only a branch would survive. Juniper wood is tough and more resistant to embolism. Piñon, whose xylem are more vulnerable to embolism, shut its stomata, opting for carbon starvation and, often, death by beetle. Such species differences are becoming key to projecting how certain forests and trees will fare.

In the aspen, Anderegg saw no evidence of carbon starvation. But he did see and hear xylem cavitation. "It sounds a little bit like popcorn . . . you can think of it as like a string snapping. You pull the string too taut and then it just breaks in the middle." In some aspen, Anderegg's team found, up to 70 percent of the vital water-conducting apparatus was blocked. "In the aspen, it seems like the damage tends to accumulate," Anderegg says. "Multiple droughts seem to hit the trees harder and harder." Such drought "legacy effects" also seem pronounced in some conifers. "We are still trying to understand why this occurs and how quickly trees can recover and which ones are better at it."

The aspen were not being undone by drought alone. "What made this drought really unique and also really important," Anderegg explains, "is that it was quite a bit hotter. It was 2 to 4 degrees Celsius [3.6 to 7.2 degrees Fahrenheit] hotter on average. This showed us that hot droughts are more lethal droughts for trees. And that really matters because even if precipitation doesn't change . . . temperature alone makes droughts more lethal." Just as sweating or panting cools animals, so does evaporation of water cool plants. If stomata are closed, the temperature of leaves increases and they can burn. Without carbon coming in, trees can struggle to make heat-shock proteins, a protective cellular mechanism they have in common with animals.

Heat also radically changes the relationship between the atmosphere and trees. Heat makes air thirstier. As the world gets hotter, "the atmosphere is exerting a more strong evaporative force on the land," says Kim Novick, a professor of environmental science at Indiana University. "Having this sort of pull from the atmosphere can be quite damaging for plants." Novick is among the growing number of scientists who look at drought with an emphasis on the role of the atmosphere and of heat, not as much on overall precipitation, which has been the more traditional approach. "We need to think about how a decrease in water supply will affect plant function," she says. "But we also need to understand how this increase in evaporative demand will affect plants."

What Novick is describing is called vapor pressure deficit, abbreviated as VPD. The deficit refers to the difference between the amount of water vapor the air can hold—its saturation or dew point—and what it is holding. Dry air has more of a deficit than humid air. The same is true for hotter air. Since the late 1990s, vapor pressure deficit has been increasing dramatically. It has been observed in the Amazon rainforest. It has been linked to an overall desiccation of trees, fueling fire risk; rising vapor pressure deficit has been implicated in catastrophic California wildfires. Every climate model projects a hotter future atmosphere, an atmosphere that may kill forests at a scale "unfamiliar to modern civilization," according to one study: by 2050, if vapor pressure deficit trends continue, all forests will experience drought stress greater than any seen in the last millennia. That may bring more frequent and intense fires to places where they are less common than in the West, such as the Great Plains, the Northeast, and the Southeast—places that are already experiencing an upsurge in wildfires. Because of vapor pressure deficit, even trees in areas with high rainfall can dry out.

Hotter drier air also undercuts what is called the enrichment effect. Rising concentrations of carbon dioxide promised a photosynthetic bonanza. Satellite and other observations in recent decades indicated that trees were growing more and that more trees were growing. Good news, because forests take in about one-quarter of the carbon emissions generated by people's fossil fuel use each year: forests have been keeping globally rising temperatures lower than they would be if that carbon dioxide stayed airborne. Trees growing more because of more carbon dioxide could mean more stored carbon. Researchers also found that in a higher carbon dioxide world, some trees showed better water-use efficiency: they could make more sugars with their "regular" amounts of water.

This optimistic scenario is not aging well. Some trees may initially grow more, but growth levels off after time. For some trees enrichment never happens because they don't have the requisite water and nutrients to do extra photosynthesizing. And if it is hot and the air is greedy for water, trees stop making carbohydrates. Vapor pressure deficit, researchers have found, has in some places canceled out any gains from the enrichment effect. Recent evidence suggests this period of carbon-dioxide stimulated growth is tapering off, says Nate McDowell, a biologist at the Pacific Northwest National Laboratory who was involved in the studies on juniper and piñon: thirsty air is overwhelming the benefits of higher carbon dioxide, growth is slowing, and mortality is rising. "It's the smoking gun," McDowell says. "It drives more fire. It drives more insects. It drives more starvation and hydraulic failure."

Most trees have encountered drought in their lives, but they now face unrelenting extremes they are less able to recover from. Between 1970 and 2018, according to one review, drought and heat had caused extensive die-off in every type of forest. Increased forest death has been observed from Australia to Algeria, from Colombia to China. In Canada, 43 percent of boreal forests are experiencing more drought-related death, causing significant releases of carbon. Drought in California has killed an estimated 129 million trees in less than a decade, and 300 million in Texas in one year alone. Forest death will likely expand and accelerate as carbon dioxide emissions continue to rise and heat continues to build. Hotter air, ever more research indicates, is more predictive of forest death than lack of rainfall, says Tim Brodribb of the University of Tasmania: hotter air is "the forest killer."

Marchetti is on the road a lot, documenting what is happening in the region. "We are going out and being the doctors and detectives of the forest," she says of forest pathologists. She sees ecology from the rocks on up: her husband is a geologist, and the two share a wealth of expertise and a truly long view. Marchetti has seen a lot of devastation, especially in areas where Douglas fir, piñon, ponderosa, and lodgepole pines are dying, where bark beetles and budworm are expanding in Engelmann spruce, and where towering cottonwoods are withering.

She also sees pockets of renewal, which is why she remains optimistic. On the way down and out of Kebler Pass, Marchetti points to thickets of Gambel oak along the road. "This could become the new normal in these areas, replacing aspen," she says. The little oaks are lovely with lobed leaves of red, orange, and gold, creating a bristly bushy forest that keeps soil on slopes and creatures supplied with acorns. "There is always going to be something successful," Marchetti says. When she takes me to a high pass where we look out over mountainsides of beetle-killed pines, I focus on the magnitude of gray death, whereas Marchetti's eye picks out the regular green presence of young conifers. If we were looking at that classic optical illusion, she would see faces, I would see a funeral urn.

Marchetti has seen regeneration in some forests where sudden aspen decline was most severe, which is

Aspen leaves and catkin

good news for many creatures. Aspen is a keystone species: an organism that weaves an ecosystem together. Aspen forests have enormous fungal variety and can host more plants than nearby conifer forests or even open meadows. Aster, phlox, delphinium, lupine, and orchid all grow alongside aspen; sedges, rushes, and mosses do too. Insects and animals follow the plants. When aspen declines, entire communities of insects, microorganisms, birds, and mammals are lost. Aspen is a foundation species as well. Because it flourishes after fire—or avalanche or mining or tornado or logging—it gives rise to new worlds, new homes. Foundation species are sometimes called the engineers of ecosystems because they build soil and hold water. Aspen excel at this because of their clonal nature: one root system to connect them all. They can share water from a spring on, say, one side of an abandoned quarry and ample phosphorus, say, on the other side.

Paul Rogers, an ecologist at the University of Utah and director of the Western Aspen Alliance, is increasingly concerned that even in places where young aspen could replace their older selves or create forests in barren terrain, they are no longer able to do so because of deer, elk, cattle, and moose. "In my estimation, browsers are the number one issue, not only in the western U.S. but around the world, in terms of the health and well-being of aspen communities, because the young ones are so tasty and so desirable," he says. It is a great time to be a grazer, and not just of aspen: few large predators remain to control wild populations and domestic livestock free range much of the global commons.

Rogers' view is increasingly shared by others in many landscapes. Kevin Griffin, a plant physiological ecologist at Columbia University, recalls a summer day in the Alaskan boreal forest where he often works, sitting down for lunch, taking out his sandwich, letting his mind wander. "I was looking across the landscape in front of me. And I just noticed . . . there was a browse line across all these spruce trees. It was so remarkable," he recalls. It reminded him of the lines deer create in New England forests as they consume the leaves they can reach: trees look shorn below, shaggy above. In the Alaskan spruce Griffin was looking at, the browse lines were close to the ground. He had seen the bones of Arctic hare nearby and an idea suddenly came to him. "I now believe that one of the key controls of Arctic treeline are those damn rabbits and not my beloved photosynthesis!" The herbivores, he says, "are having a big effect on the ecology of treeline that we have not really started to think about." Griffin is now collaborating with others to "see if we can answer some interesting questions about how a changing Arctic, a changing snowscape, could influence the animals, and how that could influence the vegetation."

Many forest managers are seeing herbivores wipe out their efforts. Whether they are planting southern species farther north in what is called assisted migration, planting seedlings after fire, replanting logged land, or trying to help forests in myriad other ways, foresters have found browsers undoing their work. "Without considering the role of browsing, climate-adapted strategies implemented today could ultimately fail and exacerbate the pressure on forests," a 2021 federal write-up noted. "These trees are caught between the devil and the deep blue sea."

Rogers has studied aspen on several continents, and he is impassioned about saving aspen stands and the tremendous biodiversity they hold. To preserve Pando, researchers fenced off areas of Fishlake National Forest, where the great clone lives, so browsers couldn't graze new growth. Rogers, who helped monitor the plots, observed that inside the fences—the ones that stayed up, most did not—aspen shoots grew and made it to saplinghood. But across most of Pando, few young trees are surviving to replace those dying from rising temperatures and falling water levels. The cycle of renewal that has been occurring for fourteen thousand years has broken. Pando, the most famous aspen stand and perhaps the world's oldest organism, appears to be dying.

Several hours after the visit to Kebler Pass, Marchetti and I are looking out at the south side of Grand Mesa, a flat mountain that extends about five hundred square miles and is full of lakes, wonderful habitat for water-loving aspen. A waterway can be traced through the countryside by following aspen's yellow lines of fall or silver-green lines of summer. At our viewing spot, a high-elevation clearing, rain-on-the-edge-of-hail begins to pick up and lightning threatens. Golden aspen look dramatic against a charcoal sky, but that contrast cannot been seen here. Bands of tattered naked trees run across slopes, rivers of dead wood flowing through live forest. The Grand Mesa aspen look even more dramatically dead than the Kebler Pass aspen. "When I was here this summer, I was like 'where are the leaves,'" Marchetti says. "This is the biggest landscape I've seen with more recent mortality."

Sudden aspen decline is chronic now. For Worrall, sudden aspen decline made powerfully clear that the effect of climate change on forests would be erratic. "People expect that because climate changes gradually over time that maybe forest damage is going to increase very gradually over time," he says. But the trees are responding to periods of extreme events—a heat wave, a drought, a hot drought—not to incrementally rising average global temperature. Forest devastation, Worrall says, "is going to be episodic, huge waves of things happening and then going away for a while . . . and then there's going to be another wave . . . but some of those changes are going to be lasting."

The connection between drought and elevation that Worrall, Marchetti, and colleagues saw in their early work ultimately led to a series of maps that remain, in some circles, infamous. The maps were generated by bioclimate models. These computer programs combine topographic information, forest composition data, past climate information, and the best-case, no-change, worst-case predictions, or "scenarios," about carbon dioxide emissions and temperature from the IPCC, the Intergovernmental Panel on Climate Change. The first maps generated by the team—led by geneticist and ecologist Gerald Rehfeldt, who worked at the Forest Service's Moscow, Idaho, office—looked at aspen and Englemann spruce. The model did well: there was a lot of overlap between what it predicted and what was being seen on the ground.

Later research using the same approach evaluated the possible future habitat for over a dozen species in southwestern Colorado, in a fourteen-thousand-square-mile area that includes three national forests. The Gambel oak future looks good with lots of new ground, as is already occurring in Kebler Pass. In slide presentations, the Douglas fir map too has lots of light blue, the color the team chose to depict possible new habitat. But on most of the maps, fire-engine red predominates. White fir, whitebark pine, subalpine fir, Utah juniper, Rocky Mountain juniper, piñon, and blue spruce largely disappear. By 2060, lodgepole pine, limber pine, and bristlecone pine are projected to lose their entire suitable habitat—and that's the optimistic scenario, Worrall notes. The models predict the near total loss of many of the West's iconic trees.

There was pushback when the team first presented the maps, Marchetti and Worrall recall. Many researchers focused on the acknowledged uncertainties of such models. But some of the pushback was, they speculated, disbelief mixed with denial. "When we shared that with foresters and the Forest Service . . . it was just too much for people to imagine, too much doom and gloom," Worrall says. "You know if you tell people that in forty years the species that you're working on . . . it's mostly going to be dead, that's just too much for people to handle."

The aspen map shares plenty of blue with Gambel oaks. They gain ground by moving up slopes into cooler areas, into places from which conifers disappear, and into areas burnt by wildfires, of which there likely will be many, many more. At the moment, Marchetti says, she thinks there is more aspen growth than aspen loss in the region. Even with those gains, though, the aspen don't fare well in the long term. The Grand Mesa aspen are already on the ground as they are on the 2060 map: dead, forty years ahead of schedule.

Subsequent studies have echoed their findings. Throughout their North American range, adult aspen are dying and not being replaced by young. A 2021 assessment of the eight most common tree species in the West found that half had significantly declined in the last two decades. The loss of common species, like aspen, is often much more ecologically devastating than the loss of a rare species. The authors of the study used a word not often seen in scientific papers: "alarming." They noted that these observations offer a "stark warning" about the future of temperate forests everywhere. Around the same time the study appeared, huge tracts of juniper, one of the trees considered the most drought hearty of them all, began dying in Utah and Arizona.

The maps are coming to look like chronicles of deaths foretold. As Worrall says, "Those kind of doom and gloom projections are starting to look pretty realistic."

Wollemi

The first leaf in my mother's tree journal is a chestnut that she collected when she was seventeen in the Pound Ridge Reservation. The park was not far from where she grew up, a gardener's daughter on a rural estate. Somehow my clever mother had finagled access to, or had owned, a horse named Alta, whom she rode regularly and who was bunked at a nearby stable; it was on a foray with Alta that she collected the chestnut leaf. My mother was considered a hellion, a wild child who got into mischief, who drank vanilla extract for a buzz, who rode bareback, who rebelled. I loved her stories of riding through woods, occasionally at night, of being fearless, of branches whipping by.

When my kids were young—seven and four—their school offered a short children's book writing class and because the books of my childhood, and of my kids' childhoods, have so powerfully shaped the way I see the world, I signed up. I cannot remember how I decided to write about my mother's childhood tragedy, but it must have been there waiting.

The story I wrote was about disobedience and strength. A girl named Minerva sneaks out after dark to ride Midnight, an untamed horse from her family's stables that she is not allowed to ride. A storm comes up. Minerva loses her grip on the horse's mane, falls, and takes refuge under a luminous birch. Midnight returns to the stables. The noise of the storm or the returning horse wakes the girl's father, who comes to rescue her in the rain. He comforts Min, celebrates her fearlessness and independence, and gifts her Midnight.

When it is fiction, you can tell your story how you want, you can change the ending—as Amy Hest, the wonderful author who was teaching the class, kept telling us because the animating event of many of our drafts was trauma or loss. As it really happened, according to my mother, she wanted to ride her bicycle with a friend and her father asked her not to go. The bicycle and friend and the roads and the woods and the meadows had a strong pull that day. When she returned, she learned that her father, prone to profound undiagnosed untreated depression, had shot himself. What she remembered—and there is no one left to fact check this with but it doesn't matter, because it is what she remembered and what she carried with her and what makes my heart ache for her still—is that her mother told her that if she hadn't been so selfish, her father would not have taken his own life.

Being outside gave my mother solace. I still have a few of the pocket-sized Golden Nature Guides that she carried on frequent rambles with me and Eric: a guide to seashells, to butterflies and moths, to birds, to reptiles and amphibians. She helped us catch and examine insects and larvae in ponds, identify frogs and toads and butterflies, collect wildflowers. *Flowers: A Guide to Familiar American Wildflowers* is particularly lovely, with pages edged in color for the different hues of flower. In *Trees*—its cover bright orange with sugar maple leaves and samaras, or winged seeds—my mother underlined an exhortation to study the trees month by month. On another page she underlined an exhortation that she clearly answered: "There is much to learn about familiar trees that can be discovered only by close observation and detailed study. First, you get acquainted with trees. Then, as you begin to look closer, you begin to know the trees."

Climate change was well underway when my mother started her tree journal. But like many things we cannot outrun, its effects were not yet so explicit. Climate change is like a trauma that keeps gathering power and force because we won't look directly at it. In 1953, when my mother was writing her first entry and taping down the chestnut leaf, atmospheric carbon dioxide levels were 312 parts per million. They had been roughly 280 parts per million for ten thousand years and had begun increasing with the industrial age. By the time my mother made her last entry in 1964, a bigleaf maple from the Berkeley campus, atmospheric levels were about 320 parts per million—higher than they had been for eight hundred thousand years. They have continued to grow sharply, reaching over 420 parts per million in 2024.

There is nothing new under the sun, the adage goes, and that is certainly true about fluctuating levels of carbon dioxide. Concentrations of the gas have shifted a great deal and many times over the planet's 4.54 billion years. The early atmosphere was mostly methane, water vapor, and carbon dioxide. By five hundred million years ago—the furthest back such estimates can reasonably go—carbon dioxide may have oscillated around 4,000 parts per million. That atmospheric concentration was already likely much lower than it had been. By then, photosynthetic aquatic cyanobacteria and green algae had been busy for two billion years, drawing carbon out of the atmosphere and releasing oxygen, contributing to what is known as the Great Oxidation Event. They converted the atmosphere to roughly one-fifth oxygen, as it still is, and flipped life from largely anaerobic to largely aerobic—the earth's first mass extinction.

By 420 million years ago, carbon dioxide levels had fallen to an estimated 2,000 parts per million. Green algae had begun to come ashore and were proliferating. The algae must have formed what Nan Crystal Arens, a professor of geosciences at Hobart and William Smith Colleges, compares to desert rock crust. "This kind of gnarly looking black, dark brown, kind of flaky stuff . . . it is a microbial community that includes fungi and algae and bacteria," she says. But it was a very thin skin: "biomass wise, it is not taking control of the climate system." Tectonics were largely still in charge. (Rocks pull carbon dioxide out of the air in a process called weathering; rising mountain ranges and subducting continental plates of early earth captured a lot of carbon, and volcanoes spewed a lot out.)

The land-scouting algae didn't stay crustal. They likely came to resemble today's bryophytes—mosses, liverworts, and hornworts—running low and plush and soft across rocks and soil and other surfaces. These early plants lacked a circulatory or vascular system and reproduced via spores that we can see in the fossil record. They had no roots, only thread-like anchoring extensions. They lived symbiotically with fungal partners, as the overwhelming majority of plants do now: theirs is a fundamental, primordial association. From these early terrestrial adventurers emerged plants with vascular systems and then plants with roots.

From that point on, it becomes impossible to disentangle plants—and the massive forms they took once they had deep roots—from climate. That's when "land plants took control of the atmosphere," says Arens, no slight to the massive contributions of marine plants intended. The oldest fossil evidence of a forest, to date, was found in Cairo, New York, in the strata of an abandoned quarry: tangles of roots from 385-million-year-old *Archaeopteris* trees, which may have reached one hundred feet. As trees became bigger, they packed away more carbon in their bodies and in the soil. More carbon was pulled out of the air, more carbon was buried away as plants died. The period between 359 and 299 million years ago is called the Carboniferous for the coal stores built by dead plants. Atmospheric levels of carbon dioxide appear to have fallen to today's level of around 400 parts per million or below. Spore-producing plants were joined by seed-producing plants, including cycads, gingkoes, and early conifers.

Then, 250 million years ago in the Permian period, tectonics took charge again. Massive volcanic eruptions filled the atmosphere with toxic gases, carbon dioxide levels rebounded to an estimated 2,500 parts per million, and some 90 percent of species vanished. After the Great Dying, as the Permian extinction is known, the surviving conifers diversified and, ultimately, became today's pines, yews, cypresses, and araucarias. Part of the Mesozoic era, which followed the Permian and is informally known as the Age of Dinosaurs, could quite reasonably be called the Age of Conifers.

Plant blindness can be found everywhere. Plants are the foundation for animal life, but they don't even get their own column in the standard geologic timescale diagram, as Katherine J. Willis and Jennifer C. McElwain note in *The Evolution of Plants*. The authors reproduce an alternative chart, published in a 1988 article, "Plant evolution dances to a different beat," by paleobotanist Alfred Traverse. "In fact, *major* plant evolutionary breakthroughs seem generally to precede similar, perhaps to some degree dependent, vertebrate land animal events," Traverse noted. The major divisions, or eras, of the geological timescale are "zoic," based on animal extinction or evolution, but they should perhaps be "phytic," based on plants instead. Credit has not been given where credit is due. The creatures holding it all together, making it all possible, are wallflowers at a self-congratulatory zoic party.

The Age of Conifers managed to keep a secret until very recently. In 1994 a ranger came across a steep, damp, cool, hard-to-reach canyon in a national park in southeastern Australia and found trees that rose one hundred thirty feet and had remarkable bark, stippled with brown resinous orbs. The conifers had a primeval vibe. They were named *Wollemia nobelis* and although they are the only tree in their genus, they joined forty other trees in the Araucariaceae family. The Wollemi—not actually pines, but sometimes called pinosaurs—had been known to colonial science only as fossils from the Age of Conifers before they were happened upon, a tiny remnant population in a remote ravine.

Much more familiar is *Ginkgo biloba*, another tree for which only one member of a genus survived. "This tree should be as exciting as a crocodile on a big city street," my mother wrote in her journal, a tree "from the Age of Reptiles." She loved gingko for its fan-shaped leaves and for its ancient story. Gingkoes are also unusual, my mother remarked, in that their pollen develops into sperm with flagella that swim through tubes inside the seed to the egg. This feature was common to many early plants, like mosses and ferns, and is retained by them today; but among seed-producing plants, it remains only in cycads and gingkoes. My mother admired the tree's hardiness too: "Somehow gingko's peculiar leaves resist fumes and soot; somehow a tree evolved in a bygone age can take our ruthless cities, creating trunk, leaf, and fruit from miserable dirt below the scorching pavement."

Along with gingko and other gymnosperms—the cycads and the conifers—flowering plants were making their way too. Little is known about the first angiosperms, except that they may have emerged before 145 million years ago, likely in what

Arens and a colleague have described as "dark, damp, and disturbed" areas, in the shadows of conifers. They were weedy and nimble, able to endure disruptions like dinosaurs and fire. Over eons, they branched into three main groups: the magnoliids, which appear to be the oldest of the lineages, the monocots, like palms, which put up a single first leaf, and the eudicots, which generally put up two baby leaves and which comprise most of the deciduous trees we know.

Then cataclysm struck again. The Cretaceous-Paleogene mass extinction 66 million years ago closed the Age of Conifers, which had been on the wane as the angiosperms flourished and proliferated. What could be called (and why not?) the Age of Angiosperms began. In the millions of years since, botanical profusion evolved, with rainforests and mad biodiversity. Some researchers point to the Angiosperm Terrestrial Revolution as driving the diversification of insects, spiders, and fungi—which, alongside angiosperms, are the most diverse kinds of extant organisms. Angiosperms make up an estimated 90 percent of land plants today; as much as 50 percent of all living species are, or depend on, angiosperms. Us too. We evolved during, and live in, the Age of Angiosperms. Plants made the world for us. Then we began to unearth their ancestors, unleashing today's great dying.

Plants are clearly survivors. All the lineages alive today have been through periods of high carbon dioxide, low carbon dioxide, the relatively stable carbon dioxide of the geologically recent era. They have been through extremes of temperature driven by atmospheric changes, tectonics, and planetary cycles: hothouse periods with palms at the poles, freezing periods when many hunkered closer to the equator. "I wouldn't underestimate the resilience of these creatures," Arens says. "There have been moments of awfulness that are way worse than anything humans can do."

Much of their success comes from being migrants. Species travel to follow the conditions they like, to find their preferred habitat, to avoid the glaciers, as hemlock did. They make the same adaptive moves many creatures—fish, butterflies, birds, people—do to ensure their survival. They just do it, from our zoic perspective, slowly. "The problem is right now that humans have made it really hard for those species to migrate," Arens says. "I mean if you're a beech tree, how the heck are you going to get across urban sprawl. Unless you get lucky and somebody carries you." Those bordering the tundra have some room and that is why the treeline is creeping up latitudes; some species are creeping up elevations toward summits. Most trees, though, cannot keep pace or do not have space.

Having survived hundreds of millions of years, the Wollemi are being undone. Two lethal infections—both species of phytophthoras (also called water molds) that may have been introduced by illicit visitors—have killed several. They have been preyed upon by collectors. Weeds, erosion, compaction, pigs, and deer threaten them. They were nearly incinerated during the brutal Australian fires of 2019 and 2020 that laid waste to a large part of the national park. Firefighters descended on ropes from helicopters to spray the trees and the area around three small groves with fire retardants and water.

Wollemi leaves

Fires are not the only aspect of climate change threatening the last sixty or so adult Wollemi. Tim Brodribb and colleagues at the University of Tasmania study, among many things, plant hydrology and have installed on several Wollemi tiny cameras and sensors called dendrometers that can record minute movements of and in trunk, leaves, and roots. Before such instruments were developed in the last decade or so, researchers generally had to study trees' hydraulic systems by cutting a stem or branch and examining it. "It's kind of like a Hydraulic Heisenberg Uncertainty Principle," Brodribb says. "You can no longer really know what was the situation before you intervened." Another approach was to observe using X-rays. "But then every time you take an image, you're also bombarding your poor tree with a lethal dose."

The new devices—and there are many varieties—can be used in real time in the field and have proved to be a revelation. "I've always loved plants and trees, but I have never really thought of them as particularly dynamic . . . in a daily sense, a minute-by-minute sense," Brodribb says. His view has radically changed: "They are super dynamic and they are super responsive and they're also very sensitive." Pulses and rhythms have become visible. When a tree draws water from the soil, its leaves shrink, like when we suck in our cheeks. When the water arrives in the canopy, leaves swell. "It's a real eye opener when you realize that you're dealing with something that's pretty analogous to animal behavior," Brodribb says. "You get this beautiful little heartbeat of the plant through the day."

And through the night. New instruments have recorded at finer resolution how much growing and rehydrating trees do at night. Some of those observations have come from giant sequoias that Brodribb outfitted with cameras during a visit to California. They "need very high humidity at night to fully recover their water status," he says. "They hydrate really slowly overnight. And just before dawn, the tree equilibrates with the soil and is fully hydrated and ready for the next day." If the giant sequoia have not been able to get enough water at night, "the first moment the sun comes out in the morning, they go and dehydrate straight away."

Nights in many parts of the world are warming faster than days—on average, one and a half times faster. In the United States, summer nights have warmed an average of 2.5 degrees Fahrenheit since 1970—Reno, Nevada, is at the high end, with summer nights over 17 degrees hotter. Nighttime vapor pressure deficit is increasing as a result. The drier, hotter night air has been linked to changes in wildfire behavior. In the West, according to one study, "wildland fire managers have reported that fires are burning longer into the night and increasing in intensity earlier in the morning compared to when many started their careers. Increasing nighttime vapor pressure deficit—a measure of the *drying power* of air—is widely suspected to be responsible for these perceived changes in fire behavior."

Hotter nights affect crops as well. Research on rice and wheat show falling production and diminishing nutritional value. "Nighttime warming poses a threat to global food security as it is driving yield declines worldwide," one review noted. Brodribb, who studies crop plants as well as trees, says he has heard the same thing from corn breeders. "The determinant of corn performance is not the daytime temperatures," he says, "it's the nighttime temperature." The many creatures—trees and other plants, humans and other animals—reliant on a period of cooler dark to recover from heat stress, or to not lose more water, or to grow, are finding less such relief.

Every tree Brodribb and his colleagues have observed so far does not do well with warmer nights. He has visited the Wollemi—"They are the gentlest of the Araucarians, no spiny bits, just doing their best in their little canyon"—to see how they are faring. The Wollemi appear to be particularly sensitive, quite unable to rehydrate by dawn after a hot night. "In Wollemi, it is humongous," Brodribb says. "They can't cope with it at all."

Atlantic White Cedar

On an afternoon in early July 2021, a few months after the Hi-Rock workshop, I sit with Bear in the small, suburban home she is renting in central Massachusetts, drinking tea in the fading daylight, waiting for a fox. She is telling me about a phone app she has been working on with a few others at Eversource, the energy company where she works as an arborist. It would allow employees to see the carbon emissions associated with an action like driving to work and then to counter those emissions with, for example, consolidating all errands into one drive. "It's a mind-shift for folks," she says. "Little things that you can personally do today to change your footprint further down the road . . . People say, Oh! I'm just one person . . . if you've ever gone camping, you know one mosquito can certainly make a difference." She is worried about the app's future because she is planning to leave the company and move to Vermont to be with her partner, Jason Lavigne. She says she will miss seeing the app come to fruition, seeing her colleagues and many of the customers she has come to know well.

She recalls a couple in their eighties who refused to give Eversource permission to do tree work—in Massachusetts, homeowners must give such permission. For six years, Bear says, they refused. The hedgerow of hemlocks the company wanted to take down, it turned out, had been planted by the couple to celebrate their marriage; the three Norway spruce also identified for removal had been planted by their children one Arbor Day. The trees were in terrible shape, all infested by scale insects; the spruce looked like "Charlie Brown trees." Bear assured the couple that she didn't cut down healthy trees, but these were indeed all dying. She was able to spare one Norway spruce that, with treatment, stood a chance. These are conversations that Bear loves: talking with people about cherished trees, understanding the history, saving what she can.

The fox doesn't appear, but Bear knows it is there. "This morning, Jason and I were making breakfast and the fox came tromping through the backyard, went over by the woodpile, and had this big gray animal in its mouth. I grabbed my binos and looked out: it was a rabbit and the fox buried it," she says. "About twenty minutes later, fox comes back with something else in its mouth and it's a squirrel. It buries it over there. I thought to myself, isn't that magical! My whole entire life I have watched kits playing in stone walls and this and that. But I've never seen a mom or a dad hunting and preparing for the nest."

Suddenly, we see the fox silhouette—so familiar, so feral—against the gray sky on a low ridge next to a sugar maple. Then it runs back into the strip of forest that winds between many backyards. Bear's neighbor recently asked her why there was a black tupelo growing near his house. Bear explained that tupelos love water so there must have been a creek or stream running through there once and, because it is slow growing, that tree must be about two hundred years old. If her neighbor followed the path where the creek had run so long ago, she said, he would come upon a massive cottonwood that, like the tupelo, likes wet feet. "It's happy! It's totally nice and tall, it's beautiful, big, and ominous. It's so fantastic. When the wind blows it, the thing just shakes and discos."

After a childhood in the woods, Bear and Melissa can read landscapes for creatures, for soil types, for tree species and forest communities. And for water. So much time running along and in creeks, playing in small ponds, and exploring the Great Cedar Swamp made hydrology second nature to them. When the twins explored the Great Cedar Swamp, the wetland was home to dozens of species of amphibians, reptiles, and insects, including the rare Hessel's hairstreak, a butterfly that looks like lichen and bark taking wing. It was home or layover to some eighty bird species. Its plant life was equally brimming. Lilies, azaleas, holly, alder, dogwoods. And of course, Atlantic white cedar, *Chamaecyparis thyoides*, also known as Atlantic white cypress—a "graceful, symmetrical conifer," writes Aimlee Laderman, a botanist who worked with the Fish and Wildlife Service and who studied the cedar for seven decades.

The Great Cedar Swamp of the twins' youth covered three or so square miles. It was by then already a greatly altered wetland. In the 1700s and 1800s, the swamp had been repeatedly logged. Colonists had learned from the Indigenous peoples they displaced of the wood's rot-resistant, insect-resistant nature. The light-weight wood was cut for shingles, boats, fence posts, and, ironically, duck and other wetland bird decoys—felling trees to make lures for creatures who would need no lures if the wetland trees were left unfelled. A Swedish visitor to the colonies in the late 1740s, Peter Kalm, noted that "Swamps and Morasses formerly were full of them, but at present these trees are for the greatest part cut down, and no attempt has yet been made to plant new ones."

As fond as the colonists were of cedar timber, they were not fans of wetlands. They rarely saw them for what they are: refugia for thousands of plants and animals and fungi, sponges for storm surges, and nature's purification system for water that makes its way underground to replenish aquifers or wends through land to join other waterways. Many cedar swamps vanished as they were drained for development or agriculture.

At the turn of the last century, the Great Cedar Swamp was excavated for peat to burn as fuel. In the 1930s, cranberry bogs were set up. In the 1940s, a portion in the center was opened by road and used as a site to test guns and explosives. It then became a testing ground for the National Fireworks Company. In 1972, V. S. Hasiotis Incorporated bought it and leased it to a related company, Cumberland Farms of Connecticut. Over the next few years, Cumberland Farms drained and ditched over 650 acres for farmland, including cornfields. Those cornfields provided some of the most disorienting experiences in the sisters' memories.

"That was one of the few times we would get afraid," Melissa says of getting lost and panicked among the corn stalks. "They were so tall you could not see the horizon."

"That scared me," Bear says. "In the forest you go from forest type to forest type . . . so you're like, okay, I know kind of where I am because I know where this creek goes. I know where the swamp is, I know where this is. . . . But with the cornfield, you didn't know."

"It was just one gigantic monoculture," says Melissa.

"It was creepy."

It was also, it turned out, illegal. In the mid 1980s, the Army Corps of Engineers sued Cumberland Farms for violating the Clean Water Act by destroying an ecologically precious wetland. The court did not favor biological hyperbole: ". . . the Great Cedar Swamp is not a critical nesting area for the Peregrine Falcon inasmuch as they have been successfully induced to nest on the roof of this very courthouse in Boston where they live by feeding on the abundant pigeon population which they catch in and above the city streets." But it easily found the company guilty.

Today, the Great Cedar Swamp is no more. There remains only an altered slice of it. Many cornfields are gone too. They were taken out of production years ago. Some became meadows. A dozen or so birds considered by the state government and the Massachusetts Audubon Society to be of conservation concern took up residence in those grasslands—bobwhite, kestrel, meadowlark, bobolink, and woodcock—as did other creatures. Those meadows were, in turn, scheduled for auction. Wetland forest became cornfields. Cornfields became meadows. Meadows seemingly destined to become houses, the terminal crop.

Dark rain-drenched boards run through the forest, sinking in mud as we step on them. The path we follow passes mosses, thickets, shrubs, and carved signs identifying larch, goldthread, sundew, cranberry, and other plants. Following the boardwalk is difficult in places where the wood is disintegrating, water-logged, slippery. In some sections, the boards have faded away entirely. "The walkway is all hemlock, which is not rot-resistant," Bill Gould says. Bill and his wife, Sherry, are leading me though Bradford Bog, an Atlantic white cedar swamp in New Hampshire. Every year the town of Bradford "has to bring in like forty pieces of this board," Bill says, pointing at the hemlock. "And I am thinking, why don't you use your own cedar and see how that works?"

Before we set off into the bog, we had stopped up the road to visit Nebizonbi, a medicinal waters site important to the

Abenaki, and thus to Bill and Sherry, who are members of the Nulhegan Band of the Coosuk Abenaki Nation. Sherry, a state representative and a founder of the Abenaki Trails Project, has been working to build a visitor center there so people can visit the culturally and ecologically significant site. But the initial plan for the center has been greatly scaled back in scope, Sherry explains, in part because the remote community likes its privacy. Farther back along the road is the estate where Jeffrey Epstein's companion, Ghislaine Maxwell, managed to hide from federal agents for a year.

The dirt and gravel road has been built up over the decades and is several feet higher than it was when Bill was young and spent time in this forest with his family. Some 1.27 million miles, or 30 percent, of public roads in the United States resemble this one in that they are unpaved, winding through rural areas. The rapidly growing field of road ecology, described in Ben Gold-farb's *Crossings: How Road Ecology Is Shaping the Future of Our Planet*, catalogues the staggering effects of roads; impacts that include altering local climate, killing millions of creatures, dis-rupting and jeopardizing ancient cycles of migration and repro-duction, and introducing invasive plant seeds and pollutants.

The raising of East Washington Road next to Bradford Bog has likely significantly modified water flow, severing streams and habitat, and may be one of the reasons this 70-acre Atlantic white cedar forest is not thriving. Atlantic white cedar need lots of fresh water, but not too much: they grow on mounds so that in the wetter parts of the year they are high enough not to be submerged. Any hydrological disturbance can be devastating. Bill has noticed other impacts too. "When the road dries, the dust it creates is incredible. That all gets sent out into the bog."

A few years ago, Bill retired from the lumber business, in which he worked as a logger and in sawmills, and he decided to do something he had long wanted to but had not had time for. "Because I have Abenaki culture and have always been from this area, I have always had a fascination with birch bark canoes . . . and another important material used in birch bark canoes is Atlantic white cedar." He got permission from Cedar Brook Farm, part owner of Bradford Bog, to harvest some trees. As he sought out and then felled a tall, straight cedar, he noticed that there was very little regeneration, almost no young cedar, and that red maple and white spruce were filling in.

Bill is seeing changes in all the forests he knows well, including those around his home. Beech are mostly gone. Blue spruce are dying. Eastern white pine are exceptionally laden with cones, which can sometimes mean that they "know they are sick and on their way out," he says, adding that the pines have been doing poorly for a while. This decline has been widely documented. In the last century, average annual rainfall in the Northeast has risen over five inches; the number of heavy rains has increased more than 70 percent, the highest increase in the nation. "All the rain we are getting," says Bill, "sometimes I think we are living in Oregon." Saturated soil can kill fine roots, injuring the root system. The damp has also encouraged the proliferation of pine-associated fungi that relish moisture. These fungi didn't used to take out white pines to such an extent, but climate change seems good for them; their populations are exploding.

A similar shift is being seen elsewhere. Over the last decade or so, more than 90 percent of the dying trees Matteo Garbelotto, a plant pathologist at the University of California Berkeley, has diagnosed are succumbing to fungi that are part of their natural microbiome. Familiar nonlethal fungi flip into aggressive pathogens. Garbelotto calls it the Dr. Jekyll and Mr. Hyde effect: "Until climate change, this was a phenomenon that would occur on a very small number of trees at a time."

Bill, Sherry, and I walk through the cedar forest, staying as best we can on the boards, trying not to trample any plants.

Atlantic White
Cedar cones

It is quiet; the damp and moss absorb sound. The trees are widely spaced and the cedar stand out, their gray bark long and shaggy, unlike that of their neighbors. They have strong presence. Every now and then, I catch a hint of their warm round tangy fragrance. We make our way to a viewing platform where we can see two peaks across a young forest where spruce are thriving. We turn back and leave the boardwalk to search for regeneration. "You're not seeing any regrowth, right? You know what I mean?" Bill asks as he hunts around.

Finally, we come to some patches where there are fewer trees, more light. "Oh look at them all," Bill says. Atlantic white cedar seedlings, close to the ground, their distinctive thick flat needles fanning out, lush and of a more muted green than the plants around them.

Our visit to Bradford Bog comes a few months into a collaboration that Bill and Sherry hope might mean a new phase, and better future, for the forest. They are working with Heidi Asbjornsen, an ecosystem ecologist at the University of New Hampshire, her colleagues, and the owners of the bog, among others, to understand cedar ecology and regeneration. The team is assessing the forest for species diversity and age range, taking tree ring cores to see how past drought and rain shaped growth, and collecting data on regeneration. Bradford Bog "is a very special place," Bill says. "To help it would be wonderful."

To Bill, harvesting some cedar trees is key to keeping the forest healthy because it creates gaps for sunlight to reach seedlings. And because cedar need disturbance, which likely arrived historically as fire, windthrow, hurricane, and as selective logging over thousands of years. In places where cedar trees appear to have been cut in the 1950s, Bill sees regeneration; in places where the forest has not been touched, he sees none. "Conservation says just leave it alone. Well, to me that ship has already sailed. We have put roads through, diverted water flows, we have done all sorts of things. . . . Now you've got climate change on top of it," he says. "Why not mitigate some of the damage we have already created?" He would like to see more integration of traditional practices with forest management. "Why is it culturally taboo to manage something for cultural purposes?" he asks. "We were caretakers for twelve thousand years. Colonials have been managing for four hundred years. Those four hundred years have been a nightmare."

The colonials arrived on a continent inhabited by hundreds of sovereign Nations and where more than three hundred languages were spoken. The land was, in many places and in various ways, stewarded. In the Northeast, some Indigenous tribes burned areas to sustain cropland and savannah and to encourage nut-producing fire-adapted trees. Newcomers were generally blind to this and other management—for cultural, economic, and political reasons. The idea of untouched land, the "pristine myth," as it has been called, has proven powerfully intractable and, for the post-colonial systems we live within, expedient. The "'virgin wilderness' narrative has been used around the world to deny Indigenous people rights to their lands," Emma Marris writes in *Wild Souls: What We Owe Animals in a Changing World.*

" 'Wilderness' thus isn't just a romantic ideal; it is also a colonial power play." Ongoing debates about the extent and character of Indigenous management reflect, at their extremes, two worldviews: humans are part of nature or are outside nature. These stances prescribe two opposite strategies: steward or don't touch. For now, don't touch predominates.

For Bill, there is no debate, and especially in the case of Bradford Bog. He says the fervent hands-off, let-nature-take-her-course approach that governs many management decisions is not feasible in most places. And, he suggests, it is driven by underlying colonial guilt: "We continue to destroy things. If we touch it, we ruin it. So let's just not touch it." But, Bill says, "maybe we can do it in a good way and use common sense."

Collaborations incorporating long-standing ecological and cultural knowledge into forest management remain relatively rare. That is beginning to change, says Michael Dockry of the University of Minnesota, a member of the Citizen Potawatomi Nation who worked with the Forest Service for many years. He points to recent examples all over the country. Fire management approaches shifting in the West with the guidance of experts from the Confederated Salish and Kootenai Tribes, from the Yurok, Karuk, and others. Twenty-eight thousand acres of forest returned to the Bois Forte Band of Chippewa for management. New joint stewardship plans implemented with the Leech Lake Band of Ojibwe in Minnesota and with the Eastern Band of Cherokee in the Nantahala and Pisgah national forests. Harvesting rights for ochan, the green headed coneflower, restored to the Eastern Band of Cherokee in Great Smoky Mountains National Park.

"Our Tribal communities have so much to offer and people from broader society are starting to recognize that," says Dockry, who prefers the phrase Indigenous science to the more commonly used phrases traditional knowledge and traditional ecological knowledge. "Tribes are managing their own lands in ways that have promoted biodiversity, promoted ecosystems, promoted sensitive species . . . which means these ecosystems are more resilient to things like climate change." Studies have shown that some of the greatest biodiversity the world over is found on lands tended to and protected by Indigenous peoples.

In Dockry's view, collaborative forestry offers the only healthy future for forests. That means, he says, "learning how to listen to each other. We're learning how to express our ideas or our needs. We're learning how to deal with past harm. We're learning how to build our own relationships as humans together for a more sustainable ecosystem and more sustainable natural resources." And it means stewardship. "Trees grow if you manage them in the right way. The forest will be regenerating and growing and becoming more healthy. And where do we see that? We look to our Native communities. Menominee in Wisconsin is where sustainable forestry started."

The Menominee Nation manages some 217,000 acres of forest—about 2 percent of the tribe's original land—and has done so for hundreds of years. The tribe notably withstood the 1887 Dawes Act by which the federal government broke tribal land holdings and communities apart, opening reservations, as was the law's intention, to parcellation and, ultimately, to purchase by nontribal members. The Menominee kept their forest collective and established a lucrative timber business. Although they survived allotment, their financial success attracted the attention of the federal government, which, in 1954, stopped legally recognizing their sovereignty. Over one hundred Nations lost federal recognition and their independence between the mid 1950s and 1960s. Over three million acres of land were seized and sold. The economic prosperity and independence that had funded education, health care, and infrastructure for the Menominee was destroyed.

The tribe was restored in 1973 and that year created Menominee Tribal Enterprises to manage the forest. The company uses sustainable silviculture, guided by the underlying ecology of the forest. One such approach is called shelterwood. Half or so of the mature trees are cut in an area, allowing seedlings light and space. Once the young trees are growing well, the remaining mature trees are logged. The approach is attributed to Chief Oshkosh: "Start with the rising sun and work toward the setting sun, but take only the mature trees, the sick trees, and the trees that have fallen. When you reach the end of the reservation, turn and cut from the setting sun to the rising sun and the trees will last forever." Although it suffers from pests, pathogens, and climate change impacts, the Menominee forest remains one of the most biodiverse and resilient wooded areas in Wisconsin.

After Bill finds the Atlantic white cedar saplings, we return to the walkway and head back toward the road, passing the plant identification signs again. Sherry mentions that many Abenaki neighbors have been surprised to learn that cranberry plants grow naturally here; she knows about wild cranberries because her mother collected them. She says that piecing together Abenaki culture and history is like reassembling a puzzle that has been thrown into the sky. Some pieces are lost forever. But every family, every person holds a different part of the interconnected whole. "It is never going to become a complete picture," Sherry says, but we "just keep trying to bring it all together."

Atlantic white cedar swamps are among the rarest forest ecosystems remaining in the United States, and among the most threatened ecosystems on the Eastern Seaboard and along the Gulf of Mexico. Never extensive when compared to some other forest types, cedar swamp forests originally covered eight hundred square miles or so, growing within one hundred twenty-five miles of the ocean in a thin band of land from Florida to Maine, and along the Gulf Coast as far as Louisiana. The famous Great Dismal Swamp of Virginia and North Carolina is an Atlantic white cedar forest. Today, there are fewer than one hundred eighty square miles.

Those closest to the shore are dying fastest. Sea-level rise and storms that push ocean water inland have led to miles of bleached Atlantic white cedar—perhaps the closest thing the East has had in the last two decades to the landscape-scale forest death seen in the West. "They are very sensitive to salt water," says Jessie Pearl, a geoscientist with the Nature Conservancy who has visited nearly every Atlantic white cedar swamp in the Northeast. "I feel like they should be better with salt water being so close to the ocean, but they're very sensitive to it." Many other trees, notably black tupelo, are dying alongside Atlantic white cedar, but unlike those trees, which can be found in other habitats, the cedar are losing what remains of their already narrow home range. By the end of this century, Atlantic white cedar coastal forests—indeed forest wetlands across the North American Coast Plain—may not exist.

While Bear and I had been chatting in her kitchen about changes in the land, New York City residents were wandering among Atlantic white cedar in downtown Manhattan. In Madison Square Park, artist Maya Lin arranged forty-nine cedar, each 40-feet tall, in her installation, *Ghost Forest*. The cedar had been cut as part of a restoration effort in a salt-water damaged section of the New Jersey Pine Barrens, where some of the most extensive Atlantic white cedar death has been observed so far. Lin's intention was that visitors would watch the trees fade and gray away as they stood in the small park. A shuddering glimpse of a landscape hard to imagine in a cityscape.

Pearl had set off in search of the remaining Atlantic white cedar forests because of Hurricane Sandy. When the superstorm hit in 2012, one of her professors mentioned that the East Coast had experienced a mammoth hurricane in 1938, but that few people remembered it, and that the destruction had clearly not informed subsequent city planning or development. Pearl started thinking about the ways paleoclimate records might help people respond to the climate crisis, particularly in New England where the weather is so variable. "The mean temperature increases of the region were slowly creeping up, and it did beg the question: well, over the past one hundred, two hundred, three hundred years, what has temperature been doing? Is this within the normal envelope of reason or is this outside of what our ecosystems and our landscapes have felt?" She wondered if a key chapter of the regional climate story might be missing because "all of the paleoclimate records prior were based on inland trees," she says, even though "our cities are along the coast and we have such a coastal-driven climate system."

For five years, Pearl traveled between New Jersey and Maine, following all leads, contemporary and historical. "If someone in 1825 was like, 'I saw a cedar swamp,' I went there myself," Pearl says. She met with members of the Mashpee Wampanoag Tribe, who care for an Atlantic white cedar forest on the southwest coast of Cape Cod and who told her about an ancient cedar forest now under the ocean. She located one swamp through an oral history—a site called Quamquissett, which she learned means Pond of Little Pines in Nipmuc. She visited cedar forests with eighty-foot trees, thick ferns, and mounds of mosses; cedar forests with small twisty trees, "like a Dr. Seuss book"; boggy ones she squelched through; ones near pitch pine woods and sandy soil. "There is a huge variety," says Pearl, whose Twitter handle @swampmonstah, was devised during this time.

In all, Pearl visited well over forty swamps. She visited the Great Cedar Swamp near Bear and Melissa's childhood home—marked in her notebook, she thinks, as VCD for "very cold day"—but she did not take cores, because the trees were too young. Bradford Bog's trees were too young as well. In some places, she visited soft mired areas at low tide to take cross-sections of intact wood in submerged forests. "I would army crawl across mudflats and I would dig them out and I would chainsaw them and I would throw them to some brave soul who was accompanying me, who would wrap it up. We would do that until the water started creeping in." Pearl found subfossilized trees that had lived for five hundred or so years, but no modern counterparts: "the oldest living tree I found was barely three hundred." She had two thousand samples by the time she was done and a tree-ring record going back two thousand five hundred years.

Pearl recalls Edward Cook warning her at the outset that coastal trees might not have a strong enough climate signal. Cook became her strongest supporter in time, she says, and their scientific stories are strikingly similar. Atlantic white cedar are like the Eastern hemlock in that they fill in a gap in the regional paleoclimate record. The coast must be understood as its own thing, the cedar say. "It has a completely different climate and has different types of phenomena. It's got hurricanes. It's got maritime storms. We've got different aspects of nor'easters," Pearl says. "These trees felt the influence of the sea."

That sea is warming rapidly. Globally, the oceans have absorbed over 90 percent of the excess heat humans generate by burning fossil fuels and felling forests. Since 1900, average sea-surface temperatures have risen about 1.5 degrees Fahrenheit the world over, with some parts of the ocean warming faster than others. The Atlantic off the coast of New England is one of them. Sea-surface temperatures there have risen twice as fast as the global average.

Warming ocean water—of which there is much more because of melting land ice—expands, contributing to sea-level rise. Over the last century, as shown by tide gauges and satellites, sea level has risen about nine inches along the Northeast coast and its pace has accelerated at a rate greater than along many other coastlines. The rate is exacerbated in areas by subsidence: some places, like Delaware, are sinking, whereas others, like Maine, are rising as the land continues to re-equilibrate after the loss of the weighty ice sheets. Certain regions are also sinking because people have sapped groundwater and soil is collapsing into depleted aquifers—depleted, in part, because wetlands, including Atlantic white cedar swamps, have been destroyed. There is no thread to pull on that isn't spliced to every other.

The Atlantic white cedar suggested to Pearl and her collaborators that sea-surface temperature and drought were linked. Their rings showed that Northeastern drought historically occurred when sea-surface water was cooler. "With changing sea-surface temperatures and climate, does that mean we are no longer as susceptible to those types of droughts? Or does that completely shift the new type of drought that's coming?" Pearl thinks it is likely the latter: "In the past fifty years or so, we've seen this uptick in extreme precipitation events in New England, but we've also seen this uptick in extreme drought events."

The cedar turned out to be one of the most temperature-sensitive trees in the Northeast. They show the cooling trend of the last several millennia as the planet spun toward what would have been the next ice age: glacial periods occur every one hundred thousand years or so as a result of regular changes in the earth's orbit around the sun and the tilt of its axis. The cedar note the cooling slowing in the 1700s, about the time Peter Kalm, the Swedish visitor to the Atlantic white cedar swamps, mused about the impact of colonial deforestation. The cedar capture the warming as it grows in speed and scale—a regional pixel in a planet-wide shift in which new human land use and then fossil fuel use cancel the earth's scheduled ice age.

The cedar show New England's rapidly warming winters—warmed by the warming Atlantic. The increasingly violent extremes of weather, the upticks of deluge and drought, are being accompanied by a fading. Like dementia progressing. The region's sharply defined seasons are blurring at the edges, losing their color, losing their character.

Ash

Soon after my visit with the fox and Bear, I meet the sisters in the parking lot of the Big Y in Lee, Massachusetts. They pull up, one in a car (plug-in electric hybrid), one in a big white van that belongs to a carpenter friend of theirs. It is outfitted with a hammock strung between back and front and loaded with gear bags, plastic bins of foot ascenders, gloves, glasses, friction savers, ropes, and a cooler of fresh food. I have brought bagels, a road atlas and gazetteer, and the audio version of the book it turns out all three of us are reading, *Braiding Sweetgrass*. Melissa and I have a three-day trip ahead, driving cross country to the University of Northern Colorado in Greeley for a workshop organized by the Western chapter of the International Society of Arboriculture. Bear will fly out in a few days.

Although we make our way through the bagels and empty the cooler, we never get to our audiobook. Careening along in a closed world allows for a particular intimacy and openness, for discussions of life, love, family, work, and if you are careening along with an arborist, trees. We talk about the trees we see in fields, forests, and picnic spots along the route—including the bleached boles and branches of an enormous number of dead ash. We talk about institutions blind to the individuals who compose them, about leaders so far removed from their roots that they can't remember them. We talk about jobs. The small arborist family-run company Melissa worked for, Shelter Tree, had been bought by a big national company that was diversifying into arborist supply gear, and Melissa had been absorbed too. The radical change in culture and workload is stressful. (Bear is worried about her sister's health. "It is not the stock market . . . you are selling lawn and garden and tree-care equipment! What the hell!") We talk a lot about food. I learn from Melissa that the best way to find a good restaurant when you are new to a town is to ask at a hair salon, a strategy that leads us to an excellent Thai place in Iowa City. (If you want the best sandwiches, she says, ask at a garage.)

Melissa tells me about Sky Farm, fifteen acres on the top of a hill that she is planting with her husband, her sister-in-law, and her mother-in-law Dorothy, nickname Besta. Each week, at Besta's instigation, they have a family meeting to talk about planning for climate change. Besta lives on the farm in a small house she designed to withstand hurricanes and tornados, a small wooden house with a sloping roof, with sides that flange down low, a house that catches the wind to cool the inside. The extended family is planting herbs, potatoes, garlic and other food plants, and dozens of trees for shade, for fruit, for resilience: ginkgo, Chinese elm, oak, maple, hornbeam. I am thrilled to hear about hornbeam, a tree I am learning about and am falling a little in love with. *Carpinus caroliniana* is a medium-sized hardy understory tree, not hugely common, with a sinewy trunk often described as fluted. Its common names bespeak strength: ironwood, musclewood. It can hang out indefinitely in the shade of larger trees, waiting for disruption and then it shoots up.

We talk about chainsaws—well, Melissa talks about chainsaws. She owns sixteen or so. "I have a chainsaw problem." ("She *really* has a problem," her husband Tom Ingersoll says. "We are seeking professional help." One of her most recent acquisitions was a Christmas present from Tom: a tiny chainsaw nicknamed Baby Shark.) She, Bear, and Tom have been teaching chainsaw classes; there is lots of demand, both to learn basic skills and safety and to learn how to care for the machine. There are around thirty-six thousand chainsaw accidents a year today, according to the Centers for Disease Control and Prevention, up from an average of twenty-eight thousand as recently as 2019. The rate seems to have been rising since Covid, the twins say, perhaps because the need for certified arborists exceeds supply in many places and therefore more homeowners are trying to do their own work, because lighter and quieter, chargeable chainsaws can give people a false sense of security, and because many people do not use vital personal protective gear.

Melissa talks about her love of cars, of tinkering with them, and of racing, something she got into through her brother. She and Bear share a love of gear, a love of knowing how to fix things, an admiration for the mechanical that opens various freedoms: freedom to take care of land, freedom of the road, freedom in trees. And she talks about how she once made this very same drive across country with a friend, years ago, in a robin-egg-blue VW Rabbit that had five-point harnesses, a racing cage, and no air conditioning because Melissa had removed it to lighten the car for speed. "We'd change up suspension and we would add in sway bars and we would add in bigger cams and we would add in exhaust systems and change out interiors and change wheels and add in roll cages. I just found it fascinating." The Sports Car Club of America racing events she describes share something with the tree-climbing competitions: precision, attention to detail, to rules, to efficiency.

We are talking about the blue VW on the last evening, as we approach Greeley. Conversation stills for a while. Melissa and I pass cattle-holding pens so long they seem infinite. Hundreds of thousands of cows standing in dirt, kicking up dust. We later share that we both had been feeling a sense of overwhelm and doom about the scale of environmental alteration. In Greeley, the smell of manure from the cattle pens mixes with the smoke of forest fires and becomes a kind of white noise background for the workshop. That summer of 2021, some nine million acres burned in the United States and in Canada; more than three hundred fires had ignited in Colorado by July, when we were there, and, later that year, the Marshall Fire near Boulder City became one of the state's most damaging. Haze from California fires reached the East Coast. Major fires burned in Patagonia, in Greece, France, and Italy, in South Africa, in Australia, in Algeria, in India.

The workshop is held in the fantastical landscape of a verdant university campus in the middle of a high dry desert during a megadrought. There are three thousand four hundred or so trees on the campus, which also serves as an arboretum: at least seventy different species, and four current and former state champion trees, including an Amur cork tree, a Kentucky coffee tree, a silver maple, and a pecan. Wherever the workshop is held, local arborists volunteer to help set up. Some are friends, some are workshop alums, some are colleagues or tree-climbing competition buddies. Some have never met Melissa or Bear or the other instructors but have heard about them through the arboreal network. What should a group of arborists be called? A grove of arborists? Perhaps a groove of arborists. No sooner do they assemble, jokes, puns, and repartee begin. Some favorite lines from such gatherings:

"Are you the new branch manager?"

"You always cease to amaze me."

"When's the best time to plant a tree? Twenty years ago. Second best answer: now."

The team scouts for trees near an open-air theater that becomes the hub of the workshop. There are some stunning ash trees that would be ideal, but they are risky because of the spread of emerald ash borer, what one expert described as "the most destructive and costly invasive forest insect in North America." The beetle—tiny, about a half an inch long, and shiny green—was first detected in Michigan and Ontario in 2002. It comes from Asia where indigenous ash species, unless stressed, can withstand its predations. Unlike the longhorned beetle, which flies short distances, the emerald ash borer is, Melissa notes, "a precocious flier," as its rapid expansion makes clear. It has been detected in thirty states, including Oregon. Some of the most far-ranging beetles were probably transported in logs and firewood. The Forest Service has ended the eighteen-year quarantine against moving dead ash, in whatever form, in part because the ban proved so ineffective.

The speed with which the beetle can kill is staggering. A seemingly healthy tree can be here one year, dead the next. More than one hundred million ash have died so far and observers anticipate that ash may become extinct in North America. The International Union for Conservation of Nature has listed five of the sixteen native ash species as critically endangered—including white, black, and green ash. The devastation is not only happening far away in forests that few frequent; it can be seen in cities and suburban areas, where shaded streets are suddenly sunny, hot corridors. When 90 percent of the elm trees died or were preemptively removed because of Dutch elm disease in the 1970s, Minneapolis and St. Paul, like many other cities, planted ash monocultures instead. Since the borer has appeared, some sixty thousand municipal trees have been cut or identified for removal in the Twin Cities. Ten thousand in St. Louis. Nine thousand in Omaha. Close to six thousand in Cedar Rapids. By midcentury, American cities may be mostly empty of ash—although some trees surely will be prioritized and chemically treated, as is true for most still-standing urban elms.

If you watch an arborist attend to a big tree, like a fifty-year-old ash, you can understand why city parks departments cannot—given traditional budgets and workforces—take care of tens of thousands of individual trees. One winter day, I had the chance to observe Bear and a team of arborists take care of a single ash. The towering tree stood alone at the edge of a field, downslope from a house. The ground was white with snow, the sky pale with the promise of more. "Ash trees have this wonderful structure, and you can tell an ash tree from a mile away," Bear said as she readied to climb, "whereas with other trees, you are like, hmm, I need to get closer." Bear and her partner arborist soon looked tiny, high in the vast tree, almost invisible even though there were no leaves and the outlines of the dark branches were sharp against the gray sky. The wind was blowing hard and the limbs swayed; the climbers were buffeted and chilled for hours. It was too dangerous to reach some of the branches that the borer had killed. Those limbs stood out even to the naive eye: they were stark, uncomplicated, simple. The still-healthy limbs were full, intricate, with lots of little twigs and branches. It took seven hours to throw lines in, climb, remove dead and damaged limbs, drag brush, and chip it. Seven hours of highly skilled, treacherous work by two small people in one giant tree.

A few years earlier, Bear's brother-in-law Tom and his crew had treated the ash with a natural pesticide that can be an alternative to neonicotinoids, the broad-spectrum insecticides that can kill not only emerald ash borer but pollinators and other insects. They treated the tree soon after a big storm blasted dead branches into the house, smashing solar panels and windows and revealing the presence of the emerald ash borer. The owners wanted to save the great ash and, fortunately for the tree and their neighbors, they had the financial means and foresight to do so. Taking out dead wood and chipping it so any larvae or surviving beetles are killed, reducing the population that might attack the intact parts of the tree, can cost several thousand dollars a visit. The owners also had been wise to schedule a follow-up pruning months in advance. In western Massachusetts, as is true many places, the wait list for certified arborists can be long. "This area is getting hammered by EAB right now, so the pressure is very high," Bear said. "When people don't remove their trees that are infested, it just creates more of a sink, more of a breeding ground. You can truly get hundreds of thousands if not billions of multiplications."

Emerald ash borer has not arrived in Greeley, but arborists there have been removing some trees to protect others. More than one hundred fifty of nearly four hundred campus ash have been cut and chipped since 2019 to keep the possible sinks to a minimum and to focus on and treat the biggest, healthiest trees, those that may have the best chance of weathering an infestation. Arborists everywhere are increasingly careful about climbing ash. "This isn't your grandpa's tree that he used to climb with bare hands," says Patrick O'Meara of High Country Landscape, based outside Denver. "Trees that have been fully affected by emerald ash borer have a consistency that is not unlike Styrofoam. That's why you have had deaths of climbers in the Midwest and those affected areas."

The Women's Tree Climbing Workshop crew passes on the ash and identifies a Norway maple, a Ponderosa pine, a Kentucky coffee tree, and two bur oaks. The pine is tall and pole-linear with ladder branches, good for ascension training. The oaks are wide and complex with long, thick branches that arch out. One was planted in 1934 and, from a distance, it looks understandable: it has a full round crown, it looks like a classic tree. But the tree is magic origami. So many secrets and hidden dimensions; it would not be possible to get to know it all. O'Meara, who is volunteering for setup with three colleagues, installs a rope that the workshop participants might use to swing from one of the oak's big branches to another. "I get to be a fifty-one-year-old boy every time I do this," he says.

Five months earlier, O'Meara was climbing recreationally with friends in a large cottonwood in Denver's downtown City Park. He had finally recuperated from two knee replacements and was thrilled to be back walking and dancing in trees. As light faded into evening, the climbers readied to descend. There was snow in the tree and it was cold, O'Meara recalls, and his muscles were not fully recovered. He did a maneuver he wasn't yet ready for and his gear failed. He fell forty feet, breaking both legs and his left arm, wrenching his right foot out of its socket, damaging his chest. "The people that I was with, I compete against them in aerial rescue, and it was phenomenal to hear some of the same things that I've heard in training come out of their mouths. I mean it was exactly how we had trained." One person took charge. Called 911. Told someone to go to the road to flag down the paramedics. Told another person to go to the parking lot and bring the paramedics to the tree. Told another person to stabilize O'Meara. "Then he turned to me, and he goes, 'and Patrick, I need you not to fucking move.'" To hear such calm and to know help was coming, "just instantly changes your mindset."

O'Meara, though, did not obey orders. He had a new $500 harness and he knew it would be cut off. So he struggled out of it. He had new $400 mountaineering boots, which he credits with saving his life. In the ambulance, "they made the mistake of leaving me alone for a sec . . . and I was able to get my boots off." He also removed a treasured tree-climbing competition T-shirt before "the guy came in and threatened me and said, 'I will put you in restraints so that you stop doing that!'" O'Meara is forthright about his accident—sometimes presenting about it at meetings—so that others might learn from it. "I was the right person to have that happen to," he says. "I'm stable, I'm married. I've got kids. I've got a support system. I've got good insurance."

His first climb after the accident was in a spruce. "A super easy climb . . . I got up there and everything felt good . . . I was happy, upset, crying . . . I am doing what I want to do . . . the universe has allowed me to be back up in this tree," he says. "And I've been in hundreds of trees since."

By Friday midday, the climbing trees are pruned, trimmed with ribbons and bells, and the ropes hang like colorful lianas in a tropical forest. Arborists' ropes carry delicious names like blaze, tango, gecko, ocean, sunburst, cherry bomb, banshee, lava, dragonfly, blue streak. Perhaps someday a golden-hued one will be called Wonder Woman. Bear says new rope models come out as often as cell phones do. "While some can be used for several purposes, some can only be used for a particular purpose," Roxy Seibel explains to the participants. Roxy has been with the workshop since 2012, twice as a participant and then as a frequent instructor. Unlike many women who seek out the workshop, she had great teachers. "I was taught by some climbers who were really on the leading edge for stationary rope technique . . . finesse kind of climbers," she says. "I had a different story than a lot of people . . . I learned with all good habits and all the safety protocols and the pride of work." One of Roxy's teachers was Tom Dunlap, credited with bringing the stationary rope system from caving to arboriculture. In this popular system,

Spruce

known as SRS, climbers ascend a single, unmoving line. Melissa and Bear want participants to learn the moving rope system, even if they have SRS experience, because moving rope can be a revelation, says Bear: "their mind just blows up because you can maneuver around the tree a lot faster."

Arborists have borrowed from caving, from the nautical world, and from rock climbing. They have tailored equipment, knots, and techniques to tree work. Knots often have several names, reflecting their different lives: a fisherman's can be a true lover's, a double fishermen's a grapevine. Rock climbers also use harnesses, but they are smaller, what Roxy describes as "a thong on steroids."

No one who entrusts their life to rope takes rope for granted and many can give detailed lessons on rope history. Some of the earliest ropes were vines and lianas—including those dangling from canopies—and woven bark. Humans have been enormously creative creating ropes: animal hair, insect silk, reeds, sisal, hemp, cotton, flax—all have been woven and braided together. Joining is at the heart of rope making: the etymological root of twine is twin, double thread, two strands. The modern era of rope making opened in 1938 with the invention of nylon. Over time, as nylon became cheaper, manufacturers created more complex ropes, ropes woven and braided around other ropes, ropes that were more static, less elastic, waterproof, less easily degraded. New materials joined nylon: polypropylene, polyethylene, polyester, Kevlar.

Roxy runs through some of the properties of the ropes that the workshop is using this weekend. There's a sixteen-strand in which the braid surrounds a solid inner core and that can take 5,400 pounds, but that ascender cams can chew up. There's a twenty-four double-braided, in which there is a second braided rope inside the outer one; it is easier to make knots with, Roxy says, but it abrades easily. There's a semi-static forty-eight strand that can withstand the wear and tear of ascenders. There are hollow braided ropes that are easy to splice but not very resistant to abrasion. There are strong, lightweight polyethylene fibers that should never ever be used on a harness rope bridge: "The core in here can turn to dust." Roxy talks about the bite of the rope, the feel of the rope, rope-on-rope compatibility, heat resistance, elongation. "This is a sexy rope," she says, pointing at coils of blue-black-white rope called frostbite.

Listening to arborists talk about rope is like being at a poetry recital. "It's a little bit of a love affair and there's a pride in that . . . arborists are definitely enamored of the ropes as much as arborists are enamored of the way a forest smells or of looking at small mosses," Roxy says. "Then there's the flash of it. Ropes are exciting . . . first of all, they're supporting you, your life. And they're in your hand. They are the thing that connects you to the tree . . . it's very romantic." Ropes are not strictly a tool. They are part of the family, she says, functional art in the spirit of tradecraft. "You have to be pretty smart and nerdy and educated about the types of rope and the fibers that the rope is comprised of . . . A lot of climbing arborists, I think, are people who maybe didn't perform as well in school but have brilliant minds. We work with physics, biology, structural engineering."

Once the workshop begins, I see that the intense experiences I and other participants had at Hi-Rock were not specific to re-en-tree after the worst of the pandemic. I get to hear the instructors talk about each person's experience, what they worked on, what they might need. They consider how the community is coalescing, how each individual learns. "Are you a doer? Are you a reader? Are you a mixture of the two? Are you slow paced or do you dive right in?" Bear explains. Are you an introvert or extrovert or sometimes one, sometimes the other?

I get to observe many transforma-
tions. Women from the arboriculture industry, from urban
forestry, from various
other professions improve
their skills, learn new
techniques, challenge themselves, overcome fears, and share
stories of sexism and dangerous working conditions, of male crews that won't
accept their authority and of the feeling that they
don't belong. Many don't feel physically or socially safe. One
woman says she cries most days on the job and another responds,
"That is what helmets are for!" A helmet of one's own: war-
rior gear that is also refuge. Many men continue to experience
women's authority, expertise, and emotion with discomfort. For
myself, and for many women I know, anger often emerges as
tears we try to hide or suppress. Righteous anger, particularly
at men or bosses, is something women remain well-conditioned
to hide, just as some men remain well-conditioned not to cry.
So many of us stuck in patriarchal socializations in which anger
is perceived as the province of men and as more powerful, even
when crying is the more courageous, honest response.

Some participants discover they had skills—throwing a
line to set up a rope system in a tree, for instance, or swinging
from one branch to another—they didn't know they had. "I
didn't realize this would be a year of personal growth in two
days," says Christine Holtz, an urban forester from Fort Collins. Some women climb trees for the first time. "I was pretty
convinced yesterday that I was not going to be able to do anything," says Dana Coelho, who works for the Forest Service in
Denver, as she made her way up the imposing ponderosa pine.

Ash keys

"This is how you change culture," she says later. "It is about building community."

Elva Martinez tells me that she had come to the workshop, driving from California, because of a redwood. Although she had never been outdoorsy, once she became a mother, she decided to take her young son camping every summer. On their first trip, she noticed a dead redwood standing alone. For the next twenty years, with only a few missed summers, she and her son returned to the same site and in that time she saw the redwood come back to life: "Now, you can't tell it apart from all the trees around it . . . but I can." She says she has been through a lot of hardship and sees herself as that tree, still standing, renewed, making a new life. For two days, she is reluctant to climb and occasionally slips away from the group. Then, on Sunday, Coelho calls for everyone to look at one of the oaks. There Martinez is, grabbing a ribbon. Huge applause rings out. She comes down, hugs Bear, beams with pleasure. She is radiant. "I kept thinking, I am going to be the person who doesn't make it up!" she exclaims. "Every time I wanted to stop, I kept going."

Shortly after Martinez climbs, I receive a text and a photo from my daughter Auden, who has been leading campers through the Boundary Waters and who has been totally out of contact. For several summers, Auden and her brother Julian had traveled to northern Ontario to a wildlands camp to canoe and portage. Those experiences shaped them both profoundly, teaching them about self-reliance, about how to thrive in a small nomadic community in physically and psychologically challenging conditions, and connecting them to being in forests and on water, to extraordinary natural beauty. Auden had trained to become a leader and had embarked on her first trip, in unfamiliar terrain, a few weeks before I traveled to Greeley. Because of Covid and travel restrictions, the camp had temporarily relocated to northern Minnesota. She and the other leaders don't know the routes and rivers as intimately as they do those in Ontario. But in the end, it is good that they are not farther north where wildfires are incinerating forests across Canada. By the end of August, some two million acres have burned in Ontario.

This destruction eclipses the six hundred fifty thousand acres burned three years earlier. In the summer of 2018, Auden and Julian and other campers and leaders had followed new routes, dodging fires. Julian had learned that if fire rings a lake, you need to capture air under your canoe because the fire can suck all the oxygen away. Auden had watched fires burn on the far side of the river she was traveling. My husband Tom and I spent weeks following wind maps and fire maps. We learned to assuage the terror of scale. If you zoomed back too far on the maps, entire provinces looked aflame. So we zoomed in close to the camp's main location and then traced the rivers whose names we recognized from the kids' stories. We tried to refrain from emailing every day. What new plans? What about Auden's route, where we could see a density of fires? Had the nightly SPOT, or satellite, pings—the all-ok—come in? We consumed news of firefighters arriving from other countries: three hundred came from Mexico to Ontario; by the end of August, over five hundred wildfire experts from Mexico, New Zealand, and Australia were working in British Columbia, some redeployed from Ontario. We learned about water-carrying planes, about fire retardants. We slept little. We were sick with fear and sadness.

This summer, the Boundary Waters are crowded with people in a pandemic surge of local and national travel, but there are no wildfires and I have experienced no conscious worry about safety while Auden has been away. But when her text arrives to say that she is back at basecamp and all is well, I begin sobbing with a relief I didn't know I was waiting to feel. I wander around the Greeley campus, visiting with trees, crying with happiness and awe. I keep looking at the photo Auden has sent me of herself and her coleader, loaded down with gear, backpacks, and wooden paddles, grinning, radiant.

When I was young, my brother Eric and I wandered free through woods and pastures in upstate New York when visiting my mother's relatives, popping out on unknown roads much like Melissa and Bear did. We ran free day and night around the Cape Cod island (only at high tide) where we spent many summers. I had always hoped that Auden and Julian would know that independence and exploration too. But I hadn't known that as they wandered and developed their love of adventure, their fearlessness, I would lose mine, becoming fearful of and anxious about things I had never considered—from the irrational (construction scaffolding), to the sensible (why not bring a helmet with you everywhere, just in case), to the visceral (heights). I wonder now about my mother worrying about me and Eric, maybe wanting to hold us back, but giving us the gift of keeping it to herself.

Whitebark Pine

"This is a very special place," Diana Six says as the small group unpacks itself from the utility terrain vehicle on a flat alpine meadow speckled with purple lupine and yellow heartleaf arnica. We are some nine thousand feet up, parked to the side of the Continental Divide Trail, which runs between Canada and Mexico, largely along the backbone of the Rocky Mountains. The sun is July bright, but there is a breeze coming up from a valley through the whitebark pine forest on the edge of the meadow. Many of the trees are tall and green, their branches irregular, arching this way and that, like thick brush strokes, like winds and gales holding still. "It is amazing to see whitebark this old, this healthy," Six says.

Six is a forest entomologist and an expert on mountain pine beetles. She is on the Continental Divide Trail near Salmon, Idaho, for two days to do field work with Dana Perkins, a retired Bureau of Land Management ecologist, and Hannah Alverson, a fire ecologist with the bureau and Six's graduate student. Much of the Continental Divide Trail runs through public land, and this high meadow and forest is managed by the bureau and leased to ranchers for cattle grazing. Alverson notes that until a few years ago, no one in her field office, which is based in Salmon, knew that there was so much whitebark pine along this section of trail and, in particular, so much thriving whitebark.

Pinus albicaulis are the aspen of high altitudes in that they are both a keystone and a foundation species. They often inscribe the treeline at elevations up to twelve thousand feet, where they can survive intense wind and cold for up to a thousand years. They can be the first to settle a mountainous rocky area, creating soil, holding moisture, providing cover for other plants, and supporting, directly and indirectly, over a hundred kinds of animals, including grizzly bears. The tree's cones do not release seeds on their own, as they do in most other conifers, but are instead predominantly opened by the Clark's nutcracker. The birds store the high-fat, high-protein nuts in shallow and far-flung caches. If the nuts are not consumed, trees can arise from the ground in clusters: it is common to see several whitebark growing tight together, some perhaps the siblings they appear to be. In this forest, we see sticky closed cones on the ground, likely downed by the wind, but we don't hear any nutcrackers. "Strange," Six muses. "Usually you see no cones with seeds in them." She points out solitary young whitebark growing here and there, and wonders whether seed predation is up or the nutcracker population is down or if perhaps the tree can occasionally make do without the bird.

Among the thriving whitebark, we also see many that are silver and weather-polished, some standing, some fallen. The dead trunks are marked by hieroglyphic-like patterns: in trees where the bark has fallen away, we can see elongated Js, with lines running out from either side of the letter's stem and, along those lines, rounded nodules. These Js are the work of the mountain pine beetle, *Dendroctonus ponderosae*. Every bark beetle has a different burrowing signature, Six explains. The patterns are beautiful, evocative: they can look like centipedes, circuit boards, neurons, tail feathers, trilobites, limestone eroded by the sea. The intricate patterns are etched in phloem. The brood chambers and feeding paths that produce a bark beetle's distinctive pattern can destroy a tree's ability to sustain itself. The mountain pine beetle is considered the most damaging of the bark beetles to date: it has killed tens of millions of pines throughout North America.

Plenty of other beetles are ruining trees too. In the first two decades of this century, according to one Forest Service count, some 59.2 million acres of forest were damaged or died from such infestations, an area close to the size of Oregon—add in affected forests in western Canada, and it becomes more than a California-sized chunk. In the West, there have been frequent beetle outbreaks in limber pine, sugar pine, piñon, Jeffrey pine, Douglas fir, subalpine fir, white fir, Engelmann spruce, and white spruce. Bark beetles have taken out more acres of forest than rampant wildfires have. Bark beetles have contributed to forests in British Columbia emitting more carbon than they store. The scale of the outbreaks has no historical precedent, at least none that anyone studying forests and beetles has yet found.

Epic gray landscapes of beetle-killed trees and orange-brown landscapes of dying beetle-ridden trees are frequently featured in photographs of the American West. But they can be found any place there are conifers. Bark beetles are consuming forests the world over—in Asia, in Europe, in Africa—and the country over. The southern pine beetle is no longer just the southern pine beetle. It is the ubiquitous beetle. From Central America to the Pine Barrens of New Jersey as well as in Long Island, Connecticut, and Maine. It has been prospering in loblolly, shortleaf, pitch pine, red pine, Scots pine, and Eastern white pine, killing millions of trees.

Surging populations of bark beetles have moved from their preferred trees—likely as they eat their way through them—to trees that used to be considered exempt. "You can't call anything safe anymore," Six says. "Now we are seeing the tough ones struggle." The initial waves of whitebark death were in Yellowstone and Glacier national parks. Then giant sequoias: elder trees, called monarch trees, succumbed in some California parks. "That has people freaked out," says Six. As did the news that beetles, having likely built up populations in piñon and limber pine, moved into and killed thousands of bristlecone pines, including one that was 1,612 years old. True to their reputation as tough trees, the bristlecone seem to have attacked right back. There appeared to be few beetle offspring.

Six tells me about the beetles' widening catastrophic impact during our drive to Salmon from Missoula, where she lives. She has been working in the field for three decades and in that time she has seen so much environmental devastation that she has come to view herself as a coroner, no longer as an ecologist. "Seeing everything you love disappearing, without people seeming to notice, it is very dire." She says she is frank with her students, many of whom study ecology to fix things. "I tell them, first and foremost, that you're not going to do it just with your science. If you don't get out and vote, you have just wasted your time." She is frank about being depressed, as are many firsthand observers of the ecological wasteland that is the moving front of climate change. "I see pretty much complete environmental and civil collapse," she says. "I don't know of anything I can do, and that is a very weird place to be in. . . . As a collective whole, we could fix this. But humans cannot act as a collective whole."

Six gets to the details of the most recent development, the bristlecones' death by beetle, as we begin to descend into a canyon and we begin to smell smoke. The Moose Fire to the northwest of Salmon has spread to over twenty thousand acres in three days and is uncontained. As we spiral down the steep, snaking road, I feel as if the small car is a dry leaf spiraling down in autumn. The smoke grows more intense. My eyes are burning. "It will be hard to breathe for a while," Six says.

From the whitebark forest on the Continental Divide Trail we can see the Moose Fire haze and we repeatedly scan the sky and surrounding mountains and monitor updates when we have a connection. The fires and the beetles and the trees are caught in a vortex of human making. For millennia, conifers and bark beetles have been doing the predator–prey dance. Defensive and offensive strategies that evolved over those millennia made the trees and the beetles excellent adversaries. The beetles—disturbance agents, in forest ecology terms—helped forests stay healthy and nimble, taking out old and weakened tress, creating space for young trees to flourish.

Several things are responsible for throwing this dialectic out of whack. Federal fire suppression policies are one. During the Great Fire of 1910, three million acres of drought-dry forest burned in Montana and Idaho, killing eighty-six people. The Great Fire was the largest wildfire in the nation's history, and it shaped the government's subsequent aggressive no-fire policy, which has been in place for more than a century now and has only recently begun to shift. "By trying to stop all major wildfires, the Forest Service had only fed the beast. The woods were full of dry, drying, aging timber and underbrush—fuel," writes Timothy Egan in *The Big Burn: Teddy Roosevelt and the Fire That Saved America.* "The years brought bigger, hotter, longer, earlier wildfires." The thicker the forests, the bigger the burn. The dense conditions that emerged because of fire suppression were new to regions that used to burn regularly. Fires were ignited by lightning and by many Indigenous Nations to manage forests and grasslands. The Shoshone, the Salish, the Kootenai, the Karuk, and the Yurok are among the many tribes who kept fires low intensity, removing saplings and brush, leaving mature trees, seeds, and fungi in the soil, ready to give rise to the next generation.

The denser forests have become over the last century, the more trees available for beetles boosted by the changing climate. Warmer weather can allow some species to produce more broods a year, as is true for the Southern pine beetle. Shorter, warmer winters also mean that beetle populations are less frequently sliced back by lethal cold. Average annual temperatures in parts of the Rockies have risen 2.5 degrees Fahrenheit in the last three decades—in Rocky Mountain National Park the increase has been 3.4 degrees—with the largest increases occurring during winter. For the mountain pine beetle, that has meant fewer freezes. The same is true for the southern pine beetle: as the number of below-freezing days has shrunk, the beetle has traveled steadily up the East Coast; in recent summers, infestation were detected on Cape Cod and the Islands. It is expected to reach Canada by midcentury. (At a certain point it may get too hot for the beetles too: when temperatures are consistently above 90 degrees Fahrenheit, Six says, "they are likely to kick the bucket.")

Some of the earliest climate-driven beetle outbreaks happened in higher latitudes, where warming is occurring most rapidly. In the 1990s, two hundred million spruce were killed by beetles in Alaska, as Andrew Nikiforuk describes in *Empire of the Beetle: How Human Folly and a Tiny Bug are Killing North America's Great Forests*. One outbreak in British Columbia was so vast that the beetles were spotted on radar; later calculations, Nikiforuk writes, showed that "about 850,000 beetles per hour were flying above the canopy . . . enough beetles in the air . . . to kill more than 1,400 trees an hour."

The faster warming observed at higher latitudes seems to be occurring at higher elevations too. "This tree sits on top of mountains, where it has been hard and cold, and way too harsh and cold for the beetles," Six says. "But now with climate change, it's warm enough for them to be all the way up to the top of the mountains. So the trees are like sitting ducks." Beetle populations can build up in lower forests—in climate-weakened host trees—and then overflow into higher trees, like whitebark and bristlecone. "The beetles act really much more like an invasive insect in the highest elevations, because it is in a new place, new species of tree," says Six.

Infestations have happened in nontypical host trees in the past. The dead trees on the ground in the whitebark forest we are visiting on the Continental Divide Trail are from a mountain pine beetle infestation in the 1930s, driven by a drought. Perkins visited these trees before, when doing her graduate work on whitebark pine's potential as a dendrochronological record. But such infestations seem to have been the exception. Drought, fire, and beetles are now regular and major forces determining forest health and expanse.

Six has shown Worrall and Rehfeldt's doom-and-gloom maps—the ones projecting a bleak future for aspen and other species common to the West—to her students. "I use this model, and the maps they came up with and the shifts, in class to show people the potential of what's expected under these different [Intergovernmental Panel on Climate Change] scenarios," she says. "More than 60 percent loss of forest in the central Rockies in just another thirty years." That shock is the first one for her students. "It's an insect and disease class," Six goes on to explain. "And so I say, 'This does not account for insects and disease.' And they're all like, 'Holy shit.' And then I say, 'Nor fire.' Pretty soon, everybody's just whoa . . . there's all this other stuff in the wings that will probably make it much worse." Climate models projecting impacts on ecosystems—called land-surface models—do not incorporate pests or pathogens. Those that incorporate drought and fire do so in a limited way, experts like Six and others note. None capture the point at which a forest has declined enough, suffered enough various impacts, that it trips over into massive mortality. "There is a possibility that you are going to hit these thresholds that will just catastrophically annihilate a million hectares of forest," says the University of Tasmania's Tim Brodribb.

Because every forest, tree, insect, drought, and fire story is distinct, no model can include all the complexity, particularly as so much remains unknown. But getting more complete resolution—incorporating more ecological interactions and floral, faunal, and fungal specifics—into projections appears critical to future management. Such detail could inform replanting efforts or decisions about whether to intervene in a beetle outbreak. Getting better and more complete resolution is also essential for understanding how much carbon will be stored by future forests. "I think many of our large-scale models are still far too optimistic because you have this fundamental tug of war between the benefits of carbon dioxide and the stresses of climate change, fire, drought, pests, and pathogens," says William Anderegg of the University of Utah. "When I think about the kinds of monsters in the closet that we don't have a good handle on for the future of our forests, I think pests and pathogens are very very high on that list."

Six loves mountain pine beetles—she has an array of beetle jewelry, art, and paraphernalia—and she speaks about them with passion. As she does every insect, animal, and tree. She and Perkins greet and compliment—"Hello!" "You beauty!"—each creature we meet during the trip: white-tailed deer, mule deer, turkeys, wasps, unidentified insects swarming a river birch on an evening, robber flies, horses, and cows. Every creature they find indoors is respectfully relocated outdoors. The mountain pine beetles are doing their evolutionary thing, Six says. "They're just doing their job, just going about their lives. We're the ones that have caused the problems."

As is true for many tree species, the changes wrought by global warming are coming on top of already existential threats. For the whitebark pine, that threat is white pine blister rust. The story of white pine blister rust is renown in ecological circles, a cautionary tale that begins at the turn of the last century but remains relevant. It follows the same narrative arc as countless other ecological stories in which humans appear.

White pine blister rust arrived in North America because North Americans of the colonial variety began to worry in the late nineteenth century that all the forest felling was leading to a timber shortage. Officials began to think about reforestation, but there were few tree nurseries in the United States at that time and so, against wise counsel, the head of the young forest service, Gifford Pinchot, turned to nurseries in Europe to grow white pines. Deforestation had occurred much earlier there and reforestation was part of an established science of forestry and timber production. Millions of white pine seedlings raised in European nurseries were shipped to more than two hundred locations across the United States. On some of them was a fungus, *Cronartium ribicola*, that had originated in Asia. Within a few years of arriving, the fungus was killing pines in many states. White pine blister rust was instrumental in giving rise to the first national legislation to control nonnative species: the 1912 Plant Quarantine Act.

Quarantines proved ineffective, as did destroying imported seedlings. The next response was to eliminate gooseberry and currant plants, which are in the *Ribes* genus. The fungus has a complex life cycle with different kinds of spores that survive only if they cycle from pine to currant to pine to currant and so on. Around 1915, with the creation of the Office of Blister Rust Control, state and federal workers began killing gooseberry and currant plants near white pines, ripping them out, burning them or, at times, dousing them with herbicides. Ribes eradication expanded after the creation of the Civilian Conservation Corps in 1933; workers dedicated to currant eradication were called "Ribes goons."

By midcentury, the rust was uncontained. But millions of currant plants important as food and income for some Indigenous Nations and farmers, and critical sustenance for wildlife, birds in particular, were gone. White pine blister rust control is, according to one article, "considered one of the greatest restoration failures in US forestry history." The combined threat of white pine blister rust, fire, climate change, and mountain pine beetle led, in late 2022, to the listing of whitebark pine as threatened under the Endangered Species Act.

Stands like this one, with so many sumptuously green big whitebark, are exceedingly rare and Six has been seeking them out. For much of her career, she studied the beetle's mutualistic relationship with fungi. Mountain pine beetle carry in special pouches fungi that ferry nutrients to them from inside the tree. "Everything runs on mutualism, everything on this planet," Six says. In recent years she has shifted her focus. Six goes out in the field now less to understand the beetles and more to understand the trees that are still standing. The survivor trees.

The first thing Six does after the hour-long commute up the mountain—through green-gray sagebrush prairie and then into forest, past dead whitebark at lower elevations, many draped in wolf lichen—is to teach Alverson how to identify the telltale yellow-orange fungus or "Cheeto dust" of the rust. They look for signs of nibbling; squirrels like to eat the fungus and can sometimes keep infection in check. They look for cankers. "No bleeding or blister or resin. I give that tree a zero," says Six. On others there is a smattering of rust, but the trees seem to be faring well, not succumbing to infection. "Persistence without resistance," says Six. "It is very dry, so the disease struggles here."

After the rust assessment, Six shows Alverson how to use an increment borer, and sampling of the survivor trees begins. Six—who has expertise in an array of fields, including microbiology, mycology, agricultural pest management, entomology, evolutionary biology, chemical ecology, journalism, and genetics—recently taught herself dendrochronology, with help from a colleague. (She says she draws the line at learning the main programming language used by the field: "This close to retirement, I am not going to spend six months learning R.") We move from tree to tree in the grove closest to the valley and then through stands farther away from the wind—and the protection it gives us from mosquitoes. The small team measures tree diameter, cores trees, and takes plugs of phloem and a handful of needles for genetic analysis. I follow Perkins, who gives me a helpful conifer-identification mnemonic: "Pines are prickly. Firs are flat and furry and friendly. Don't shake hands with a spruce." The wind is swaying branches, a wild soft sound. The smell of the pines is sharp and dry.

This site is the fourth one Six has looked at to understand the whitebark pine survivors. She has looked at their growth rates and has found that the slower growing the tree, the less the beetles seem to like it, for as-yet undeciphered reasons. This pattern has been seen in other tree species, as has the opposite: "slow-growing ponderosa are almost always nailed by the beetles." She has looked at their chemical protections. Those results were mixed and didn't suggest that the survivor trees had a special defensive signature. With her students and colleagues, Six continues to look at growth rates and defenses, but she has added in another analysis. Beetles must assess a tree for the robustness of its deterrents: "Can I get in?" But, Six says, that is not the only thing beetles have to consider: "Is it going to be worth it?" That might come down to nutrition. "You have a gazillion beetles flying around and they are running out of places for food and they are just missing trees four feet away? I don't think so."

Six is collaborating with ecologist Amy Trowbridge of the University of Wisconsin-Madison. Much of Trowbridge's work has been on chemical defenses in drought-afflicted piñon: she has chronicled how carbon starvation during drought ultimately limits piñon's ability to fend off bark beetles. She and Six are looking at whitebark, hoping to "get as comprehensive as we can in terms of the whole kit-and-caboodle of what a bark beetle smells, sees, tastes and why that leads to choice and success," Trowbridge says. They are evaluating the starches and sugars involved in whitebark's metabolism, chemical production, and levels of nutrients like phosphorous and nitrogen. "Beetles can somehow make it through those defenses and there's something else that allows them to just be very successful in these trees. Maybe that is the fact that there's lots of sugars," she says. Trowbridge hopes a clearer chemical picture will extend the suite of chemicals and physiological traits that hyperspectral biologists—who interpret the nuances of reflected wavelengths from canopies—can detect with drones, small planes, and satellites. Maybe that could "give land managers a better sense of when trees might need some sort of active management."

Six too hopes this research leads to better management. Maybe survivor whitebark pine, she posits, don't have the food beetles and fungi need. Or perhaps the enduring trees are more drought tolerant. Or both. "These trees may have what it takes for climate change, as far as more drought, because they're still growing, maybe they need less water. . . . And they come with

Whitebark
Pine cones

this added aspect that beetles don't like them for some reason." Right now, Six and other forest experts note, many survivors—of drought, of insects, of disease—are typically cut after widespread die-offs in a controversial practice called salvage logging. Six would like to see some forests instead left alone to naturally recover after the "natural selection events that are picking off trees that can't live in our new world and leaving behind those that can," she says. "I think there's a lot of potential in our forests to deal with what we are facing right now . . . to buy us some time, or them some time."

At the end of the second day, the wind has become stronger and as we drive down the mountain, we can see a huge cloud formed by Moose Fire smoke hanging like an ominous slab. Such massive clouds can create their own weather and wind, in turn spreading the fire that created them. We learn that two seasoned helicopter pilots have died fighting the fire.

In Salmon, the smoke is thick and ash is falling. The wildfire is one ridge away. Six has been through fire; she has evacuated her home three times and expects to again, as fire is no longer an if but a when. "It is a terrible way to live, being scared of losing everything every year." She figures that we can drive back to Missoula the way we came if we leave before dawn the next morning. So we do, "heading to Mordor" in Six's car. The road runs along the Salmon River and across the water we see fire burning in the dark. Trees in flame, flames tumbling down slopes.

I have been sending regular updates about the expanding fire to my family. After we emerge from the valley, I send them pictures of Six driving, the flames framed by her window. Auden texts back to say we are "wayyyy too close." Julian points out that something seems to be shifting:

> Mom
> R u okay
> That doesn't look sage
> At all
> If I was there in that car
> And u were the one who wasn't there
> You'd probably get so scared/mad that you'd start
> hovering above the ground
> Especially if I wasn't wearing a helmet like the
> driver is clearly not

PART III

Woundwood

In September 2021, five months after my first workshop, I return to Hi-Rock to climb again. I am irritable as I begin the drive from New York City to Massachusetts, irritability that I recognize as nervousness about climbing, about facing my limitations and showing no improvement (I had not practiced anything, not a knot, since May), and about the pandemic. Melissa and Bear had again required proof of vaccination, a timely negative test, and that we all stay masked when indoors. But I am still fearful of sharing a room, which we hadn't done during the first workshop. At the last minute I decide to stay with friends in nearby Hillsdale, New York, instead of bunking at Hi-Rock.

My buddy is also new to climbing. Within a few minutes of learning the basic system, she is high in the hemlock. I struggle with the hip thrust all over again, feeling dismay and disappointment, and feeling old. Instructor Kate Odell eyes me with compassion. "We're going to start you right away on the foot ascender tomorrow," she says. "You deserve to have some fun too." Kate has driven from New Hampshire where she works as a climbing arborist: "I'm just kind of living the dream because I am on tree crew pretty much all the time." The first afternoon passes quickly. In the dark, the long road out seems especially long, unfamiliar, unsettling.

As I drive back to Hi-Rock early the next morning, fog hangs low above mowed fields, hugging trees. I see a peregrine falcon and a belted kingfisher, one of my mother's favorite birds, and I miss her fiercely. In addition to loving trees, she loved birds. She would save up for years for birding trips; she went to Iceland to see puffins and to the Midwest to see prairie hens. Most of her birding was done in New York City, though, with a group of birders, some of whom are the stars of Marie Winn's *Red-Tails in Love: A Wildlife Drama in Central Park*. That so many species could visit or live among great buildings, that people could be quiet observers amid the frenzy, and that she could see a beautiful creature that others had missed as they darted by, brought my mother great joy. With her, I had sought out saw-whet owls and observed red-tailed hawks and peregrines. We had watched great-horned owls swoop at dusk out of pine trees, shadows emerging from shadows.

When my mother's language lost its detail, she would say, "I don't need to know their names. I just love to look at them." When being outside brought too much geographical disorientation and anxiety, she cut photographs of birds from calendars and brochures and placed them around her apartment. At some point deep into her dementia, she had a bad fall and was admitted to the hospital where she had spent much of her professional life working as an administrator. As I walked along Amsterdam Avenue to visit her, a red-tailed hawk landed on the lowest balcony of a fire escape ten feet away. "Que linda," someone sighed. I imagined the hawk was my mother or that the hawk had come for her. At that very moment, I discovered when I arrived at the hospital, a substitute home aide, who did not know about my mother's do-not-resuscitate order, was pulling her out of death. Many more years of dementia followed.

I had worried that my memories of my mother in her dementia would be the stronger ones, that they would lie on top of my other memories and suffocate them. But in the years since her death, it is as if the dementia is a thick layer of dust slowly blowing away. Many of the memories that have returned are about being outside, about noticing, and about trees. The names of the trees in New York City's Riverside Park that she insisted Eric and I learn. The tree-identification page from a magazine taped on the refrigerator: vibrant yellow, orange, and red fall leaves jazzing against a royal blue background. The stories she read to us about forest folk, real and imagined, and of powerful life-saving trees. The story about the lone pine and its companion in Ludwig Bemelmans's *Parsley*: "And when the old tree and the stag were together, weatherbeaten the one and gray the other, it was difficult to tell which were the antlers and which were the barren boughs." About how the pine saved the stag from a hunter.

Kate gives me a green ascender that can work both on the right or left foot. I like the idea of one that I can shift from side to side, so one leg doesn't get too tired. Arborists often use a foot ascender on one leg and a knee ascender on the other. They stand straight and each step moves them up the rope. From a distance it looks as though the climber is ascending the air.

Kate helps me set up a pulley system. She loops a short friction hitch cord that has a spliced eye at either end around the falling side of the line. She ties either a Michoacán or a Knut, I don't catch which. She catches the rope along the metal wheel of the pulley, clips both ends of the hitch cord to another part of the pulley and attaches the setup to my harness bridge. She then clips the end of the other side of the rope, the climbing side, to the pulley system. Although I have not set up this system myself yet, I am surprised to find that I am largely following what Kate is doing; it has a logic, it feels familiar. I take a photograph of the setup and admire its elegance. Then I get rid of the slack by pulling the falling side of the line out and away from the base of the pulley.

Liftoff can be awkward, particularly for newbies. Climbers sometimes tighten the rope as they jump; some lift one leg off the ground as they get rid of the slack. That transition, the first liftoff, is graceful when the instructors do it—athletic, acrobatic, balletic. Bear says she feels the same excitement she did as a child every time she begins to leave the ground, a sense of amazement that she is about to be in a tree. I take up the slack, teeter, and, unable to control the pendulum I am, crash into the trunk.

As I start climbing, I have to reach down and pull on the falling side of the line as it comes out of the foot ascender so I can advance. Higher up, gravity pulls the rope. It flows out of the cam and pools on the ground. I have both gloved hands on the rope above the friction hitch. I step down, the rope moves through the pulley, the hitch relaxes as my weight shifts to the ascender from the harness. I push the knot up the line and make sure it catches. It does. I stand in the air to catch my breath. Another few steps. Another few breaths. Every few feet, as I rest, I tie a slip knot below the ascender, pulling my boot up to reach the falling end of the line. My hands have memorized the slip knot. The rhythm of stepping, of making sure the knot catches, of catching my breath, of tying the slip knots, has kept me focused on the act of climbing, not on the tree and not on the height. When I stop and look, I realize I am way above the waterskiing sign and several feet above the trillium—the high platform suspended between the hemlocks. I am forty feet up.

There is a green ribbon on a nearby branch; I untie it and stick it inside my shirt and later tie it to my backpack, where it has remained ever since. After some frustration, I release the rope from the ascender so that, as Kate warns, I don't go "ass over teakettle." I squeeze the friction hitch to descend. I have no intention of visiting the trillium; the nearest edge is far from the trunk of my hemlock. Relatively far, that is, maybe a few feet.

But as with limb walking, I find myself doing things I didn't anticipate, things I am absolutely opposed to doing. With Kate's guidance I push out from the trunk while squeezing the hitch knot. It is scary. If I release too fast, I will plummet, maybe missing the trillium. If I release too little, I won't go anywhere and will crash into the trunk, as is my wont. I release softly, I push out, I am in the air. I swing over and down into the trillium. I am sitting between the three hemlocks. Kate is beaming at me from the ground and Bear is beaming at me from one of the hemlocks. From my seat, I see the expanse of the lake. Fear is gone—no dizziness, no buzzing in my shins. I feel the wind cooling my sweat. I feel the slight rocking pull of the hemlocks holding the trillium. I am clipped in, but I feel unclipped, free in the trees. I feel amazed, strong, grateful to be so high in these hemlocks. I feel a surge of deep happiness and power.

Getting to the trillium can do that. "It wasn't that I was afraid. I wasn't afraid. It just felt like, I can't do this. And Bear wouldn't let me off the hook," says Gina Colelli, a trauma therapist who met Melissa and Bear when they were teaching a chainsaw class at the Berkshire Botanical Garden in Stockbridge, Massachusetts. She had signed up for the class because her former boyfriend had refused to teach her how to use a chainsaw. "That's how you get to be seventy years old and take tree-climbing classes, because you're full of piss and vinegar," she says. Shortly into the chainsaw class, Colelli learned about the workshop and enrolled that day. "I hadn't climbed a tree since I was a kid and I thought this would be really wonderful. I could climb a tree again," she says. She had felt immediately drawn to the twins: Melissa, who exuded confidence in everyone; Bear, who seemed to have a self-contained intensity that was like a furnace, in Colelli's words. "I don't always get to be with other women who are strong like that, strong and loving and kind and compassionate."

At the workshop, Colelli, who has always been athletic and practices yoga, says she couldn't get the climbing movements. For most of the weekend she felt as though she didn't belong. "I couldn't pull myself . . . I couldn't figure out that motion," she says. "I just kept on saying to her, this isn't going to happen. I can't do this." Bear listened and waited.

Colelli burst into tears when she swung into the trillium. "The heart of it, the nugget, was I didn't realize that I had lost confidence in myself. And when I had that experience, I became acutely aware that there was an aspect of me that had dimmed, almost died, and without knowing it. I think it may be a big part of the aging experience, too. There's something very nice about getting comfortable in a routine and not pushing anymore. . . . And that experience burst me wide open."

In the afternoon, I climb a red maple, get another ribbon, and ring a bell to a round of applause. I do it all much more slowly than my buddy does. She is a climbing natural. But instead of feeling acutely what I can't do, I feel acutely what I can.

The maple is wonderful to climb. The three boles that make up its lichen-mottled trunk braid together, creating many choices, many routes. A few of its leaves have turned red, but the canopy is still abundantly green and the tree doesn't look ready for fall. In this maple, as in many other deciduous trees, the cambium can keep producing new cells until a few weeks before leaves start to change color, whereas in the three nearby hemlocks and in most other conifers, the cambium began to stop creating cells after the summer solstice. Falling temperatures are a principal fall-to-winter signal for some species. Hours of light are a signal for others. Even hours of artificial light. As Peter

A. Thomas writes in *Trees*, "the branches of a Norway Maple immediately around a streetlight hold their leaves for much longer than the rest of the tree, since they perceive the days as still being long."

As life is slowing for winter, trees are busy recycling as well as getting rid of things they don't need. They reabsorb chemicals and nutrients from their leaves and store them in the trunk and roots. They shuttle toxins like heavy metals or nonessential elements into dying leaves, so they can be discarded. Chlorophyll breaks down, reflecting less and less and finally no green light. The carotenoids—chemicals that shield chloroplasts from ultraviolet light and from heat stress—reflect more oranges and yellows. They are the source of aspen's gold. Of the amber, lemon, honey, canary, chrysanthemum yellows of sycamore, birch, Norway maple, gingko.

A small number of trees, about a half a percent of the world's species, produce anthocyanins, compounds that reflect light in the red wavelengths. This Hi-Rock red maple is one of some eighty species in Massachusetts to do this, including sugar maple, copper beech, northern red oak, and sumac. The Northeast—New England and Canada—is one of few places on the planet where a high percentage of trees turns red, according to Thomas; the other regions are in East Asia. Why some trees produce anthocyanins is not fully understood, but it may have to do with signaling danger—noxious!—to coevolved insects that traveled with the trees during ice ages.

The timing, extent, and vibrancy of fall foliage are shifting and becoming less predictable. New rainfall patterns seem to play a role. "If it's very warm and wet, then they keep their leaves much longer," says Richard Primack of Boston University. "If it's extremely wet, they might lose their leaves earlier because of fungal damage." Rain is one of many variables that scientists are beginning to tease apart to understand how autumn is changing and what it means for forests and trees.

Most work in the field of phenology—the study of seasonal changes and cycles in plants and animals—has focused on spring. The data come from sources like the Smiley family at Mohonk, who marked the arrival of spring peepers, katydids, and spotted salamanders as well as the flowering of shadbush, red trillium, marsh marigold, and mountain laurel. Perhaps best-known in New England are the observations begun by Henry David Thoreau in 1851 and that continue today. Comparisons of long-term and recent observations show disappearing creatures and shifting habits. Trees are, generally, flowering and leafing out sooner—in the Northeast, about eighteen days earlier on average—although within this overall trend there is great variability. "Eighteen days might not seem like a whole lot, but it can make a big difference for other plants and animals that depend on the appearance of these leaves, and whose schedules may not have shifted in the same way," writes Primack. Understory plants that during Thoreau's time took advantage of the "spring light window" before the trees above them leafed out, have lost much of that window. Many populations appear to be dwindling.

One of the biggest concerns about shifting flowering or leaf-out times has to do with what is called phenological mismatch, with disruptions to food webs and to reproductive cycles that could cascade through ecosystems. This disruption is taking place in Alaska, where Pacific black brants—a kind of goose—are arriving in their spring feeding grounds earlier, feasting on sedge before it has fully grown and reproduced, causing a decline in sedge. The larvae of an endangered butterfly, the Karner blue, that feed on blue lupine have been emerging before the lupine and may be declining. The European pied flycatcher is migrating as per usual but arriving to find oaks already leafed out and no winter moth caterpillars, which feed on young oak leaves, to eat.

Biologists are also worried that if plants bloom before pollinators are ready there will be less reproduction and then fewer pollinators, and so on in a vicious cycle of diminishment. About 90 percent of plants rely on animals for pollination. But "concrete definitive evidence for phenological mismatch between plants and pollinators . . . remains surprisingly elusive," says Nicole Rafferty of the University of Melbourne. Rather, she notes, there are subtle mismatches. One oft-cited study describes a Japanese poppy that is flowering earlier but whose bumble bee pollinator has not appeared earlier, which has led to reduced pollination and fewer seeds. Rafferty and her colleagues found something similar in greenhouse experiments. Induced warming led to earlier flowering but did not lead to earlier bee appearance. The earlier flowers were small, had less nectar than is typical, and produced fewer seeds. "It's not like immediate local extinction of these plant populations, but longer-term consequences in terms of their reproductive success, fitness, and population dynamics," Rafferty says.

Pollinator mismatches likely have not been widely observed for a few reasons. "Pollinator mismatches can be hard to document because they are ephemeral," says Theresa Crimmins of the University of Arizona and director of the National Phenology Network. "So if you are not looking in the exact right place at the exact right time, you might miss it." But also because evolution has built in great plasticity and redundancy: many pollinators can suffice, few plants rely on one. Among trees, it appears figs are the most pollinator specific: each of the more than seven hundred species of fig depend on a particular wasp or set of wasps. Most flowering trees are pollinated by insects but some rely on wind. They are anemophilous: anemone, from Greek for "daughter of the wind" or "wind flower." Conifers, for their part, are all anemophilous. It is a wonderful word to think about when you are high in a hemlock in the wind: the tree as the child of that wind, the tree as a flower.

Trees are reproductively flexible and many can vary the sex of their flowers from year to year or in different parts of one tree. Red maple flowering strategies are especially flexible, as Primack has observed. For five years, he visited red maples in a swamp near his home. For reasons of too much water and too many rocks, they didn't grow tall. "They're mature trees, probably quite old trees, but they're very short," he says. "And so it is very easy to study the flowers." Maples are known in the botanical world for their reproductive complexity: some make flowers with pollen, some with pistils, some make self-fertilizing flowers, some do one thing for a few years and then switch. Red maples do all that and more: some produce flowers with pollen in one part of the canopy and flowers with pistils in another.

Red Maple samara

Spend time in or under or near just one tree. It is like the Big Bang. A universe unfurls.

In the evening I sit on a bench near the fire with Moulis, who is also back for her second workshop. We have not been each other's groundies in practice, but we share a deepening climbing kinship and excitement about each other's accomplishments. In the last three months, Moulis has started working with a trainer and has gotten stronger—she pulls a sled with weights across the floor. Sometimes her daughters jump aboard. She too has reached the trillium, which was her goal for the weekend. She is finally up in the trees that led her to become an arborist. "I am back to enjoying things in a childlike way," she says. "I can take time and I can notice everything. I can smell the fresh air and I can listen to the wildlife. It is seeing the insects and hearing the birds. And seeing the tree and respecting it, and understanding how strong it is. And being happy to be up there. It's also not something I ever thought I would be doing when I was at my sickest point." She tells me about the free library she recently put up on her street. "You have to start somewhere," she says, adding that neighbors have already starting borrowing books.

She shows me pictures of her daughters. When she was four, Rita had wandered out of preschool a few times to find trees, and Moulis says her recreational climbing now centers around Rita rescue: "When she climbs too high, I have the chance to climb up and get her down." A teacher had recently sent home a rebuking note saying that Rita, now five, keeps picking up dirt and detritus on the playground. "To her, it is plant collecting and soil sampling," Moulis says she had to explain to the school. Her older daughter Jenevieve is learning an array of knots for Cub Scouts and has let her leaders know that she won't eat any foraged plants—including dandelions, which she loves—unless she knows that they have not been sprayed with pesticides.

Moulis also shows me pictures of a diminutive American chestnut in the woods near her house. Her daughters know its story, how special it is. They know that the chestnut was wiped out. The annihilation began in the 1820s, when chestnuts in the South began dying because of a root rot called ink disease, caused by an introduced phytophthora, a water mold like the ones killing the Wollemi. Then came the blight. Between 1904 and 1954, an introduced fungus, *Cryphonectria parasitica*, killed an estimated three to five billion American chestnut trees. "Enough trees to fill nine million acres. Enough trees to cover Yellowstone National Park eighteen hundred times over. Enough trees to give two to every person on the planet at that time," writes Susan Freinkel in *American Chestnut: The Life, Death, and Rebirth of a Perfect Tree*. Moulis's daughters know that the little one near their home is what most American chestnuts are constrained to become now: a small tree emerging from the lingering roots of a stump, a sapling that will not likely make it to adulthood.

The tree is very special to Moulis. Her mother worked at a nursing home called Chestnut Point and she remembers going to work with her and looking for spiky chestnut balls on the grounds. "I would just gather and play with them. And, you know, they kind of hurt, but they were also friends," she says. "I was an only child." In first grade, she got one to germinate. "It didn't survive the winter, but I took that tree around like it was a little friend. I decorated it for Christmas. I really loved it."

In recent years, Moulis has helped maintain an American chestnut in front of the Phoebe Griffin Noyes Library in Old Lyme, Connecticut, as part of a pro bono program her company has participated in. Using a bucket truck, volunteers put every flower in a small white paper bag, trying to prevent the wind-born pollen of chestnut species from China and Japan, which are more resistant to the fungus, from fertilizing the flowers. If the flowers aren't protected, "then you're going to have a hybrid," Moulis explains. After about a week, volunteers remove the bags and paint the flowers with pollen provided by the American Chestnut Foundation. The flowers are covered up again for protection. The burs—the spiky chestnut balls, each containing several seeds—are collected in the fall and planted in a nursery.

The Old Lyme chestnut tree is renown, the offspring of two American chestnuts that survived the blight. It was planted in 1990 and has so far not been killed by the fungus. Although it made it beyond saplinghood, the tree doesn't look like an iconic American chestnut: *Castanea dentata* could reach twelve feet in diameter and one hundred feet in height. This chestnut is on the squatter side and has a shrubby aspect because of the profusion of sprouts emerging from the trunk; many trees grow such epicormic shoots when stressed by disease or environmental conditions.

The first page in my mother's tree journal is labeled *Castanae dentata*, but my phone app and a friend who is a chestnut maven tell me it is not an American chestnut, rather a European chestnut, *Castanea sativa*. My mother has the identification wrong, but other details right, particularly the legacy of the blight: ". . . they still struggle to live, and perhaps the next generation will see the sucker-switches from old roots overcoming the deadly malady and turning into trees again."

When I was in my twenties, my mother asked me to accompany her to visit the man who owned the estate she had grown up on. We taped our conversation with him, but I can't find the cassette. I remember we talked about the book *Design with Nature* by Ian McHarg, and that my mother asked him about her father. She knew he had spent a lot of time with her father when he was a boy. He said that yes, he had loved to follow her father around. That her father knew how to fix anything, from structures and stone walls to ailing flowerbeds and landscapes. And that he seemed to know about everything: birds, plants, animals, and trees. He was a naturalist and a gardener. My mother started keeping her tree journal five years after his death.

I tend now to foreground what my mother made from her trauma: to look more at the green shoots, less at the gray stump. Renewal arising from blight. My mother was the first of her family to go to college. She thrived in a city after growing up rural. She traveled. She was open-minded. She loved trying new things. Even after getting a degree in public health and settling into a career as a hospital administrator, she studied to get a real estate license and took sailing classes in New York Harbor—I recall that she got some kind of license or certificate for that as well. She studied Chinese brush painting. She became a potter. Even as she grappled with loss and deep wounds, she gave me and Eric her huge love and warmth. She took us to a small neighborhood library every week when we were little and read aloud to us every afternoon, her breath like ice cream, she put so much sugar and milk in her coffee. She pointed us toward the pull and beauty of ocean and forest. Toward how we were not ourselves without them.

Across the lawn from the trio of hemlocks and the red maple are thick woods where more challenging ropes are set up, where climbers use their lanyard to move over and between branches or where they move between trees. It is the graduate school division. Near those woods, a three-trunked hemlock, or perhaps three hemlocks that grew from seeds on top of each other, has climbing lines installed. The hemlock stands close to a red oak. The four trunks have similar widths and the trees have similar heights; their branches cross and intertwine in places. They look like siblings who get along, who reach across each other at the dinner table and pay no mind.

On Sunday, Rachel Vanicek and I pair up and climb in this stand. Vanicek works on plant health at Bartlett Tree Experts, a large national company, and she comes from a family of horticulturalists and farmers. As we climb, she tells me about one of her professors, a pioneer in urban tree research, who believes we should embrace certain nonnative trees, because they often coevolved with and have resistance to many nonnative pests and diseases. Vanicek also tells me about a new disease. She indicates a beech across the road and tells me that something called beech leaf disease is harming the trees and that people don't understand a great deal about it. Neither of us knows then that an epidemic is looming.

I set my own pulley system. My fingers are coming to know the knots—particularly the Knut and the Michoacán. I check my configuration against the photo I took when Kate set up the system the day before. I am feeling more confident. When something doesn't feel right, as Melissa and Bear instruct, I take the whole thing apart and start anew. The one thing I cannot get is the carabiners, which are triple-action double-locking auto-closing: pull, twist, push. Arborists do this with one hand and a satisfying click. I need two hands and am constantly dropping my carabiners or getting my glove stuck in the mechanism.

I use the foot ascender and climb the biggest of the little hemlock trunks until I reach the place where the oak stretches across and blocks my path. Bear is nearby, helping someone in the advanced program in the woods, but she is also watching me and Vanicek. (Some participants have noted that Melissa, Bear, and the instructors seem to see everything and be everywhere all at once.) She suggests I undo the ascender and try a mini hip thrust—in a crouch, like a frog—to get over the oak branch. The mini hip thrust works. I am elated. I cross over the branch and keep climbing. I reach a ribbon. There is a bell above the tie-in point, but I don't feel confident enough to move that high—it would require using a lanyard. There is a ribbon far out on a branch as well, but the angle is tricky. Vanicek navigates both challenges, looking strong and at ease.

Bear encourages me instead to climb the tree freely—to use the rope system as backup and to scramble around. I can't. Something about moving away from the gear freezes me. I have a sense that I could start at the bottom of a tree and climb as I did when I was a child, or I can climb the way I've learned from Melissa and Bear, but it is one or the other. I cannot move between these two states of being. In trusting the gear, I feel separate from some instinctual, older understanding of myself in a tree. But in trusting the gear, I have been able to climb, overcome a fear of heights, and see trees in a new way.

Bear asks me to look closely at the hemlock, really look. Many of the needles are yellow with tiny brown insects peppering the undersides. Elongate hemlock scale, as these insects are called, appears to have been inadvertently imported from Japan in the early twentieth century. They can feed on over forty species of conifer—including pine, spruce, cedar, yew, and fir— but prefer hemlock. Traveling via Christmas trees, among other routes, hemlock elongate scale is now established in about fifteen states. (American Christmas trees are shipped far and wide. A shipment of pines to the Caribbean appears to have contained a different scale insect, the pine tortoise scale, which has killed more than 95 percent of native pines in Turks and Caicos.)

Scale alone don't always take down a tree. But they settle in stressed hemlock, those experiencing drought and warmer temperatures. And in those already suffering attack by the hemlock woolly adelgid. Bear and another climber had spotted adelgid high in the trio of great hemlocks the day before. She asks me if I see tiny white puffs, like little cotton ovals, near the scale. I cannot. Woolly adelgid landed in Virginia in 1951, traveling on a hemlock imported by a nursery. The adelgid is minute, about a half a millimeter, but prolific. As noted in *Hemlock: A Forest Giant on the Edge*, ten adelgids can produce thirty million more within two years. They emit a woolly waxy cover and use a stylet, or sharp straw-like mouth part, to feed on a tree's sugars. Since it arrived, the tiny hemlock woolly adelgid has been remaking hydrology as it fells old-growth forests. It has, so far, hit a northern wall of cold in Maine. It may also hit a wall of damp: a recent study found that increased rainfall was linked to increased fungal infection of the adelgid.

I settle into a fork in the hemlock where there is a nook filled with acorn shells and humus, dead vegetation becoming compost. I release some rope and lean back against a branch. I can see the lake and the inlet where beavers have a lodge. I can see how this one tree is woven together with the others in this little group, these sibling trees. There is such intricacy and intimacy, such support, such leaning on each other. I feel as if I am in on a secret.

The workshop is over. Everyone breaks down their gear, packs it up. Some help the instructors take the ropes out of the trees and remove friction savers. We share about our experience, collect our gratitude bags, choose an item from the giveaway table. Moulis selects a signed copy of the *Tree Climbers' Guide*. With Roxy's help, I select a length of lanyard rope. I am slowly building a kit. At the May workshop we had each been given a climbing line. Before this September workshop, I had bought an orange helmet, gloves, and safety glasses that could fit over my regular glasses. I peek at the notes in my gratitude bag before I start the trip home. Vanicek thanks me for letting her "geek out" about tree disease. Moulis has written that she is so proud of me for getting to the trillium and ringing a bell.

Suffused with strength, delight, and a sense of connection with trees and an amazing community of people, I drive back toward New York City. As I get closer, the darkness settles in, the traffic increases, the drivers seem mad. It is hard to hold on to the feeling of the trees––of the bark, of the strength. But I do. And it is on this drive back from Hi-Rock that I begin to talk with my brother Eric again.

A few months before the pandemic, Eric died by suicide. He had been living since his twenties in the Pacific Northwest. He loved how close nature was to Seattle, how easily he could get out of the city to hike, kayak, or snowboard. In 2017, six months after our mother died, he reluctantly moved back to New York. For many years, he had worked in healthcare tech. He was a wonderful manager, as I have learned from people who worked with him. He put other people first, tried to make things work for them, to support them. But when he was abruptly fired— one of those blindsiding inhumane "corporate restructuring" escort-you-from-the-building firings—by the company he had devoted much of his professional life to, he lost confidence. He was not able to find another stable professional home, or to support himself. That meant too that he was no longer able to outrun some history and some illnesses of body and mind that he seemed to be able to keep at bay when he was immersed in and distracted by work. He came back to New York City in distress and a great deal of pain. He kept a lot of that pain secret from almost everyone who knew him. He struggled for nearly two years. People loved him so deeply. He didn't let anyone see all the pieces. His agony became unbearable to him.

His death made me feel pain that I thought might vaporize me—a kind of pain unlike anything I have ever experienced. And perhaps because he kept so much of his inner life and pain hidden, because his death was so shocking, because of the guilt that can never be fully released by most people who lose someone to suicide, I couldn't feel his presence anymore. He was the only person who knew the same things I knew, who was of my soul. But since his death in November 2019, nothing animated him for me. My mother's pre-dementia presence manifested in the appearance of her favorite birds or by being in and appreciating a tree, but I couldn't find or feel Eric. For the first time, almost two years after his death, in that drive back from Hi-Rock in September, I had a sense of him. I imagined him sitting in the passenger seat and could talk to him.

There is another picture of me and Eric that I had not been able to look at often since he died because it was too excruciating. It was taken by my mother during a visit to Seattle. Eric and I are sitting on the floor. He has one arm tightly wrapped around my shoulder, and we are leaning into each other. Like the sibling trees.

That night I dreamed about the place where Eric and I spent our childhood summers running wild in dunes, avoiding the sharp darts of beach grass, exploring the expanse of low-tide mud flats, of creeks, of marshes, of the high-tide line and the rotting salty smell of eelgrass baking in the sun, popping with flies and sand hoppers. The two of us a world unto ourselves. We knew the same secrets about the landscape, we knew where to find refuge and magic. Then, in the way of all dreams, I was no longer on the land but in the ocean, feeling the force of two powerful currents entwining, knowing they were rip tides, but they were not scary, rather something to be a part of.

Beech

Like many forest pathologists, Robert Marra of the
Connecticut Agricultural Experiment Station has
mostly studied fungi. He's looked at the fungi that
cause boxwood blight and Dutch elm disease. Fungi
that kill salt marsh grasses. Fungi that cause cankers
on oaks and birches. The chestnut blight fungus.
"I mean, there's some bacterial diseases, and there's
other weird things like phytoplasmas," he says. There
are the phytophthoras so deadly that "they giggle
when they think about fungi." Generally, though,
"most of us work on fungi." Because of that, there is
a kind of template for understanding arboreal fungal
diseases, like white pine blister rust: a recognizable
pattern to how they move, how they weaken or kill,
and, sometimes, how to address them. But there is no
template for Marra's current focus: beech leaf disease.

In 2012 a biologist working for Lake Metroparks—a
collection of parks in and around Cleveland, Ohio—
noticed that beech leaves were looking odd. Some
were small and shriveled. Some were dark and thick

between their veins: with the sun shining through them, they appeared to be striped. He sent pictures to researchers at Ohio State University, including Enrico Bonello, who was immersed in work on two proliferating arboreal threats—emerald ash borer and sudden oak death. Bonello said he didn't have the capacity to tackle something else just then and tried to forget about it.

But more reports of unhealthy and dying beech came in and, in 2014, Bonello, the Metroparks biologist John Pogacnik, and others visited some of the parks and saw the banding, the stunted leaves, and the dying, denuded beech trees. "At that point we didn't even know what to call it," Bonello recalls. "So let's call it beech leaf disease, you know, just for lack of imagination." Bonello canvassed folks in the field. "Nobody had ever seen anything like that before anywhere. So that was really cool. And concerning. And disconcerting."

Meanwhile, beech were dying in other states. Beech leaf disease seemed to be on the move, although, as Marra and others note, it could be that it was finally being detected because it had a name and foresters and arborists were actively looking for it. To some it seemed a viral or perhaps bacterial infection. Then, in 2017, David McCann of the Ohio Department of Agriculture saw through his microscope swarms of little worms swimming out of beech leaves. He sent them to the federal nematode laboratory, which is in Beltsville, Maryland, where researchers determined that the tiny worms were related to a species that had been discovered on beech trees in Japan. The nematode was named *Litylenchus crenatae*, subspecies *mccannii*, in honor of McCann, who was thrilled, calling it the coolest thing that had ever happened to him.

The Department of Agriculture has a nematode lab and collection—one of the largest in the world, with millions of specimens and an exhaustive database—because some nematodes are essential to healthy soil, whereas others feed on crops such as carrots, potatoes, soybeans, sugar beets, corn, and toma-toes. Those latter nematodes cause an estimated $157 billion of global crop loss and damage a year.

Nematodes are everywhere. They live in dirt and oceans and freshwater. They live from Antarctica to the Arctic. Perhaps the most famous nematode is *Caenorhabditis elegans* or *C. elegans*, the first animal to be fully genetically sequenced and one of the principal model organisms for biology. Such model organisms—the best-known are yeast, mice, fruit flies, zebra fish, and the tiny plant *Arabidopsis*, or thale cress—provide a way of studying biological processes that can be extrapolated to other creatures. Typically, they reproduce quickly in laboratories and have rela-tively small genomes, so certain genes can be "knocked out" of commission and the impact of that loss observed. The minute roundworm *C. elegans* has been working as a model organism since the 1960s and has helped researchers learn about cancer, about aging, about neural networks; it has contributed to at least three Nobel prizes and thousands of discoveries. It is the only nematode that has been so extensively studied. *L. crenatae mccan-nii* is not going to overtake *C. elegans*'s fame, but it is well on its way to becoming infamous.

A nematode that destroys the foliage of trees is a new phe-nomenon in North America. "We have never dealt with a foliar nematode of a tree before," Marra says. The nematode's origin story, and a great deal about its habits and movements, remain a mystery, one Marra has devoted himself to solving. The nema-tode may have come from Japan because its close relative is not causing systematic tree death there, which suggests the beech trees there coevolved with the worm and have some resistance. And because the genetic sequences of the nematodes first found in Ohio, then in New York, in Connecticut, and everywhere else it has been identified in the United States so far, seem quite similar. The nematodes are not clones, but their genetic diversity doesn't seem as great as it would be if they had a long evolutionary history in North America.

A North American nematode that arrived in exports to Japan in the early twentieth century shows the same pattern. It moved from Japan to China, Taiwan, and Korea, and to Portugal. From there it moved to Spain, apparently relishing dry hot weather. It has been described as "the most destructive disease in pine forest ecosystems worldwide." The pine wilt nematode, *Bursaphelenchus xylophilus*, gets into pines via local bark beetles; death often arrives within months. The genetics of that nematode are hugely varied in its home range. "Whereas in Japan and Europe, they're just large clonal expansions," Marra says. "Nobody here cared about that nematode because it wasn't a problem . . . in Europe and in Asia, their native forests of pines are being wiped out."

Deciduous forests in winter are often a study in grays. There is little color, aside from evergreens and dangling dry yellow-brown leaves the winds seem to have missed. Beech are among the trees that retain some autumn foliage, a phenomenon called marcescence. The leaves may deter moose and deer from eating young twigs and buds; they may catch snow and hold moisture into the spring; they may drop and return nutrients to the soil at the time the tree most needs them. Or marcescence may be a vestige, a habit formed during the early days of trees, when most were conifers and kept their leaves year-round. For now, marcescence retains its secrets and the winter woods retain flashes of color and something for the wind to rustle and play with.

Looking at trees in winter can be comforting. Their defoliated raggedness looks seasonally appropriate. Perhaps those bare branches will leaf out fully. Perhaps that stain is damp, not rot. Perhaps things are not as bad as they seemed over the hot dry summer. Perhaps those persistent beech leaves mean no nematodes reached that tree. "In the dormant period, it is not as obvious which beech trees are affected," says Moulis, whose work as an arborist in Connecticut has brought her into contact with many beech.

Moulis worries about what each spring will bring. "When I started hearing about it a couple of years ago from the ag experiment station in state, I was not expecting the impact and how quickly it would affect these trees. Now I'm getting calls almost every day to come look at the tree that suddenly died next to the power lines. There are so many beech trees. These American beech trees were perfectly fine last year and now they're completely defoliating." At one of her sites near Madison, Connecticut, Moulis remembers a favorite route. "It used to be like completely nighttime driving that road," she says. Now, "you look from side to side and you see beech trees, the trunks are still standing and . . . there's just a couple dried curly malformed leaves. It's so alarming to drive down a street that used to be completely shaded and now it's sunny."

Marra is one of the ag experiment station staff who put out that word in 2019. Now, he says, "I live and breathe beech leaf disease." Each year, more counties in more states report the disease. It has been detected in Michigan, on the western shore of Lake Erie across from Cleveland, in Ontario, in Maine, and in Virginia. An infested leaf can contain hundreds of thousands of nematodes that swim out through the stomata if there is water on the leaf. "You have those nematodes packed inside the leaf, like it's a subway car. It's rush hour. Then you put water outside of a stomate and it's like opening the doors of the subway and they spill out. So now you've got thousands of nematodes just on the surface of the leaf and all it takes is a blue jay or a finch or a squirrel or a mite or a rain drop," Marra says. "They are sticky. They stick to things."

The nematodes overwinter in beech buds, eating nascent leaves. Fewer leaves, less photosynthesis, fewer nutrients, less growth, and, soon, no life. Marra is seeing in forests what Moulis is seeing in towns. Beech are intricate, complex trees; the silhouette of a beech is full of branches, busy and rich with leaves. American beech, the only endemic beech, is *Fagus grandifolia*: "big leafed" could be said to refer not only to the size of the leaves, but to their sumptuous abundance. *Casting Deep Shade* is the poet C. D. Wright's meditation on beech. In some forests, beech leaves make up most of the foliage—or used to, Marra says. "The moment you step onto a forest floor, you say, Why is there so much light? Something looks weird and wrong here. It's June and the forest floor is brightly lit and you look up and you realize, Oh, this is wrong."

Marra finds the nematode fascinating, which gives him the energy, stamina, and curiosity to research it. Some scientists have hypothesized that the nematode may be working in conjunction with some agent—perhaps a bacterium. Marra is of the view that the nematode is acting alone, particularly since a series of tests called Koch's postulates were completed. Koch's postulates are a critical forensic tool for pathologists. They were developed by nineteenth century microbiologist Robert Koch, whose work was central to the acceptance of the germ theory of disease. Put concisely, the postulates require identifying and isolating the suspected cause, seeing if it gives rise to the same disease in an unexposed plant or animal, and re-isolating it from that plant or animal. The postulates were "satisfied" at the federal nematode laboratory, Marra says.

Right now, Marra is studying the genetics of the tiny worm. He will travel to Japan with a team of Forest Service researchers to collaborate with scientists there. It is an international flight he is loath to take. "My friends will vouch for me that I'm agonizing over the idea of flying to Tokyo . . . because I belong to this group called No Fly Climate Sci," Marra says. "I am circumspect about when I do travel and how I travel and why I travel, you know? Is that something I really need to do?" But collecting nematodes from Japanese beech trees, seeing what the worms are or are not doing to beech in a different, and perhaps original, habitat is essential for understanding genetic variation and life history, which may, in turn, be able to help American beech. "I feel blessed and honored and grateful that I have this kind of passion to do it," Marra says. But "it's not that I don't break down in tears when I go into a forest and see what's happening and think, What have we humans been doing?"

What we have been doing is moving things around. At first slowly—and, in the first millennia of our floral–faunal relocations, often with good results for our diet and well-being. And then with increasing velocity, volume, variety, and havoc—often causing the extermination of people and species. For long-lived trees, international trade is often a catastrophe.

For geologic, evolutionary, and climatic reasons, parts of North America, Europe, and Asia share many tree families. A pest traveling from one place can often find its tree of choice where it arrives. But the new tree generally lacks the chemical protections that its relatives have had time to develop against that pest at home. In addition, the traveling pests often were not accompanied on their international flight or sea voyage by the predatory organisms that normally keep them in check in their place of origin. In China, the American white moth (known in the United States as the fall webworm) and the red turpentine beetle are major tree and plant pests, whereas in the United States, trees evolved in tandem with those insects and they have not tended to do long-term damage.

Many imported plants and trees become welcome parts of the landscape, particularly in cities and suburbs. But others can have adverse effects, and sometimes forests are lost to recently arrived plants. Vines like bittersweet entomb and suffocate trees. Forests can be replaced by shrubby tangles and brambles. Grasses—including cheatgrass and guinea grass—supplant trees, contributing to cataclysmic wildfires like those in Maui in 2023. Invasive plants can alter forest biodiversity. One of Hawaii's most famous trees, the 'ōhi'a—also called the Pele tree, for the goddess of fire and of volcanoes, because of its vivid red flowers—is dying from two introduced infections. It is commonly replaced by albizia, a fast-growing import from Papua New Guinea and Indonesia that does not sustain Hawaii's endemic creatures.

The pace of introductions has not abated. When the Asian longhorned beetle arrived, it was the first major wood-boring insect to cause havoc: thirty-five different landings have been recorded in North America and twenty-six in Europe since the 1990s, and the beetle is still burrowing into maple, willow, horse chestnut, elm, still requiring teams of spotters and climbers like Bear and Melissa. Now the longhorned beetle is one of many destructive wood-boring insects. Research in the early aughts estimated that between 1860 and 2006, about four hundred forest insects from elsewhere were identified in the United States, with 14 percent of them causing "notable damage." In the last decade or so of that period, a greater proportion of the arrivals, some 44 percent, caused severe damage and a significant proportion of them were borers.

In addition to borers, there are defoliators, including winter moth, browntail moth, and spongy moth. There are piercers and suckers: elongate hemlock scale, hemlock woolly adelgid, spotted lanternfly, to name a few. There are the mighty fungi. Those that have already reshaped the landscape—chestnut blight, Dutch elm disease, white pine blister rust—and those doing so now. There are the imported phytophthoras, the water molds, that have not been numerous—although they are increasingly taking up spots on the ever-lengthening catalogue of threats. They are the mixed martial art champions of arboreal pathogenesis: *phytophthora* means "plant destroyer."

And now, the nematode.

As soon as beech leaf disease appeared in Connecticut, Marra responded to a Forest Service call for monitoring plots and set up eleven sites around the state. One midsummer day, he checks the one just north of New Haven, where the ag station is based. A few minutes into the forest, we notice our first beech. It has barely any leaves; those it does have are pale and floppy, missing their protective waxy cuticle. "Oh my god. These are all beeches. Geez. Wow," says Marra, stopping short. "It is all happening so fast . . . I started this plot three years ago . . . and this tree here had a full canopy." We pass another beech that has darker thicker leaves, streaked with brown and curled up, claw-like. Not a single beech along the trail looks healthy. Most are barely hanging on. "People have said to me, 'Are you depressed all the time?'" he says. "And I say, that's my baseline."

We leave the trail and hike into a small area where several trees are marked with blue flagging and several others have number tags. Marra records data for all the trees over five inches in diameter in the circular ten-meter plot. He records extra details about the beech, describing patterns of mortality in the crown and leaves. He checks each beech for both beech leaf disease and another infection. Well before beech leaf disease arrived, American beech were struggling, just as whitebark pine were struggling with white pine blister rust before the mountain pine beetles ascended. In the late 1800s, a scale insect arrived in Nova Scotia on a shipment of European beech. The holes created by the insect allow entry to resident fungi that can kill the tree.

Beech bark disease, as it is called, is why many beech forests are already full of weedy beech saplings. Marra sees no sign of beech bark disease on the beech we see. But the nematode has crippled them: almost no canopy, only a few leaves on some of the lower branches. They look erased.

In most reports about future forests, there is usually some good news. In the projections Worrall, Rehfeldt, and others did in Colorado, for instance, they predicted Gambel oak and aspen would occupy some areas emptied of other species. Beech and ash looked to be among the climate change "winners" in the eastern part of the country. As recently as 2018, a year before Marra set up his plots, a Forest Service report about the Northeast noted that some projections of future climate might be favorable for beech and ash; in a familiar world, they would fill in for species able to survive farther north—sugar maple and hemlock, among others. A different forest for sure, but a vibrant forest and one with creatures. Beech nuts have replaced part of the food gap left by American chestnut, which are in the beech family. Some forty animals, including black bear, marten, fox, raccoon, and turkey, rely on mature beech, one of the only trees in certain areas to produce what is called a hard mast, a periodic wealth of nuts that sustain and regulate wildlife populations. Beech start to do this when they are forty or more years old. But trees disappeared by disease cannot fill in gaps. And ancient masting patterns and schedules that preserved both beech and their dependents are now being deranged by climate change.

The beech we see around us are not dead. One is putting huge resources into growing epicormic shoots: little bushes of branches are emerging all over the trunk, trying to ramp up photosynthesis. Marra says that tallies of tree death—this number of beech trees, that acreage of ash—is not the most important metric to him. "People say to me, How much mortality are you seeing with the beeches? And I say, none. But that doesn't mean they are not in serious decline. And you should be really interested in what's declining," he says. How is the forest composition changing? Can the emerging forest still provide food and shelter and mutualism? Is it overrun with invasive plants that can't support the wildlife? "We have never had a foliar nematode disease of trees. We have never had 424 parts per million carbon in the atmosphere or changing weather patterns in way that trees have not evolved to respond to. And invasive plants," says Marra. "People need to get out into forests more."

After the trees have been assessed and he has searched in vain for beech saplings, Marra downloads data from the humidity and temperature monitor. It is attached to a small wooden board that is, in turn, attached to a tree about ten feet up. The board is hard to distinguish from the bark. "I took a piece of beech bark into Home Depot and matched the color," Marra says. "I did that. Yes."

We stop chatting to listen to a high-pitched bird call and I realize, as if I have been slapped and with a terrible hollowed-out feeling, that although I have heard music and voices from the nearby Quinnipiac University sports complex, I have not heard birds calling until that moment. "It is very *Silent Spring*," says Marra. America's once most-abundant bird, the passenger pigeon, relied on beechnuts. John James Audubon's portrait of the species has a pair arrayed on a beech, according to naturalist Donald C. Peattie. It is not difficult to imagine that the tree too will soon go the way of the bird.

Beech leaf disease is such a new phenomenon that the science is unfolding in real time. "They don't even know where it's coming from," Moulis says. "We don't even know how to fight it." How beech will fare over the long-term remains unknown. Experimental treatments are being tested, but it is early days. Neither

Marra nor Moulis has seen infected beech trees come back to robust good health—most die, a few linger with few leaves—but Moulis has observed that European beech, *Fagus sylvatica*, do not seem quite as hard hit as their American relatives. John Pogacnik, who first noticed the strange banding on beech leaves in 2012 and catalyzed the eventual identification of the nematode, has been tracking beech since his discovery, even into retirement. "My job as biologist was to visit each park. I usually did it from mid-May or so when the birds and everything else starts coming out and would do surveys of everything." He has seen so many changes to Ohio forests after four decades of observing them that as we walk through one of the Lake Metroparks, we don't even get around to beech leaf disease for a good long time.

But we do talk a lot about worms. Invasive earthworms. Pogacnik points to bare soil on either side of the trail. "Look at the ground here. Do you see any leaf litter?" he asks. "This is where there's a nightcrawler hole. What they do is they pull the leaves into their hole and they eat them. . . . When you look at the ground, you don't see leaves and you see all these just piles of leaf skeletons." Colleagues have told him that they have visited worm-affected woods after dark and have heard hundreds of nightcrawlers chewing; he can't confirm, but says it is believable. We can see deep into the forest in many places—there is no understory, no leaf litter. "You should not be able to look into this forest and see for fifty feet," Pogacnik says.

When glaciers covered much of North America during the last ice age, earthworms were killed off. Some species survived, mostly in the Southeast, and have been slowly working their way north since. Meanwhile, some seventy species have come from afar. They can cause compaction, water runoff, erosion; they can change the pH of soil; they can alter or destroy fungal–plant relationships; they can consume the seeds of many trees, and expose their roots to the air. "Try to find a red maple seedling here that is more than a year old," Pogacnik says. "Red maples, which are thriving in most places, are absent here." Worms also eat the seeds of smaller plants; and without those plants to feed on, deer and other herbivores consume saplings.

In a few places along the trail, Pogacnik notes dense patches of woodland aster and goldenrod. He and some friends have discussed planting local native flowering plants like these in forests degraded by earthworms. Asters and goldenrod provide food for birds and pollinators, and they provide some cover for ground-nesting birds such as ovenbird, whippoorwill, woodcock, meadowlark, indigo bunting, and hermit thrush, and habitat for amphibians that have lost their damp leafy ceilings to earthworms. Many native forest floor plants can resist deer, withstand worms, and forestall takeover by invasive plants.

We see beech, many with shriveled leaves. "But they're alive," Pogacnik says. Then the path curves and we begin to follow the loop back to the trailhead. Pogacnik is clearly searching for something and is keeping it a surprise. "Now, here we have something different," he says finally, and there is happiness in his voice. "That looks quite good, doesn't it? This has been like this for probably ten years." It is the most magnificent beech I have seen since learning about beech leaf disease. A few crinkled leaves, a few leaves brown at the tips, a few concessions to the nematode. But the canopy is thick and full with wide green leaves, a profusion of leaves, an abundance of leaves, casting deep shade.

Oak

Even in the late afternoon soft light of early summer, the trees along I-95 look miserable. Bear has been driving for nearly twelve hours. She left western Massachusetts in the early morning, stopping to help a snapping turtle out of the road before she'd gotten much underway, and stopping a few hours later to pick me up at a Starbucks just off the highway in Oakland, New Jersey, where my husband has dropped me off. She calls it a day when we reach Richmond, Virginia. My ride with Bear includes the pursuit of good food, mechanic-level detail about the cars and motos that pass and memories of cars and motos past, and stories about trees along the way. We see dead elms. We see dead ash. We see trees suffocating in mulch piled up against the trunk—the root flares of these "volcano trees" can't breathe and such trees usually die young. Uncounted millions of trees are misplanted and volcano-mulched in this way, Bear says, and are lost every year. She points to a few tall red pines that look alone and uneasy in a section where the interstate is being widened: "Oh those trees will be just fine. Just take all their friends away. Those trees aren't going to fall on the highway."

Bear has left Eversource and has been directing the Women's Tree Climbing Workshop full time for about nine months. The pandemic had made acutely clear that life is short. And, she says, the workshop is all about letting go of fear. So how could she not do the same and leave the safety of her secure job? Although it seems Bear does not need a pandemic to push her to take risks and try new things. In addition to being a forester for a time, as well as an arborist and a tree warden, she has been a cook, a baker, a FedEx driver, a forest fire fighter, a wilderness trail worker, a house painter, and a town clerk. She is studying to become a yoga instructor too. The sisters have trademarked the workshop and ordered an official van— license plate WTCW. Bear ordered from Amish carpenters a tiny house with lots of windows ("I am very phototropic. I was a plant in a previous life.") that could serve as her office and where the climbing equipment could be stored safely, away from mice, damp, and sunlight. Neither the van nor the office had arrived by the time this June 2022 road trip came around. The white U-Haul rental she is driving is stuffed top-to-bottom with gear that was being stored in a shipping container on Melissa and Tom's farm.

With Bear full-time, one of the twins' goals is to increase the number of workshops held each year, from a total of two or three to one almost every month, as seasons and instructor availability allow. Another goal is to offer nonbinary and gender-inclusive workshops and to do workshops in new regions, opening the training to people who can't travel far, because of time, money, or family. Elfand—not Elf-land, as we keep saying, at first by mistake, then for the fun of it—North Carolina is one of the new sites.

We arrive at Chestnut Ridge, a 362-acre camp and retreat center with forests and a lake, the following morning. "Don't bring the chestnut back," Bear says as we drive in, talking about American chestnut restoration efforts. "We had our chance. Just let things be now." The parking lot is already filled with volunteer local arborists. The team today includes two former workshop participants, Amanda Whitten and Tana Byrd. They start looking for trees that would be safe, fun, and challenging to climb. "Think about yourself as an absolute beginner: What used to terrify you?" Bear asks. "Think about that when you are setting the lines, putting in the bells and ribbons." Two large lovely white oaks, *Quercus alba*, already have thin ropes in them—leftover from a camp activity—that could be used to pull up the much thicker climbing lines. One oak has a weeping canker at the base. Bear asks if oak wilt has been seen in the area, and the locals say not yet.

Most of the leaves in my mother's journal are oaks. She has several from the East Coast. A red oak from South Salem, New York, has a color pencil sketch of its acorn: "notice very shallow cup, large acorn"; a black oak from the same place has sharp-tipped lobes that "bear a tiny bristle" and its acorn has a "deep cup and scales which tend to stick out." Most of the oaks are from Berkeley. A silk oak with "feathery foliage." A coast live oak "with wide-spreading heavy, thick branches forming a broad, round crown." A gently lobed English oak, "a lovely shade tree." A Mexican oak, which has a suggestion of points at the end of the leaf, like a wave just beached. A turkey oak. "In landscaping the world, nature has used more kinds of oak than any other tree," my mother wrote. She was right.

There are about four hundred thirty kinds of oak, one of the largest varieties in an arboreal genus and they are among the species most common in, and central to, ecological richness. There is "good evidence that oaks shine brighter than other plants in their contributions to biodiversity on the national level, the regional level, and even the level of a single yard," Douglas Tallamy writes in *The Nature of Oaks: The Rich Ecology of Our Most Essential Native Trees*. "Oaks support more forms of life and more fascinating interactions than any other tree genus in North America." Some two thousand three hundred species of mosses, animals, fungi, and lichen rely on oaks; in the United States, the oak-reliant count includes more than five hundred kinds of butterfly and moth. The loss of oaks ruptures habitats, shatters diversity. One-third of oaks globally are endangered and many others are in decline because of all the usual suspects: deforestation, climate change, insect pests, herbivores, and pathogens.

In the western United States perhaps the greatest current threat is sudden oak death, which has killed millions of oaks, radiating from California's Marin and Santa Cruz counties, where it arrived on imported rhododendrons. Some of the critical work to identify the cause of sudden oak death—*Phytophthora ramorum*—was done on the Berkeley campus, where a collection like the one my mother made is no longer possible. The disease has crossed north into Oregon, south into Big Sur. The map of affected counties grows every year. The water mold seems to appreciate the warmer temperatures and rain patterns of climate change.

In the eastern part of the country, oaks are dying from a different major disease. The oak wilt map is another map in which the shaded areas of loss seem unreal in their extent. Two dozen or so states east of the Continental Divide have lost and are losing hundreds of thousands of oak—as well as acorns, habitat, woodland diversity, and street shade. The disease has recently spread into Canada. Oak wilt, which was identified in Wisconsin in the 1940s, is caused by the fungus *Bretziella fagacearum*, which travels as spores on beetles and between the touching roots of infected trees. Pruning oaks between April and July can invite the wilt, because young beetles on the move seek raw, open wood. The fungus forms masses in xylem, preventing water from moving to the canopy. The United States has ninety-one species of oak, fifty or so in the East, and none seem safe: red oaks and those in their group—including live oaks, pin oaks, scarlet oaks, black oaks—die most quickly, sometimes within weeks; white oaks and those in their group—such as swamp chestnut oak, bur oaks, post oaks—often die within a few years of infection.

The white oak canker Bear has identified is not wilt, rather something that can be treated if needed. Bear taps gently around the base of the trunk with a rock, listening for rot. There is none. A maple, two hickories, and a chestnut oak next to the white oaks also seem perfect climbing trees. "Hickories are stronger than oxen. They are honey badgers," says Melissa. "They can weather an intense storm no problem. They might look a little messed up, but they will be fine." Several shortleaf pines down a slope of lawn and near a fire pit are too far away. But on the lawn near the white oaks are two enticing pecan trees that would be perfect for teaching how to throw a line into a tree. Bear is particularly brilliant at throw line. She swings a sixteen-ounce throwbag attached to a thin line until it reaches the right momentum and then she lets fly. Almost every time, the weight sails though the branch union taking the long thin line with it. A rope can then be attached to the thin line with a clove hitch.

The arborists start pruning, taking out dead wood, but not too much: they leave habitat for birds and insects as well as conditions that an arborist will encounter at work. They put in the bells and ribbons, the hammocks, and the trillium. They make sure the tie-in points are at strong branch-trunk unions. It is hot, about 90 degrees. I sit in a gazebo's shade and listen to arborists sing and watch them move up and down, in and out of the canopy, some in the oaks, some in the pecans, like spiders on silks, while tiny gray spiders run across the picnic table, my laptop, and my arms.

After two days of setup, the participants arrive, choose their bunkbed in Falcon, one of the camp's cabins, and the introduction circle begins. There are arborists who don't know any other women working in the industry and are looking for guidance and a community, for mentors. "It is a bitch working only with men," says one. Some are here for additional training—or for basic training they never got. Some are considering arboriculture as a career. Some are here because they heard it was a healing experience. "I know what you need," says another, quoting her sister, a workshop alumna. "It has been a hard year."

Under the sweeping long branches of the white oaks—some broad limbs stretch out as far as the tree is high—the instructors start, as they always do, by reviewing safety. The industry standards for arboriculture and related gear are "written in blood," says Tana Byrd, "so people's kids come back from work." Arboriculture is an old science and art, but a young profession and its first safety standards, which remain voluntary, emerged only a few decades ago. In 1965, eighteen-year-old Jeff Hugg was nearing the end of his second week as an arborist on a job near Johnstown, New York, his hometown. He had apparently taken so quickly to tree climbing that he was given a solo pruning assignment. He died a few minutes after starting work: a 4,800-volt electric line ran through the first tree he climbed. His mother, Ethel M. Hugg, an elementary school teacher, fought for safety standards and her advocacy led in 1972 to the first occupational safety standards for arboriculture, which are called ANSI Z133. "Doesn't surprise me one bit that it was a woman who led the fight for standards," someone says. Bear peers inside a helmet to look for the manufacture date and to see if it has another rating, called ANSI Z89.1, which governs head protection; she declares the helmet retired and now a pot for petunias.

Tana is wearing the latest in ANSI-rated eye protection, funky glasses that don't look like protective gear—they come in cat-eyes, aviators, blues, pinks, greens, yellows. "If you like the way you look in your stuff, you will wear it," Melissa says. It is Tana's second time as an instructor and she radiates energy. She started working as an arborist in Texas when she was in her twenties. Someone she knew did tree work, she says, and "I started working for him and he kind of drank a lot. And he got 70 percent and I got 30 percent. I was kind of like, the heck with this." In 2014, she started her own company, bought her own equipment, and "just started ripping and tearing." A few years later, she saw an advertisement for a Women's Tree Climbing Workshop in Texas. "I thought, there has got to be an easier way," she says. "It saved my life, just for the simple fact of the skills it taught me—and not just in a tree, but in life in general."

Tana says she can still remember the wrong boots she was wearing at that first workshop, tying her first Blake's hitch, the smell of the rain in a gorgeous and grand live oak, and the encouragement and empowerment. "I had never been on rope and here's all these people looking at me . . . and I remember coming down from that rope feeling like 'Oh my gosh, I am, I did it, I am a professional!'" She remembers showing Melissa and Bear pictures of herself at a job site. The photos were "of me and my kids taking this huge cottonwood down with no helmets and chains. I was climbing with no rope, free climbing. I had no training." Her kids were both under ten then and often came with her to work. "I was a single mom, so it was kind of like my only option . . . we just had to survive." After she did the workshop, she had shirts made for her business, T-N-T Tree Care and Landscaping: a photo of her on the front, sitting in her harness and helmet, thumbs up, huge smile.

The group breaks in half for gear inspection, with Melissa leading one section and Bear leading the other. Stacey Sherrod, who is in Melissa's group, says she has never inspected her gear before. Others murmur the same. They have not looked for outdated gear, for a small notch that could compromise a rope, for a rough spot on a metal ring that could fray a rope, for a weakness in a bridge or one along the seams where the D-rings attach.

Arboriculture is highly dangerous. According to annual analyses by the Tree Care Industry Association, there are some 239 injuries per 10,000 tree workers as opposed to 89 per 10,000 for all industries lumped together, and 17 deaths per 100,000 tree workers as opposed to 3.4 to 3.8 for all industries. The association notes that the statistics are hard to interpret because the types of tree work are not consistently or clearly defined and because the data are poor. The figures are also considered underestimates because the Bureau of Labor Statistics says there are 63,700 workers who do tree removal and pruning in the United States, whereas other estimates put that figure closer to 290,000—including many solo operators and many who are undocumented. Beginning in 2021, the Occupational Safety and Health Administration started a series of national programs to reduce accidents and death. Arborists fall from trees, like Patrick O'Meara did. Or they fall from bucket trucks, cranes, or ladders, they get dragged into chippers, cut by chain saws, hit by falling limbs and falling trees, electrocuted, or struck by passing cars. There is no record of the injuries and deaths that occur specifically because of failed gear.

Melissa turns one of Sherrod's carabiners over and tells her the lock isn't working smoothly anymore, which could be dangerous if she needed to open it quickly. She does it in song, something she and Bear do from time to time. For Bear it usually means things are all right; for Melissa, the opposite. "I love how you turn into an opera singer when you don't like something. It just fills me with joy," Sherrod says. "When she sings in opera, I am like, 'Yes, what are you saying, I am listening! What are the holy words?'"

The next day, Nicole Benjamin-Harden has the group look closely at the white oaks to think about which branches are strong, what is good for the tree. "Think about how these branches can protect you," she says. "It is like when kids are climbing on us, it can be annoying. But if they are cute and sweet, we enjoy it. Think of it that way." Nicole is a friend of Tana's—they started a group called Guardians of the Canopy in Charlotte, North Carolina, to teach kids about trees, climbing, and arboriculture—and she is instructing for the first time. She is a rugby champion and a national tree climbing champion and will be heading to Denmark in a few months to compete in the international tree climbing championships.

Nicole used to do water quality monitoring for energy companies, but had "a young life crisis," and started working with the trees she has loved and climbed since she was young. When she was seven, she used a ladder to get into a towering pine near her home in Minnesota. She took the family camera with her and shot an aerial photograph of the house from the top of the pine, then replaced the camera in the drawer where it was kept. When the film was developed, she says, her parents couldn't mentally process the image—they even wondered for one crazy moment whether somehow Nicole's first grade teacher had borrowed the camera and done aerial shots of students' houses. Shortly after, Nicole—also unbeknownst to her parents—installed and camouflaged a rope in the pine so she didn't have to use the more visible ladder.

Nicole says that trees and tree work saved her life. She says that family complexities led her into some dark places, but that the first arborist company she worked for paid for her to see a counselor. She learned how to recognize the age layers within herself, the small child, the pre-teen, the teen, the twenty-something. "So when I would face things that would make me uncomfortable or would be triggering or whatever, I was figuring out which Nicole do you fall back into and why?" Being up in trees keeps her calm and centered. "All the voices just go quiet and I lose track of time," she says. "Sometimes I wish I would have found this much earlier in my life, because I was already 31 when I started to work. But at the same time, I'm grateful. It just waited to come along."

This group of workshop participants is quick to get everything: many of them have some familiarity with ropes and climbing, although that was not reflected on their applications. Melissa and Bear have consistently found that women tend to underestimate their skill level, often describing themselves as beginners when they are advanced. "Your self-descriptions are not accurate," Melissa says. "You are only novices in your minds." Many also often express concern that they are taking a spot away from someone who needs it more. The instructors are soon helping these participants with more than the basics. Ribbons are disappearing as climbers reach them and pocket them. And many bells—which were a goal for the next day—are rung before lunchtime. People are laughing in the hammocks, laughing in the trillium—applause is ringing out regularly, as someone reaches a new height or perfects a new technique. Sherrod rejects the hip thrust after discovering that she is excellent at foot lock. "Just because I am not good at the hip thrust, doesn't mean I am not a good climber!"

White Oak leaves and flowers

Bear is coaching Louise Hosburgh, who is from Kentucky, has a donkey named Petey and a horse named Sassafras Roxane, and who started climbing a year before.

"I want you to get it better than that," Bear says. "When we are scared, we scrunch up. Stretch out your left leg, Louise."

"It is always a weird death-gripping when I don't know what I am doing," Hosburgh says as she follows Bear's guidance, tries to relax, extends her leg, and starts walking along a limb.

"I am in love!" She hugs the white oak. "I am not going to be able to sleep tonight, thinking about all this and the possibilities! I am a real arborist!"

"You rang not one, not two, but three bells!" exalts Bear.

"How do we get more of this in the world?" Nicole asks of no one in particular.

That night, the group gathers around the fire pit near the short-leaf pines. So many frogs are singing, a knot of frogs, so loud and full and intoxicating—although it is troubling that they appear to be moving toward the chlorinated swimming pool. Sherrod says that the day has been gourmet, that she gives it a chef's kiss, and that she is going to go cry in her sleeping bag because she is so happy and tears are an excellent exfoliant. Sherrod, who had started as an arborist immediately before the workshop, later tells me that the workshop taught her to pay close attention to safety, to her crew, and to herself: ". . .being able to be there for my team and understanding what they need and when they need it. And being more outspoken. I have had a very strong increase at being able to communicate my concerns on a job site."

Sherrod describes the joy of being able to analyze how to deal with a massive tulip poplar that a powerful wind had blown onto a house in Nashville, Tennessee, during a spring storm. The family had "watched the tree come up from the ground and then set back down, and then come up from the ground and set back down," Sherrod says. Finally the enormous tree fell, crashing through two bedrooms. The family was unharmed; they had fled the house when they saw how the wind lifted the tree. When Sherrod and her team cut the trunk—which was partially decayed but "nowhere near dead"—it springboarded: the roots pulled at the base and the huge stump snapped back into the hole in the ground. It was a highly dangerous situation that required great care and communication. It went smoothly, Sherrod says, because her team talked the whole complicated process through and in a new post-workshop way. "I'm definitely a lot more open with them and talking to them," she says of her colleagues. "I was already really good about encouragement because that's something that I need, but I'm a lot more active with it than I was before."

When it is her turn to speak in the circle, Nicole says she regrets not asking the participants to stop saying sorry: "Women are always apologizing for just being. Maybe we could say sorbet or sherbet instead?"

Tana says she has not been able to stop crying because Melissa and Bear, without mentioning it, put the T-N-T Tree Care and Landscaping shirt she made after her first workshop on the swag table. Sherrod and Avalon Collier had discovered it and initiated a modest bidding war, which Sherrod won. Tana tells me afterward that the shirt represents who she used to be. She has gotten sober. She has traveled widely—including to Hawaii and Ivory Coast, where she assisted a primatologist with field research. She is getting her horticulture degree. She and her son were the first mother–son combo at a tree-climbing competition. She will present at the Women's Forest Congress in a few months on a panel, Women as Catalysts for Change. All this since that Texas workshop.

Melissa and Bear "took me under their wing," Tana says. "So when I say they saved my life, it wasn't just for the trees, or just with my kids, or how I handled my life. But it literally was a 360 because there was a seed that was planted in me, and they kept watering it."

The group gathers again at the end of the workshop, in the cafeteria. The counselors from Chestnut Ridge are gathering there too and a racket builds as they drag coolers around and set up tables while the kitchen staff begins dinner prep. Against this backdrop of noisy chaos, the instructors share their highs and lows. Nicole says her high is that she knows she could call anyone in this group at three in the morning from a roadside anywhere and could count on them to help her.

The participants have picked a number out of a helmet and, in order, walk up to the giveaway table to choose something. On this table is a particularly hefty prize: an entire bag of gear, more than $1,000 worth, donated by the company where Melissa works. Collier—who has fought wildfires in Montana, cleared trails in New Hampshire, and who told her boss that she wouldn't attend the workshop unless her only female colleague, Sherrod, came too—has pulled number one. She walks up to the table. She takes the bag of new gear. "Sorbet," she says. "One thousand times sorbet."

Most of Collier's recent arborist work has been removal, taking down dead and storm-damaged trees in and around Nashville. There is little pruning or planting going on these days, she says, because there have been so many storms and so much extreme weather-related damage. In the last few years, she has noticed spring coming earlier and the magnolias and other flowering trees—cherries and red buds—responding by flowering earlier. The warm days are then often followed by freezes, and the flowers brown and die and fall. Southern magnolias seem to be faring particularly poorly, unaccustomed to cold snaps right on the heels of the first flush of spring warmth.

"At the very beginning of March, I mean, it was insane. We had a 70-degree day and then it cooled off overnight. And then next day it was negative. Like it was below zero." It was so cold, many southern-adapted shrubs and trees died. The company Collier was working for at the time called off jobs because it was too cold to work. Then summer heat arrived. "Before we know it, we are not going to be in zone seven anymore," she says. "We are going to be pushed up to zone eight. Zone nine. Within my lifetime." The Department of Agriculture sets thirteen hardiness zones, roughly mappable onto latitude, that are determined by winter temperatures averaged over a thirty-year period. In the newest map, issued in 2023, many sites have shifted north by five degrees.

Collier says she has seen populations of insects fluctuate, particularly in the last few years, and she is worried about it. "When people finally put it in a cycle of how one thing affects the other thing, then it really hits home. Then you can start painting a picture," Collier says. "But mostly, people don't like to do that because it's too scary. . . . And sometimes I wonder if we can't even care about each other, how are we ever going to come together to address the environment we live in and have been poisoning for so long?"

The ropes are out of the trees. The ribbons, bells, hammock, and trillium are out too. The gear is lugged in many trips, some in the camp's little red wagons, over to the van, where Bear repacks— and no one interferes with her system. She has, Melissa says, "Tetris brain." Nicole nestles into a small hollow at the base of one of the white oaks. She leans her back into the embracing tree and thanks it.

Bear and I start the drive north. At our first coffee stop, which is at a fast-food sprawling mall-ish area, Bear gets out her shears and kneels in front of a maple sapling in the parking lot. It had been tethered to three stakes for stability. But no one came back to check on it and the tree looks tortured. Thick canvas-like straps cut into its trunk. Two branches have been nearly severed from the trunk by the straps—the cambium is dying. Bear cuts away as much as she can and tries to pull out the rest of the strap, but some is too deep. She cuts the bonds of another maple too. The maples are no longer being completely dismembered and choked by the cords, but they will likely die soon—they are the wrong species for a hot parking lot and their leaves look too pale. "They are very unhappy here," Bear says. She had liberated a cherry tree at the U-Haul place at the beginning of the trip. Like Melissa, she often sneaks out at night to undo damage—to liberate trees from suffocating volcano-like mounds of mulch, trees that she has seen suffering and dying when she passed them during the day.

Magnolia flower

We talk about the southern magnolia haunting us. Over dinner, one of the workshop participants had shared pictures of a magnolia, about seventy feet tall, perhaps one hundred years old. The photos showed a vast, complicated, beautiful tree, a tree of enchantment, an epic tree, its branches so intricate and wild and mythic, it seemed a tree that brought the world to life. Magnolias were among the earliest flowering trees to appear—they arose roughly one hundred twenty million years ago, before bees, moths, and butterflies had evolved, and so they rely on pollination by beetle, drawing them in with humongous fragrant flowers, which, in some species, emit heat that volatilizes the nectar, ensuring the scent drifts as widely as possible. Southern magnolia, my mother wrote beneath a color pencil drawing of a creamy water-lily-like flower and a nine-inch leaf that has come loose of its tape, "is so heavily leafed that it forms a tower of leaves, and the trunk is hardly seen."

The photos we were shown turned out to be before shots. The tree was felled by an arborist crew soon after: it had been in something's way. "I had to leave the table. I felt sick," Bear says. "You've just killed a sentient being, you have no right."

Arborists must do what their clients demand—or not work. They may try to explain why a driveway should be moved so an ancient tree can survive. Or why an addition or a pool could go somewhere else so as to not destroy a healthy grove. Or why pruning should only be done at certain times. Melissa tells customers, for instance, that even if they want her to, she is not going to prune their elms when the trees are in full leaf and most vulnerable to the beetle that carries the deadly fungus. "I'd love to prune your elm tree, but I am going to wait for a few months because this is the time when your tree could be more susceptible than ever," she says. Likewise, she won't treat with pesticides in the early spring as trees are blooming and bees, hornets, flies, and other insects are pollinating. It is "the whole web," Melissa says. Like many arborists, she talks to people about trees when she is in the post office, the grocery store, anywhere, to anyone who will listen. Sometimes those conversations lead nowhere. People mostly still don't foreground trees. But sometimes the trees are seen as integral to the whole.

In 2017, four artists bought singer, composer, and Civil Rights activist Nina Simone's childhood home in Tryon, North Carolina, to save it from demolition. They have been working to restore the small house and create a museum there. The trees are as important to the restoration and the honoring of Simone as the house, including the magnolia that extends over one corner of the roof. "It's such a beautiful tree. It was incredible to see it," says artist Julie Mehretu. "There is something about it being there and living over time, and having been witness to a certain type of time, and being this guardian of the house."

Protecting the enormous magnolia meant releasing it. "It was covered with vines that were starting to choke it out," says Nicole, who spent a spring day with a colleague removing kudzu, wisteria, and grape vines—gobs of vines like a giant nest, she describes, vines that filled an entire dump truck. The branches are now no longer constrained.

Like many trees, magnolia can move at night. Recordings of birch, cypress, cedar, oak, maple, and other tree species made with laser scanners reveal that branches move, sometimes by many inches, sometimes assuming new configurations by morning. Species vary greatly in their nocturnal bending and stretching. Southern magnolia has the most unusual and evocative pattern. Over the course of one night, the tree's branches trace the same movement three times. Like a Buddhist prostration, like a dancer practicing her choreography, like a refrain.

PART IV

Aerial Roots

A year after my last workshop, I return to Hi-Rock for a third time. It rains in thick sheets during most of the drive from New York City, but the downpour stops as I reach Bash Bish Falls State Park. The woods, countryside, and sky have that sharp clarity and saturated color of sunshine after a storm. There are dead limbs on both sides of the muddy road into camp, haphazard stacks of birch branches, leaves browning, from a recent pruning.

In the eighteen months that I have been visiting Hi-Rock, many things have changed. The old-fashioned carved-letter waterskiing sign on the biggest hemlock has been replaced with a less charismatic painted one that says, "Ski Dock." Some of the workshop's emphasis has changed. When Kate Odell leads the tree biology section she talks, as one instructor always does, about checking the base of trees, looking for rot, listening to how the trunk sounds. But this time much of her talk is also about climate change and the pests and diseases thriving in stressed trees. "I see a lot of secondary issues, insect and disease issues, that typically in the past would not be a problem," Kate explains to me. "You look in all the literature I have on them and it's like, 'Takes advantage of stressed plants.' Everything is stressed."

The trees at Hi-Rock have changed too. Near the sibling trees, the beech tree Rachel Vanicek pointed out is dead from beech leaf disease. The little red oak to the side of the main lodge, the site of my first failed hip thrust, looks scrawny and unhealthy. It has lost the fullness of its crown to spongy moth. Moulis, who is also back for this September workshop, tells me it is a good thing I missed the one a few months earlier in May. "We were pulling spongy moth caterpillars off of ourselves," she says. "They were basically raining down on us."

Lymantria dispar caterpillars are an old pest with a new name. The first change made by the Better Common Names Project of the Entomological Society of America was, in 2022, to retire "gypsy moth" and to adopt the French colloquial name, based on the sponge-like appearance of the egg masses. (The group is looking into renaming other insects, including the Asian longhorned beetle: many names "inadvertently create associations between invasive pest status and groups of people.") The caterpillars escaped during a storm from the home of Étienne L. Trouvelot, despite the netting he had apparently draped around his backyard. Trouvelot had obtained them from Europe in the 1880s with the intention of breeding a hearty silkworm that could fill gaps in the fabric market left by the Civil War and a silk-worm disease. Since he had a lot of oaks—for a while, anyway—on his property, he reportedly chose a caterpillar that would feed on oak leaves. A century and a half later, spongy moths are going strong, adapting to hotter weather and benefiting from drought because it kills one of their fungal predators.

Hi-Rock's great hemlocks have also declined since my first visit, but not because of spongy moth. What with the oaks, maples, and birch, the caterpillars have had plenty to eat. "I remember them being more full, these three hemlocks," Moulis points out as we stand in a circle around Kate. "They are declining." Kate has noticed it too: their canopies are thinning. "If I am standing underneath, I should not be able to see the sky," she

says. "Over a year-and-a-half, these trees have just nose-dived."
The twigs now all have the white fuzz and brown spots of hundreds of thousands of insects feeding.

When the instructors set up before the workshop this time, they had to remove dozens of dead branches from the three hemlocks. Bear says the trees move differently. When wind hits, foliage and branches usually catch it and in their sway and dance, diffuse it, spreading its force throughout the tree. Now the wind is hitting the trunk straight on. In a gust, Bear says, it feels as though someone shoved the tree in the back. The wind is strong and chilly off Plantain Pond as Kate talks about the trees' woes. I yearn to be in the hemlocks, to feel the wind as they do, even if it is rough.

My first climb happens quickly. It feels natural to reach for the pulley, carabiners, and friction hitch cord on my harness. I clip a carabiner—without dropping it—to the eye at the end of the climbing line so that side has some weight on it and isn't pulled out of my reach while I work on the falling end. I decide to tie a Knut. The movement flows. I bring the hitch cord in front of the line, loop it around once, bring it under and then over itself, loop it around the line three times. I push the end through the first loop. I have a recognizable Knut. I dress it: aligning it so that it looks like a knot from the "picture books," as *On Rope* describes it. Then I set it, making it firm and tight.

But the Knut feels too tight, it looks a little pudgy. I tie a Michoacán instead. The knot still looks bulky and is holding too tight. Kali Alcorn, who has traveled from British Columbia to teach this weekend, lends me a thinner hitch cord. I tie the Michoacán again, testing its grip on the line and then adding another loop to make it hold more tightly. I am improvising, adding or subtracting loops to get the right amount of friction.

I don't have to think this all through. My hands have acquired some fluency. I set up the pulley system. I take up the slack on the line. I sit in the harness, swinging a few feet above the ground, to test the system. Everything holds and feels secure. I don't sway wildly. I don't slam into the trunk. I put the falling end through the foot ascender I have been sure to borrow from one of the gear bins.

Soon I am up the hemlock, well above the trillium. The legendary climbing champion Wenda Li, who is instructing at the workshop for the first time, is smiling at me from below, and I feel so proud of my knots, so agile, and filled with glow. Wenda suggests I stop climbing with the rope and instead climb the branches —it is what she loves best, she says, free climbing, yet tied in and safe. Wenda has been climbing for decades. She discovered that she loved trees during high school in Toronto, where she was an academic urban kid, she says, part of a first generation Chinese Canadian family that emphasized study-ing. She saw an advertisement for a one-month Outward Bound program and, seemingly out of character and a bit surprised at herself, begged her father to let her do it. For the first two weeks she hated it. She hated canoeing, hated portaging. Then she was left on an island for a three-day solo. "You are looking at ants, you are looking at the wind. It made me present," she says. "I discovered that I needed to be connected to trees."

Wenda decided to get a degree in forestry. She soon became disillusioned with that work, as Bear and Melissa had, because the job she found involved timber sales and forest razing. She applied for a position pruning in Toronto parks. One of the tests was climbing a tree. "It was only thirty feet high, but it was an epiphany. I knew the second I got up in the tree. I felt confident. I felt grounded." On the ground, though, her job was terrible. She describes bullying and being viewed and treated as a quota, as "a diversity requirement for the city." As she got better, she says, the abuse got worse: she had become more of a professional threat. She developed an ulcer. "If you experience this day after day, year after year as an adult—this humiliation—it destroys your self-esteem."

In 1993 she found her way to an International Society of Arboriculture jamboree, found her people, and quit her job. She applied to a private tree company. "Before I signed on, because I had spent so many years not being my authentic self, I put everything on the table," Wenda says. That included being open about her education, about how much she knew about trees— something she had to hide at her other job—and about having a female partner. "I hadn't honored my integrity. I had sacrificed my morals. It was very damaging." Now she tries to be open about most things, she says, including stage-of-life details in an industry oriented toward men and young people: she will travel from this Hi-Rock workshop to an Arborpalooza conference in Idaho to present the first-ever session on menopause. Trees, says Wenda, saved her life. It is a phrase I hear again and again from instructors, from participants.

Even with Wenda's encouragement, even knowing her story, I can't move from the rope system to free climbing the hemlock. This challenge, this movement between what feels to me like two world views, two ways of being, seems something I can't overcome. I descend to let my groundie have a turn.

Later that day, I visit the hemlock again. I tie my system and it feels intuitive and I climb, up and up and up, and suddenly I am at the tie-in point in the biggest hemlock. I can for the first time see where the rope goes through the friction saver. Even though they use friction savers, the instructors are careful to keep changing the tie-in points in the trees we climb repeatedly. "I think of myself as being here for a very short time on the earth, but trees are here for a long time. We will damage that tree and kill the limb if we keep using the same tie-in point," Melissa has explained. The strategy seems to be working; I see no damage, no rubbing on any of the branches.

I see a bell about five feet above the tie-in point, near the tip of the tree. When I last climbed at Hi-Rock, in the small cojoined hemlocks and oak, I was not able to strategize or to feel confident enough to reach anything above my tie-in point. Now, I feel safe and at home and so lucky to be up in this tree. I trust my equipment, my knots, myself, and I trust the hemlock. I ask Melissa if I can go above the tie-in point. She says to use my lanyard. I feel for it on my harness and clip one side to a D-ring, throw the other around a branch union above me, and clip that side to my other D-ring. I am tied in twice. I climb up and ring the bell.

Usually when a bell chimes, calls of congratulations erupt from groundies, from climbers, from instructors—I remember that from climbing in the red maple. Moulis had told me that her goal for the last workshop had been to swing into a hammock and to ring a bell, and she had sent me a video of one of those huge celebratory moments. When I ring the bell at the top of this hemlock, though, there is no sound in response, except a slight wind sigh. The breeze and the sun feel wonderful. I can see almost the entire lake and the uninterrupted forest around it. I am elated. I realize that I didn't need to ring the bell and am relieved no one heard it. I have wanted to be alone and unremarked in the hemlock, to be as unnoticed as it is possible to be, a person high in a tree.

Some of the hemlock branches are flush with tiny cones. Hemlock cones are, like all cones, geometrical wonders, but hemlock cones are especially stunning because they are so delicate-looking, so small: usually under an inch. Hemlocks produce both male cones, yellow berry-looking puckered orbs of pollen, and female seed cones, which emerge green and become brown. I would like to think this is a good sign: these trees are reproducing. But more likely it is a "distress crop," an abundance of seed that a dying tree uses its last resources to make.

I apologize to the hemlock for knocking off some lichen and bark along my climb, and I sit in the tree's embrace for a long time. I feel delighted and so am surprised to start crying in an intense fusion of joy and sadness. Joy about sitting in the great hemlock. Joy about my strength and ability. Joy about being outside and around people who care for each other and for whom the connections between trees and people are as vivid and clear as a great ash's branches against a gray winter sky. Sadness about so much loss. Not being able to share with my mother: Oh, This Tree! This Amazing Exquisite Extraordinary Tree! My brother never able to fully find refuge or relief in the places he loved and in the people who love him. That all of us, who each experience such loss as part of life, seem willing to lose and give up so much that we don't need to.

Sadness about saying goodbye to this hemlock. I had gotten up early that morning to spend time with the hemlocks, to stand with them, to trace their roots around rocks and through the clearing between them. As I had left them to go to breakfast, the sun came over the low mountain on the far side of the lake and it seemed too bright too fast. There is almost no hemlock canopy left to catch and diffuse the light.

Two months before I make this climb—although I didn't know it at the time—dendrochronologist Edward Cook returned to the Tionesta area of western Pennsylvania to visit the hemlocks he hadn't seen in four decades or so. He was with several colleagues, including Neil Pederson of Harvard University, who studies forest ecology. It was a difficult day. They spent many hours searching, passing through clear cuts. The forest was unrecognizable to Cook: there were so many dead beech trees, so much disturbance. Pederson felt saddened as well. "I am walking through a graveyard," he says. "Adelgid is on its way . . . the mature beech are gone."

The group made their way through thickets of beech saplings knowing that they too would be gone soon: they saw evidence of beech leaf disease in two places, following right behind the devastations of beech bark disease. "So that national landmark forest is doomed," Pederson says. Old-growth forests are not permanent, he adds, but "to me personally they feel as though they will always be there." Seeing forests change so radically during his lifetime has been devastating. And, he says, he was worried about Cook.

Pederson kept reliving in his mind a trip he had taken with his doctoral advisor, the late Gordon Jacoby, cofounder with Cook of Columbia University's dendrochronology lab. Jacoby had gone to revisit a tree in Mongolia. "It was the first old Siberian pine that he had cored that showed global warming in Mongolia, and it turned out that it was a stump and someone had cut it and it was gone," Pederson says. "I just didn't want to deal with that again. I couldn't deal with someone at the end of their career going back to see one of their favorite trees and . . ."

In the last hour of daylight, they found the hemlocks Cook and his friend had cored forty years ago. "I had to run away, because I started crying and I was just like, Oh my God, he's reunited with his trees, you know," Pederson says. "They're not dead."

That the Tionesta hemlock were thriving despite woolly adelgid was a surprise. Another team of dendrochronologists had gone to a different site in the region where Cook had also found hemlock in the 1970s and those trees were gone. Cook discovered after the trip that the Pennsylvania Department of

Conservation and Natural Resources has been treating the Tionesta hemlock, something that can be done with individual trees around homes and along streets, but that is extremely challenging to do in a forest. The department has been trying to save hemlock for about two decades.

It is an enormous undertaking, requiring a big and consistent budget and lots of trained people, and it entails the use of pesticides, which many states opt not to use. "Pennsylvania, historically in this program, has been willing to kind of do almost whatever it takes," says Sarah Johnson of the department's Bureau of Forestry. There are "key functions of hemlock that cannot be replicated by any other species." Where hemlock forests have disappeared, waterways heat up, embankments erode, and populations of birds plummet, including the black-throated green warbler. And the blackburnian warbler. And the hermit thrush. And the Acadian flycatcher. A tree is not just a tree. A forest is not just a forest. Both contain and sustain multitudes.

Johnson says that in the long term, the bureau's goal is to use chemicals less or not at all and to manage instead with other methods, including biocontrol—breeding and releasing non-pest insects to prey on pest insects—as well as genetic selection. A biocontrol program is underway: a fly and two beetles, one from the Pacific Northwest where they feed on a native woolly adelgid, have been released in some places. Johnson says she sees a lot of the beetles in the forest. "They're reproducing really well. We can find them very easily. They're moving very well," she says. But so far, in her view, "they're not helping trees very much." The second strategy, genetic selection, is moving slowly.

That slow movement is frustrating to Ian Kinahan, an ecologist with the Massachusetts Department of Conservation and Recreation, who studied lingering hemlock—survivor or, technically, "field resistant" trees such as the whitebark pines Six found on the Continental Divide Trail. Kinahan too sees lingering trees as an important part of the solution to the pest–pathogen–climate trifecta. A lingering hemlock may have the right genetic stuff to deal with adelgid and, if so, perhaps its offspring could help replenish forests. In the early aughts, Kinahan's advisor had put out a request for community scientists to alert him to any lingering hemlock. About one hundred thirty such trees were identified. A team collected twigs from some of those trees, got them to root, and raised them to saplinghood in a greenhouse alongside other hemlock. Then they released some adelgid. The insects liked the lingering trees a lot less than they did non-lingering hemlock.

After that, the promising hemlock were settled in forests in seven states. The last time Kinahan checked, about four years after planting, the trees "had significantly higher survival and they grew better and looked healthier and had lower pest densities—including lower densities of scale insects—compared to the susceptible trees at all those plots." But Kinahan says he has met a lot of resistance to the idea of resistance. "I was just banging my head against the wall trying to communicate this information to the community," he says. Kinahan was happy to learn that the Forest Service is beginning a hemlock resistance program led by geneticist Jennifer Koch, one of a small group of researchers devoting their professional lives to studying lingering trees—in fact, Koch credits one of her lab technicians with coining "lingering." "I didn't want to use 'survivor' because they might still all die"; and a totally "resistant" tree is rare, she says. Lingering seemed most apt. Persisting could be nice too.

Koch's first lingering tree research was on beech, studying trees that had been discovered surviving in places where beech bark disease had swept through. She and colleagues at the Forest Service's Delaware, Ohio, facility created a system of identifying and propagating these beech, raising them in a nursery, harvesting pollen, breeding, developing bioassays, and tracking lineages.

After their first cross of parent trees, they found half the offspring to be highly resistant to beech bark disease. "You never want one hundred percent resistance," Koch explains. "You usually see super high levels of resistance when you have single-gene resistance, and that's easily overcome, especially by fungi that mutate rather rapidly, more rapidly than the trees." Koch and her team began to collaborate with, and receive support from, state, private, Tribal Nation, and nonprofit partners, including the Holden Arboretum in Kirtland, Ohio, a two-hour drive away. Then beech leaf disease appeared in nearby Metroparks and at Holden. "We had to stop because of the fear of spreading the nematode," she says. "One of the biggest letdowns of my career . . . now all of that work is at the mercy of this disease."

Koch and her colleagues have also been breeding ash, primarily green ash, one of the most vulnerable to emerald ash borer. A colleague who had been tracking and predicting ash mortality had "mentioned that there were these few oddball trees that didn't fit her model at some of her sites. There were trees that still hadn't died," Koch recalls. "That's when we got interested." Her team made their first collections from lingering ash in 2009 and have had success identifying trees whose defenses kill lots of larvae—the pattern of

Emerald Ash Borer tunnels

resistance seen in ash from Asia that coevolved with the borer. "They still get attacked, but they are able to recover."

Resistance research takes tree time. It is labor intensive at all levels, from the laboratory to the forest, and requires savvy about molecular biology, genetics, entomology, pathology, ecology, forestry, and horticulture. Researchers get up close and personal with every tree and for many years; for Koch that has led to the development of severe skin allergies to every species she has worked on, and she carries latex gloves and a barrier ointment with her everywhere. Trees have to be planted in near and faraway field sites—these should include zones that might better suit the tree in the future, so they could be candidates for assisted migration. They must be closely monitored. "If you plant it in a place where it doesn't get enough water or it's in shade and it needs sun, then it's really stressed and that resistant tree can still become susceptible," Koch says. The archive at her facility is not boxes and file drawers of papers; the archive is a forest of trees with detailed genealogies.

The Forest Service has run resistance breeding programs since the 1960s, and the biggest operation is led by Richard Sniezko at the Dorena Genetic Resource Center in Cottage Grove, Oregon. Dorena is also the site of the department's tree-climbing training school—where wildfire responders and research climbers are taught. As has been true for many academic and industry-based tree genetics programs too, much of the focus was initially on timber species, but the scope then broadened. There have been results with white pines showing resistance to white pine blister rust and with other species, including Sitka spruce, loblolly pine, Port Orford cedar, and koa, a Hawaiian acacia, showing aspects of resistance to everything from water molds to weevils. Overall, though, the field, many note, has generally not been well funded.

American chestnut breeding programs stand out as the exception. Passion and love for this tree have driven exceptional public support for, and dedication to, its revival. One of the main forces behind these efforts, the American Chestnut Foundation, was founded in 1983 and has supported several strategies for bringing back the tree. Experts have been crossbreeding surviving American chestnut with blight-resistant Chinese chestnut, *Castanea mollissima*, over several generations to achieve a hybrid tree that is mostly American chestnut. Lingering American chestnuts have been bred with each other, as Moulis and others were doing by bagging, protecting, and pollinating the chestnut outside the library in Old Lyme, Connecticut; this approach is the one favored by the American Chestnut Cooperators Foundation, formed in 1986. Both organizations have investigated biocontrol: deploying viruses that can attack the blight.

The American Chestnut Foundation also supports genetic engineering. Researchers at the State University of New York's College of Environmental Science and Forestry developed a variety called Darling 58, which includes a wheat gene that produces a blight-neutralizing enzyme. Darling 58 was submitted in 2020 to the Department of Agriculture for approval to distribute in the wild, which would mean it would be exempt from the tight regulations generally governing transgenic plants. The effort suffered a setback when the American Chestnut Foundation learned that the strain was not faring well at some test sites. It turned out that the variety being tested, as well as the one submitted for federal approval, was not Darling 58, but Darling 54. In 2024, the American Chestnut Foundation withdrew funding from that effort.

Even so, financial backing for American chestnut resurrection has been consistent and substantial across decades, meaning uninterrupted research and progress. In contrast, federal agencies typically provide multiyear grants that are not necessarily renewed. That situation is changing. Koch says she is beginning to see forest geneticist job postings and more nurseries, breeding programs, and seed banks being established. The North American Forest Genetics Society, which includes experts from Mexico, the United States, and Canada, held its inaugural meeting in 2022. Genetically informed breeding "is a necessary part of combating climate change and keeping healthy forests," Koch says. She sees resistance and biocontrol as working hand in hand, as they do in nature. "These biocontrol agents, they're usually associated with plants that also have resistance," she says. "You have this ecosystem that has evolved so that the trees and the insects and the parasitoids are all in balance."

Tree genetics is a universe unto itself and is not always best understood in comparison with animal genetics. Unlike other plants and animals, trees can have enormous genetic variation within a single tree, especially if they are long-lived. The meristem of one branch may develop a mutation that every subsequent cell produced by that meristem will carry. Meanwhile, on another branch, perhaps a different mutation has occurred. Researchers studying Sitka spruce found one old-growth tree with one hundred thousand differences: many needles, branches, and portions of trunk were genetically distinct from one another. One tree can be many trees. In the Hi-Rock hemlock, the branch I sit on might be genetically distinct from the branch my foot rests on, from the branch hosting the lichen I am entranced by, from the branch my hand holds.

Trees can also have enormous genetic diversity at the species level. Some species have genomes that are fifty times as large as any animal's. Also, unlike many animals, plants often have more than two copies of a chromosome in each cell. At one end of the spectrum—the record holder for the moment, notes Kew Gardens' Illia Leitch—is a fern with ninety-six copies of its genome in each cell; near the other end are quaking aspen, which can be triploid, carrying three copies. Plant polyploidy, as multiple sets of chromosomes are called, gives plants extraordinary genetic range and nimbleness—some mutation or some combination of genomes might solve an emerging problem. Diploid aspen seem to be more drought resistant than triploid aspen, for example. Many trees show great genetic variation both within a population and between populations, variation that reflects their migratory history, where they waited out glaciers or hot house times, how connected they were to other trees across the landscape, how they reproduced, who was eating them.

Eastern hemlock genes reveal their travels north from several southern refugial core populations. After the glaciers receded, some hemlock headed more centrally, toward today's Indiana. Others, including ancestors of the Hi-Rock hemlock, traveled along the Appalachian Mountains. The southern, the central, and the northern populations diverged genetically, as would be expected. Some of these lineages also reveal a pattern perhaps best explained by the hemlocks' rapid near disappearance five thousand years ago. Eastern hemlock pollen vanishes from sediment records at that time, throughout the continent, likely because of infection or infestation, or both. A few trees lingered, genetic studies show, and, over several thousand years, restored hemlock populations. All the hemlock we know today are, in essence, descendants of those lingering hemlock.

The Hi-Rock hemlock do not look as though they are car-

Hemlock cone

rying a solution in their genes. They don't look like robust lingering hemlock. Melissa says the trees will be unclimbable soon. After that, the trio of big hemlock will need be cut down for safety. I hope the wind has carried their secrets away, whispering them to hemlock in the nearby woods.

As we settle around the fire on Saturday night, we are unsettled by a huge white light low in the sky over the lake. Too big and too slow to be a plane. Too big and too fast to be a star. It casts a fan of rays above and below; it looks like a luminous steampunk angel fish. We decide finally that it must be a satellite, but it is an odd beginning to the evening. The rest of the world is encroaching.

During the share, the ratio of topics has shifted, as the trees have shifted and the tree biology session has shifted. It seems to me that people are talking more about the climate crisis. There is, as always though, celebration of accomplishments and a sense of elation. Wenda says the participants' experiences recall a poem she used to know by heart and that she paraphrases for us. I find the exact lines later; they are by poet Patrick Overton and, of course, from a collection called *The Leaning Tree*:

> *When we walk to the edge of all the light we have*
> *and take the step into the darkness of the unknown,*
> *we must believe one of two things will happen—*
>
> > *There will be something solid for us to stand upon*
> > *Or, we will be taught how to fly.*

Serenity Smith Forchion, one of the participants, asks Bear and Melissa whether they have a secret language (no, they say) and whether they can communicate without talking (yes). Smith Forchion can be so direct because she too is an identical twin.

In the years I have known Melissa and Bear, I have moved from not being able to tell them apart to not being able to understand how people can't tell them apart. There has been one visual cue. In that time, Bear's hair has gone from below waist length to an inch long. Ever since their mother became ill with cancer and lost her hair, Bear has grown her hair out and then cut it to donate it. With a helmet on, however, hair length is not a twin diagnostic. "We will not take offense if you mix us up," they say at the outset of most workshops. But I have never asked them directly about how their experience as twins may have shaped the culture of the workshop, the way they teach, the connection they feel to trees, the way they approach the world. Smith Forchion's question opens a space to do that.

"Everyone was constantly trying to compare us and pit us against each other," Bear says.

"Society does it all the time."

"They are like, 'Who's better at this and who's better at that?' And we immediately look at each other and are just, 'She is.'"

People are so curious, Melissa says, and don't know how to talk or ask about being identical twins. So they start with, "How are you divisible. How are you not the same thing."

As they are telling me this, moving thoughts back and forth between them, they often ask, "May I speak for us?"

When they have floundered in their lives, they say, it was when they were apart and not moving through the world together. "We have always been a we," Bear says. "Never an I."

On Sunday morning, Smith Forchion offers to be my buddy and we ask Melissa for permission to climb together in the largest hemlock. Around us, people are setting ropes and preparing to climb at a waking-up pace, but I am itchy to get moving. I don't want to lose any time in the hemlock. I put on a foot ascender—always shall I climb with an ascender—and because my legs are tired, I put on a knee ascender as well. Smith Forchion is reluctantly trying a foot ascender for the first time. She says she doesn't like using any extra gear when she is in trees because it makes her feel separate from them.

We climb to the top of the hemlock. It is warm and the sky is light gray, overcast. I ask Smith Forchion—who, I learned the previous evening, is a world-famous aerialist—how she came to be in this tree. Smith Forchion and her identical twin sister were born in Massachusetts in a log cabin that their parents built. Their father was a forester and owned a sawmill on two hundred acres of woods where many friends also built log cabins. "It wasn't quite a commune," Smith Forchion says, "but it was definitely a collective way of living." The twins ran wild and spoke in their own language and, like Melissa and Bear, who were born two days earlier the same year, made trails and built forts. "We were just sprites in the woods, running around in homemade clothes and missing a shirt or pants or whatever it was. Sort of latchkey kids, but in the way of the woods being our home." They climbed maple, cherry, oak, hemlock, feeling as comfortable above the ground as on it. Serenity remembers as a child dreaming about flying out over fields, forests, and a valley, seeing the vast intricate landscape unfolding.

At a Club Med in the Dominican Republic, where their mother was attending a medical conference, the twins met their first trapeze and were smitten. In their late teens they worked for Circus of the Kids—a social circus, Smith Forchion explains, one that teaches self-empowerment, team building, and emotional tools, in addition to mad circus skills. Circus of the Kids was followed by Ringling Bros., Pickle Family Circus, and Cirque du Soleil.

The trees led them to the circus and the circus led them back to the trees. After years of traveling, the sisters settled in Brattleboro, Vermont, founded a company and a school, the New

England Center for Circus Arts. Once back in the woods of their childhood, Smith Forchion began to study a silviculture textbook her father gave her. She works closely with a forester to figure out how to best steward the several hundred acres of woods she owns, when to log, when to leave things be, how to manage for climate change and insects. She has grappled with what to do about the imminent arrival of emerald ash borer. Should she cut all the ash before they become infested, when the timber is still worth something—"those logs could send my kid to college"—and before the trees become hazards? Or should she leave the trees to become food for the forest and perhaps ensure genetic diversity: "maybe it's that one tree that has resistance." In the end, she decided not to cut. "I'm going to leave it there in case it might help the forest a little bit."

She also felt a pull to dance in trees. In aerial work, Smith Forchion doesn't use a harness or a safety rope. Trapeze artists know ropes, knots, and attachment points inside and out. They set up their ropes and check them, needing to see and trust that they are secure before they can move into the air. But aerialist systems are different from those that arborists use, and Smith Forchion knew she needed an expert. "I didn't have the skill set to do it . . . . We tell people never, ever work off of trees unless you have a certified arborist," she says. "I want to learn how to do this myself, because I think it's important for safety that I understand how this works . . . . But I need someone who can say, 'Yep, we can do that,' or 'No, that's not safe either for me or the tree.'" She began collaborating with arborist Mark Przekurat, who is famous for his rope-splicing class, Fid & Fibers, and who told her about the Women's Tree Climbing Workshop.

Smith Forchion was hoping to stay "incognito," as she puts it, while at the workshop. But it is hard to be incognito when you climb the way she does. Everyone this weekend has paused to watch her. She has a fluid grace in a tree that seems to slow time and expand it. Up in the hemlock together, we look at the needles and the bark, and we talk to the tree. For an instant I want to name the hemlock, but a name wouldn't be big enough. Perhaps the tree should be naming us. We see lots of woolly adelgid and scale. We see a tiny spider when it moves in the lichen that it matches exactly. Smith Forchion reaches for two ribbons on a limb, and I take the one attached to a bell, which I don't ring.

We had spoken the day before about how my vertigo was gone. Smith Forchion had asked how my fear of heights had dissipated. It had to do with coming to trust myself and the gear, coming to trust other people, finding creativity I didn't know I had, like using the lanyard to overcome an obstacle, finding ways of becoming unstuck. Feeling my adventurous self again. I remembered that the last time I had climbed was when I was eight months pregnant with Auden and had scaled a twelve-foot or so chain-link fence—big bulk, belly, and all—so I wouldn't miss a train. I had also explained that I still could not move between relying entirely on the gear and climbing free like a child.

Aerialists recognize that there is a space where you are not of the ground or of the air, Smith Forchion says. It is in that space that she has to think the most, be the most careful, the most intentional. "I find one of the hardest places for my students to find their grace is in those moments in between those places. So you might have someone who's a fabulous dancer or a great acrobat, and they can do the ground movement. But then transitioning from ground to air feels like they're being pulled or ripped from one dimension to the other . . . . It's that moment when your foot is peeled off the ground and you're reaching, you're agonizingly trying to reach back down to the earth while you're also being pulled up into the sky. There's a story that can be told in that moment."

I hug the trunk, then grab a branch and start to climb from one limb to another without tension on my rope, without feeling the tug from the umbilical cord of safety. I feel my full weight and how heavy I am. The tree is no longer lifting me but holding me. I feel the strength in my arms and my legs. I feel a lightning streak of fear, fleeting, terrifying. Then I feel right—— completely right and true. I am back in a thickly gnarled apple tree in an abandoned orchard near my grandmother's trailer home in the Catskills—the apple tree I used to imagine living inside. I am lying on a long limb hanging over a lawn that Eric is playing on somewhere in South Africa. I am sitting next to Eric in a tree in Riverside Park, on a branch that loops down to create a comfy bench. I am inching up a trunk in a magical twilight garden as fireflies come out and flowers glow and grownups don't know where I am. I am watching my son Julian smiling, lounging in the high crook of a dogwood. I am watching my daughter Auden fearless, high in a white pine. I am free and in every tree I have ever been in and I am in this hemlock.

As we descend, I dance a bit. Serenity shows me how to lean back and stretch my arms. Someone takes a photograph as we do this and captures what I come to think of as the three stages of tree climbing. Near the base of the hemlock, one participant is hugging the trunk with arms and legs, bear-like, beaming. Farther up, I am nearly horizontal, smiling, relaxed, the falling end of the line loosely held in my right hand. Above me is Smith Forchion, nearly upside down doing a split, laughing in her element.

Getting up into the canopy revolutionized our understanding of trees. Nalini Nadkarni remembers her first glimpse of the overstory in a cloud forest in Monteverde, Costa Rica. "It was just loaded with these canopy plants, and there were birds and monkeys," Nadkarni says. "I was asking my professors, What's going on up in the canopy? And they basically said, 'We have no idea. There is no safe way to get up there.'" It was the late 1970s and Nadkarni had started a doctoral program in forest ecology in the Pacific Northwest, working with a soil scientist studying fungi–root associations. This kind of research was novel then, Nadkarni notes, and it was exciting. "But it was all lab work and I thought this is not for me, this colossal number of test tubes." She wanted to be out in forests. Trees had provided a rare safe place for her as a child. So she enrolled in a course offered by the Organization for Tropical Studies and traveled for two months between different field sites in Costa Rica.

When she returned to the University of Washington, she told her advisers she had decided to study epiphytes in the canopy. "To me, it seemed a place of discovery and that is what scientists are supposed to do." The response was not enthusiastic. "They thought it was just Tarzan and Jane stuff." Undeterred, she turned to a graduate student who had been climbing trees in Costa Rica. "I just sort of got on my knees and said, 'Please, I'll do anything. Just teach me how to climb trees.'" After some training, Nadkarni returned to her advisors and said, "I know how to get up there now!"

As often happens in emerging areas of science, it was an era of convergence, of many people arriving at the same idea at the same time. For decades, most researchers studying forests had been groundies: they recorded and analyzed what they could see of trees and forest ecosystems, but the high forest—where photosynthesis, the heartbeat of the planet, and thousands of plants' and creatures' lives were unfolding—remained unexplored. In the 1960s, ecologists working at Oregon State University began to study the canopy in towering Douglas fir, but to do so they often felled the trees, ultimately pulverizing everything they hoped to study. In 1970, Diane Tracy, a student and rock climber, suggested to her professor, William Denison, that researchers use rock-climbing strategies to get into the two-hundred-foot trees. As Jon Luoma describes in *The Hidden Forest: The Biography of an Ecosystem* and Denison describes in a *Scientific American* article, "Life in Tall Trees," Tracy and another student, Diane Nielson, pioneered approaches that reshaped forest ecology. Among the first findings to come out of the new frontier was the critical importance of lichens: canopy lichens absorb nitrogen from the air and carry it to the forest floor when they fall, providing vital supplies of this essential nutrient.

Denison's article—with illustrations of women installing beams and using a system that included mountaineering hardware—inspired Nadkarni at a pivotal moment. Her professors were vigorously encouraging her to stay on the ground: there are so many "questions on the forest floor, why do you even have to go up in the canopy?" But she reached out to Denison and embedded with the researchers in Oregon for a while, ultimately convincing one of her advisors that she was on to something important. In the canopy of bigleaf maples, Nadkarni was stunned to find a huge array of epiphytes—plants living on other plants—and a root network. Some maple branches had produced aerial roots to gather nutrients and moisture from the rich humus of decaying plants and animals that lay in niches and nooks, atop branches and in the hollows of trunks.

Over time, she found trees all over the world that root into compost high in their branches. That compost supports insects and epiphytes; sometimes a quarter of a tree's mass is other plants, sometimes much more. The epiphytes are, in turn, important to birds, providing food, nesting materials, and water. Canopy research—using caving, rock-climbing, and arborist techniques as well as cranes, walkways, towers, and balloons—is now fundamental to forest ecology. "I think of it in terms of when people invented scuba gear," says Nadkarni. "There were these amazing insights that we were able to get that we couldn't have gotten if marine biologists didn't have access to that free movement of being able to understand and observe."

Nadkarni, who recently retired from the University of Utah, is often back in Monteverde, studying how climate change is affecting the cloud forest with a team of collaborators, including Sybil Gotsch of the University of Kentucky. Climbing is critical to Gotsch's work too; she has invited arborists to Costa Rica to train local conservationists as climbers. Their research is revealing that epiphytes, so central to hydrology and biodiversity in cloud forests, are extremely vulnerable to drought and the absence of mist.

Gotsch also climbs recreationally to feel rooted. "I don't think you need to be a religious person to have this kind of feeling. But if you've ever, even as a tourist, gone into a massive old cathedral and you look up. And you know those cathedrals with the ridiculously high ceilings, I believe, were designed so that one can start to feel this connection with the spirit realm or with God or with whatever we think is above us," she says. "I feel that same kind of feeling in my chest when I get to the top of the tree, like this awestruck, overcoming emotion. That's a very centering feeling." I am not surprised to learn that one of Gotsch's teachers is a close friend of Nicole Benjamin-Harden, or that soon after Louise Hosburgh finished her Women's Tree Climbing Workshop at Chestnut Ridge in North Carolina, she started working with Gotsch. Nor am I surprised when, independently of me, my daughter Auden and Bear and Melissa meet while visiting different friends in Ohio. That mycelial network, as Melissa and Bear say.

The radical change of perspective that came from Nadkarni and many others who ascended into the canopy has been mirrored by the radical change in perspective that has come from looking underground. The life beneath trees has opened in similar ways. Roots from neighboring trees have been shown to keep stumps alive and to pass nutrients to each other. Over the last few decades, researchers have also begun to reveal the intricacies of mycorrhiza, the fungi living in symbiosis with roots. Some of the most famous work in this realm has been done by Suzanne Simard, a professor of forest ecology at the University of British Columbia. She found that Douglas fir seedlings accessing the adult fir fungal–root network grew faster than those that didn't. She has observed fir sharing carbon with understory birch, and birch sharing carbon with young fir. Other researchers have observed carbon move between alder, spruce, pine, larch, and beech, as well as the movement of chemicals that can alert trees to the arrival of pests. This network is what Melissa and Bear noted that trees on Petersham Common lacked. A universe of symbiosis and mutualism that pesticides destroy. That chemicals, such as nitrogen fertilizer, harm. That infernos impair.

Some scientists, including several of Simard's collaborators, rue the now widely used metaphor of the wood wide web because the published evidence for fungal networks distributing nutrients or of parent trees or neighbor trees sending care packages to young or struggling trees remains scant. And because it is not a professional norm to attribute anthropomorphic values to observations, as Simard does. She urges a philosophy and view of the nonhuman natural world that "begins by recognizing that trees and plants have agency. They perceive, relate, and communicate. . . . They cooperate, make decisions, learn, and remember—qualities we normally ascribe to sentience, wisdom, intelligence," Simard writes in *Finding the Mother Tree: Discovering the Wisdom of the Forest*. Trees are simply doing what trees do, fungi are doing what fungi do, the pushback goes; sometimes the dance between plants and fungi that has been going on since algae first came ashore looks like altruism, sometimes like competition.

Above, beneath—and around. Interdisciplinary studies are also documenting and quantifying what many people intuitively understand when they are close to and among trees: trees and forests benefit our physical and mental health, and not only by providing oxygen, taking in carbon, managing water, removing pollutants, as some do, and keeping us cooler. Trees have been shown to bolster people's immune and cardiovascular systems, to lower blood pressure and blood sugar levels, to reduce stress hormones, and to alleviate depression, among other benefits. Trees, and some of the compounds they release, can do this for us whether they are growing in a forest, a park, or an ungenerous portion of dirt in a sidewalk. The field is young and, as with most every realm, there are gaps and nuances; effects clearly vary with the particulars of person, place, and tree. But the recognition of the connection between trees and human health is driving the expansion of urban canopies. In the United States, such expansion includes providing trees and green space denied to people by racist policies and redlining. In Korea and in Japan—where the term "forest bathing" was coined in the 1980s—spending time in forests is part of the public health system. Japanese doctors prescribe shinrin-yoku. There are designated healing forests throughout Korea. Other countries too increasingly are integrating forests and trees into public health programs.

Whenever trees and forests are closely observed or observed with a different perspective, something remarkable is revealed. The life of the canopy. The life of the roots. The life around and in trees. Pulses and rhythms. The ones Brodribb and others see in the minute movements across the day or through the night. Branches that dance. Signals that rush through a leaf when it is bitten by an insect. That trees have both chemical and electric signaling systems like animals was first described—and, for a long time, rejected—in the research literature by biophysicist Jagadish Chandra Bose a century ago. Bose held a view, and used language, strikingly similar to Simard's. "These trees have a life like ours . . . they eat and grow . . . face poverty, sorrows and suffering," he wrote. "This poverty may . . . induce them to steal and rob . . . they also help each other, develop friendships, sacrifice their lives for their children."

People who care for trees often share a quality of lyricism. They have an ability to see the past and the future in tree time while being acutely aware of the present, like having a satellite view and looking through a magnifying glass simultaneously. This ability to scale, to move nimbly up and down across time or space, to see from different vantage points, to see tree and forest both, to see individual and community both, to recognize different ways of knowing, is essential to facing the climate crisis. We need to change our view and not fear radical transformation—not stand frozen at the edge of a precipice we will fall off if we don't step back. Climbing offers "a different way to look at the world," says Reiko Matsuda Goodwin, a biological anthropologist at Fordham University and a workshop participant. It opens "up a different perspective to look. But not only looking outside, looking inside too. To think about what's good for you, what's good for the world."

A few months after I dance with Smith Forchion in the hemlock, I stand beneath an enormous London planetree on the Smith College campus in Northampton, Massachusetts, where I am observing another workshop. London plane are a cross between *Platanus occidentalis*, the American sycamore, and *Platanus orientalis*, whose home range runs from southeastern Europe to Iran. They are one of the most common trees in New York City: some eighty thousand line walkways and promenades, their trunks massive and knobbed, their outer bark peeling in patches. The trees were a favorite of Robert Moses, and of city planners the

London Plane

world over. Riverside Park, near where I live, has hundreds of them. They anchor the park, giving it grandeur and shade.

I remember the sense of excitement about getting a tree identification right when I was with my mother and Eric in Riverside Park. I feel that still; when I can identify a tree without my phone app, I am thrilled. The health of the tree was not part of our identification ritual, which is a particular subset of plant blindness: see the tree, ID the tree, but don't reflect on how it is faring. In fairness, the park's trees were generally doing better a half century ago, and we climbed them regularly. I was reminded of that one late afternoon a few years ago when I saw a boy in a small tree, stretched out along a little branch, chatting with friends on the ground below with such euphoria and elation. It is a rare sight; the city parks department now prohibits climbing trees.

London planetrees are hardy like many hybrids. They have survived to magnificence in cities because of that robustness: shaking off air pollution, road salt, heat, drought, and closet-size allotments. They have been less vulnerable to certain pests and pathogens, likely because one of their ancestors had met a variation of the insect or disease before, somewhere along the long evolutionary road. But when I look at the park's London plane now, I see they are having it rough. Some have thinning canopies. Many have dead branches. They seem plagued by infection or infestation. All look as though they could use more soil, less compaction—particularly those whose roots are pushing up pavement. I wonder about the effect on their roots of the rain ponds that now form and linger for days after storms. These trees at least have been spared what appears to be London plane kryptonite: saltwater flooding.

The London planetree and anthropogenic climate change were born at the same time. A British visitor to the colonies in the early 1600s collected sycamore seeds, one story goes, sailed with them to England, and planted them in his London garden near other trees from afar. Another telling is based in Spain. Somehow, though, trees from one side of the Atlantic met trees from the other side and a new tree emerged. Then it too traveled. It is like a parable. People take things that are not theirs to take. They break the world. Sometimes, something resilient emerges. As Gabriel Hemery and Sarah Simblet note in *The New Sylva: A Discourse of Forest and Orchard Trees for the Twenty-First Century*, "Planes, especially London plane, are likely to benefit from climate warming. They will become increasingly important to us as we seek to cool down towns and cities during hot summers without expending energy." Then, as ever, the downbeat: "the burgeoning number of diseases affecting the species is deeply concerning."

Perhaps the future rings of London planes will come to show that we changed our habits and turned the tide. That we each struggled—as participants do in the workshop—to discover how we might best provide care, and in what way and at what pace. Perhaps the future rings will show that the heat leveled off and, eventually, ebbed. That seasons became distinct again. That the trees grew into their full selves, their roots stretching out as far as they needed. That the trees were mulched and got an infusion of nutrients. That, well-fortified, they staved off many pests. Perhaps their good health will reflect the resilience created by diverse kinds of trees joining them.

The planetree on the Smith campus has recently been mulched—a whole golf cart full—and is less girdled by pavement than its New York City relatives. Its trunk is wider too, its canopy broader and more arching. It is a champion tree, and the participants who climb it joke that they are champion tree climbers. It is the first time I am using my own gear: I have invested in a foot ascender, harness, pulley system, and lanyard. I adjust the harness, hook the pulley system and carabiners to the

right places. Melissa helps me arrange my lanyard, to
daisy chain it and make sure its pulley mechanism
is facing the right way. I struggle a bit to
get the straps on the new ascender tight.

London Plane
seed pod

Soon I am higher than the surrounding buildings, a few feet below
the tie-in point. I can see low mountain
ridges in the distance. I sit on a branch. I free climb to another.
I sit in a fork. The tree is immense, arching this way and that,
like many trees in one. Its bark smooth from afar, stippled with
eddies up close, white, brown, and polished gray. Pale green
leaves are unfolding from buds alongside hundreds of seed pods,
small yellow globes dangling from stalks. A big wind sweeps in.
I stand on a branch, hug the trunk, and sway. The tree is holding
still and moving at the same time. I feel as though I am rising
and falling with the breath of something vast.

Just after I descend, a red-tailed hawk lands on a nearby
lamppost.

I am no longer scared of heights in the way I was, no longer
immobilized by fear. I can tie several knots—I see them when I
close my eyes, feel them in my fingers—and can set up a pulley
and feel confident. I can ascend a line and free climb once aloft. I
can feel grounded above and regrounded when my rope returns
me to the earth. I have my own system of aerial roots to rely on.
Aerial roots like those Nadkarni found within the canopy. Like
those that some trees, including yews and ficus, send down from
the crown to weave another thread into the web of soil, water, and
fungi, to steady themselves.

I will always need to climb with others and to rely on someone to set a line for me. And I cannot do what my climbing
partner and buddy Moulis now can. "I started not being able

to climb at all, which you remember. I had to use the lanyard crawl. It was a struggle to get up the tree," she says. Now she has a certificate in aerial rescue, is qualified in tree risk assessment, and can use the single rope technique. "I'm very proud of everything I have learned. It's not just about learning how to climb trees, but it's also how it has helped propel me forward, both in my life and my career."

She graduated with honors from Naugatuck Valley Community College with an associate's degree in horticulture. In a graduation picture, her youngest daughter Rita is dancing on one side; on the other, Jenevieve is hugging her mom's arm and grinning. Moulis is wearing green safety glasses. She is studying for her bachelor's in conservation and urban forestry at the University of Massachusetts Amherst, leading study groups for women working toward their certification. She has her eye on a doctorate in plant pathology. "You can't get discouraged just because it is so hard at the beginning," she says. "You have to keep going back and fine-tuning everything."

Moulis still works full time as an arborist, but she left the utility company to join a friend's residential tree-care business. It's stressful because they both have kids and mortgages, but it is less stressful than being on the growing number of storm shifts, during which utility arborists remain on call for days to do emergency tree response during power outages. "I've done a couple hundred hours a week . . . I didn't know it was possible to work that many hours in a week." Seeing Bear leave her secure job and then, in early 2023, Melissa leave hers was a big part of Moulis's decision to "step into the unknown," she says. She returns regularly to the workshop. The trees and the workshops help her care for her daughters and her family. "I need to fill my cup. I need the love and support of the community that I am just so grateful to have," she says. "Climbing trees and being around trees, it is the way I ground myself. It is my meditation."

My mother's tree journal is a meditation too. It was her way of paying attention and perhaps a way of connecting with the father she lost. The assemblage of leaves at the back of her journal—the ones she didn't name—didn't call to me when I started this book. I was more interested in the stories she had told about the trees she met than I was in the stories she hadn't. Eventually I opened the acetate sheet and spread the leaves out. Some are trees she had already described: red oak, coast live oak, camphor. Others she had not: swamp mahogany, scarlet oak, hawthorn, plum, and witch hazel. Also aspen, cedar, and beech. Without knowing I was doing so, I have filled in some of her journal pages.

I left my mother's unidentified tree unidentified for many years too. At one point, I felt resolve and got the envelope containing the catkin wrapped in tissue out of the three-ring binder and packed it between cardboard panels inside a waterproof plastic bag and took it to Florida. By looking at old documents, I had been able to figure out where my mother's relative lived in Sebring in 1994 when she collected the flower from the unknown tree and wrote, "I haven't been able to find the tree yet." I bring it with me to Bradenton, Florida, which is eighty miles or so west of Sebring. I imagine driving to the address and finding the tree. My other thought is to go to the Marie Selby Botanical Gardens in Sarasota and to find someone who can identify the catkin. Or to show it to the arborist I will be staying with.

I was tagging along on a trip with Bear, Melissa, and Tom, who had decided to celebrate the twins' birthday with a visit to Florida to help an arborist, Tammy Kovar, whom they met at one of the workshops, do some bromeliad restoration. Bromeliads are a type of epiphyte. It is a working vacation with a whole new set of trees and things to do in them. "I feel like a brand-new arborist," Bear says at one point. Kovar lives in a house in a tidy planned community, with broad lawns, solitary palms, and identical white mailboxes set precisely the same distance from the street. The road through the compound curves around, but nothing about the place is organic. It feels girdled and baked.

Except Kovar's property and that of her neighbor, which are several degrees cooler and where a chaos of plants, trees, birds, squirrels, fruit, snakes, anoles, and butterflies nearly spill over the property boundaries. It reminds me of Daniel Pinkwater's picture book *The Big Orange Splot*, in which Mr. Plumbean is ostracized by his neighbors for having a messy house on a neat street—until his neighbors transform and personalize their homes as well. The neighbors in this tidy community do not seem to be responding in kind, so far.

Melissa, Bear, and Tom spend a day affixing bromeliads to a live oak that had lost most of its epiphytes during Hurricane Ian. The oak looks much livelier by evening, teeming with small bushy bromeliads. They spend a morning helping a crew move a twenty-five-foot persimmon tree that Kovar rescues from a property about to be converted into a housing development. They spend an afternoon chain-sawing, hand-sawing, and dragging out invasive or infected plants, clearing space in the snarled tangle that covers about a third of the land between Kovar and her neighbor's homes. They remove trees infected by a bacterium destroying the citrus industry. They remove camphor, carrotwood, rosary pea, Chinese tallow, Surinam cherry, arrowhead vine, Brazilian peppertree, Chinaberry, and bamboo. Over six hours they drag brush and fill a 490-square-foot trailer five times. Florida is one of the states losing the most endemic biodiversity to imported species. The days are long, intense, hot, draining.

When I am not observing or dragging brush, I return to spend time with a monkey puzzle tree that was damaged during Ian or perhaps another of many hurricanes. Its branches and crown have been sheared off and it looks dead. On the ground lie broken branches densely studded with small brown prickly tri-angular leaves. The branches look like long thin elongated pinecones twisted on a bias. They are mysterious and perfect. I have met a new tree, *Araucaria araucana*, my first araucaria, in the family of Wollemi, unlike any tree I have met before. It feels like a major discovery, like delight and giddiness. A reminder that there are still so many unknowns to chance upon. I pack a branch to bring home and, later, put it near the picture of Eric and me at Mohonk. Eric faced what the trees are facing: too many profound hardships hitting all at once with no respite. Being in trees, knowing they are wrapped around their history, embracing their earlier selves, has given me another insight too: Eric and my mother as my heartwood, supporting me from the inside out.

Monkey Puzzle leaves

When it comes time to leave Florida and I face the last chance to identify my mother's tree in the state she found it, I find I don't want to. I carry it around in my backpack and take it out a few times, but I can't bring myself to find the answer. I don't drive to Sebring. I don't go to the botanical garden. I don't ask Kovar. It is as if my mother asked me a question and that if I carry it with me, I remain more connected to her. Or that I want to leave my quest unfinished. But it doesn't feel right to know yet.

On a spring afternoon more than a year later, in a downpour that lasts eight hours, I visit with Melissa and Bear at Sky Farm, and it is the right time. They are directing the workshop together full-time, figuring out how to earn a living, maintaining the workshop's core while growing it, teaching other classes and new groups, including teenagers at a summer program in Boston called Speak for the Trees and people entering the green job, urban forestry workforce. The twins can do more arborist work together again and Bear is regularly at Sky Farm, where the family is still planting gardens and trees and where Tom and Melissa plan to start building a house soon—informed, as is to be expected, by the skills Melissa learned at a two-week post-and-frame construction class she recently took.

I open the envelope and gently unwrap the white tissue paper. The little sprig of something that, I realize, my mother collected exactly thirty years earlier, to the month. This little sprig that she wrapped with care and kept with her, that she puzzled over. I anticipate that Bear and Melissa will glance at the catkin and immediately name it. But that does not happen. There is silence for a while. Bear thinks she saw it once at an arboretum and has a memory of meeting it. "It was one of the trees I was so excited about when I first learned about it," she says, but the name has slipped away. She starts scrolling on her phone through the arboretum's web site. Melissa gets a well-worn reference book from her office, *Manual of Woody Landscape Plants*, and starts paging through. A huge chestnut leaf falls out. Bear shows Melissa one possibility, a Leyland cypress.

"No."

"But I'm close."

Bear shows Melissa a Kashmir cypress.

"No. Not quite," she says. "I think you are on the right track."

They look at my mother's tree under a magnifying glass.

"The needles are puckered. That could just be desiccation," Melissa says.

I look at it under the magnifying glass. When I first opened the envelope so many years ago, I thought it was a flower, a catkin. Now I look carefully and see a very fine array of tiny pale green silvery brown needles, intricate, woven, unusual. It is a conifer not a catkin. Something seems familiar.

Melissa asks Bear to send her a high-res photo.

"We know it is not a bald cypress," says Bear.

My mother's Sebring, Florida, tree is not a common conifer—at least not one well-known to folks from the Northeast. I feel a strange pride that her leaf is posing a challenge, that she knew her trees well enough to know that this was out of the ordinary. That she really did leave a mystery. That she sampled in the correct way.

"What is neat about this is that it was plucked off right at the twig," Melissa says. "Which is really cool."

The rain is plinking on the roof. It is dark outside. The shades are down. It is warm and light and cozy inside. Some ladybugs are taking refuge from the storm, wandering across the walls. A woodcock calls.

Melissa finally turns to her phone's tree ID app.

"Oh it might be this . . . interesting. I am going to do it one more time. . . . It feels right."

It is a Norfolk Island pine, *Araucaria heterophylla*—in the same family as the monkey puzzle tree, in the same family as the Wollemi, which were discovered the same year my mother collected this leaf. This araucaria is endemic to three islands in the southern Pacific Ocean, in the Australian territory of Norfolk Island, nine hundred miles northwest of New Zealand. Colonists—commencing with captain James Cook—and settlers have put the tree through a lot, as always, trying to make a timber go of it, clearing it for farms, importing pests. The International Union for Conservation of Nature listed the species as vulnerable in 2011. But its current population trend is "increasing." It can reach over one hundred fifty feet in the wild, is common in Florida, and thrives—without becoming weedy or displacing resident trees—in many warm places the country and the world over where people have carried it and planted it and cared for it and often given it as a house plant present.

"It's rather suiting," Melissa says. "It's a gift tree."

Epilogue

On a mountain in central Massachusetts are some hemlock groves that swirl and undulate. Some of the trees curve out and away from the ground in a gentle swell and then grow straight. They rise sinuous and orient themselves toward the light. Decades earlier, again and again in these groves, a low branch became fixed to the ground, perhaps by one that fell from above or perhaps the lower branch was heavy. In time, the branch sensed the earth it rested on. It sensed the moisture in the soil and created roots. In time, the tip of the branch grew toward the light, curving up and away from the ground, rooted now at a new point of beginning. As more time passed, the portion of the branch between the new tree and the old decomposed and fell away and there were two trees where there had been one. They are the same tree. Rooted, it grew. Rooted, it touched the earth. Rerooted, it grows again.

Acknowledgments

My first profound thank you is to Bear LeVangie and Melissa LeVangie Ingersoll and their families for opening their lives to me, for giving me so much time, patience, and kindness, and for sharing their wisdom and approach to life. I am both more rooted and more free for knowing them, part of a new constellation. An enormous thank you as well to the entire community of the Women's Tree Climbing Workshop, a remarkable group of people I have been fortunate to spend so much time with; an especially big thank you to June Moulis, Roxy Seibel, Tana Byrd, and Nicole Benjamin-Harden.

Thank you to the extraordinary friends who supported me in so many ways. Lynn Berger saw there was a book in what I was talking about before I did. Lynn, Elly Eisenberg, Sarah Lilley, Amy Schatz, Gisela Winckler, and Tali Woodward read an early draft and made excellent suggestions. Max Rudin gave brilliant advice during several tight deadlines. Huge gratitude as well to Jen Barden, Ed Bell, Susanna Blackwell,

Marie Doezema, Anne Georget, Sarah Hansen, Hilary Harris, Ben Harris, Alyson Martin, Gary Marks, Maceo Mitchell, Alice Naude, Ulla Pors Nielsen, Stephen Saxl, Gavin Schmidt, Pamela Smith, Alisa Solomon, Andie Tucher, and Patricia Wynne for their care, humor, enthusiasm, and tree stories.

Huge thanks to Laura Briscoe, Tim Brodribb, Dani Cardia, Christiane Fashek, Halley Harrisburg, Illia Leitch, James Lendemer, Marilyn Neimark, Michael Rosenfeld, L. B. Thompson, Patrick Overton, Cary Quigley, and Sara Wicks for their help and generosity. To Hannah Fairfield and George Etheredge, who shaped and made possible my first story on this topic. To Janelle Retka, who saved me by stepping in to help with research, and to Alex Hodor-Lee for his beautiful photographs, taken minutes before a rainstorm set in. Thank you to arborist Steve Adams, who first talked to me about what he is seeing in trees and who set me on this path. To my wonderful colleagues at Columbia University's Graduate School of Journalism. And to my students, who every year teach me new things and show me how to see the world more fully and deeply.

Writing in the first person and writing about my family are new to me. But this book feels right and true to me now and that is in great part due to my extraordinary good fortune in having a genius, wildly creative, hilarious agent, Anna Sproul-Latimer of Neon Literary, who pushed me to return to my creative writing roots, to see the poetry and the imagery in the material I was collecting. There is so much of her in this book. I am also enormously lucky to have met the artist Ellen Wiener, who took a risk on me, and created the beautiful works of evocative power that enliven these pages. Every conversation with Ellen is a joy and a discovery—"big weather," as she puts it.

The brilliant Tom Mayer put such care and attention into this book at every scale and at every stage: diagramming structure and arc, pushing me to take risks, to go deeper, to say more with less. His line edits are as genius as his structural edits, as his big-picture ideas edits. I am beyond grateful to have had the chance to work with him again. A huge thank you as well to my copyeditor, Marjorie Anderson, and to the entire team at W. W. Norton: Lauren Abbate, Nneoma Amadi-obi, Steve Colca, Sage Gilbert, Jason Heuer, Erin Lovett, Susan Sanfrey, Beth Steidle, who created the beautiful interior design, and Steven Attardo, who designed the stunning cover

Writing a book is, as my father-in-law Bob Naiman said last time I wrote one, a whole family activity. Thank you to the entire Greenspoon-Kronstadt-Naiman-Nesbet-Sand-Sugg extravaganza. To my dad, Ralph Holloway, for the tree news and books, and my gardener stepmom, Daisy Dwyer, who adored all plants. And to the core of my world: my husband and children. I could not have done this book without the love, care, kindness, hilarity, inspiration, insight, and brilliant comments of Auden Naiman, Julian Naiman, and of Tom Naiman—who read, edited, and refined every draft. We all miss Weezee and Eric so much. During the pandemic, we also lost my brother Benjamin, another force for good and care. To all the forces for good and care.

Note on Sources

This book began to take form when I was reporting stories for *The New York Times* about climate change in Yellowstone National Park, in Phoenix, Arizona, in New England's forests, and in Maine. The research for those stories and many of the people interviewed for them informed my early understanding of what climate change is doing to trees and forests. That understanding deepened over the years through reading books, reports, articles, and an ever-expanding wealth of peer-reviewed studies about trees, forests, and climate. Many of those materials are listed in the bibliography. Several excellent, informative tree-related podcasts are listed in the bibliography as well.

I interviewed dozens of researchers and experts who gave generously of their time and knowledge. Thank you to: Sandra Albro, Hannah Alverson, William Anderegg, Nan Crystal Arens, Heide Asbjornsen, Nina Bassuk, Barbara Bentz, Enrico Bonello, Tim Brodribb, Faith Campbell, Jeannine Cavender-

Bares, Charlie Cogbill, Alexandra Contosta, Edward Cook, Theresa Crimmins, Miranda Curzon, Anthony D'Amato, Michael Dockry, Susan Frankel, Matteo Garbelotto, Bill Gould, Sherry Gould, Sybil Gotsch, Leigh Greenwood, Kevin Griffin, Richard Hallett, Dan Herms, Maria Janowiak, Sarah Johnson, Steve Kannenberg, Rachel Kappler, Lisa Keith, Ian Kinahan, Jennifer Koch, Kenneth Kunkel, Gigi Lish, Sean Mahoney, Samira Malone, Suzanne Marchetti, Robert Marra, Nate McDowell, Julie Mehretu, Constance Millar, David Mladenoff, Nalini Nadkarni, Kim Novick, Katherine O'Donnell, Jessie Pearl, Neil Pederson, Dana Perkins, John Pogacnik, Richard Primack, Nicole Rafferty, Paul Rogers, Diana Six, Paul Smith, Richard Sniezko, Valerie Trouet, Amy Trowbridge, Yana Valachovic, Marcus Warwell, Angela Waupochick, Tony Waupochick, Murphy Westwood, Laura Williams, and Jim Worrall.

Thanks also to Keymah Durden, Dave Hester, Sharon Lilly, David Meshoulam, Tracey Miller, Jack Ostroff, Tom Saielli, John Scrivani, Krystal Sierra, and Jack Swatt.

I interviewed or had conversations with over a hundred people involved with the Women's Tree Climbing Workshops as instructors, organizers, setup crew, or participants—both at workshops I took part in and at ones that I observed. Many people—those named in the text and those who are not—shared deeply personal stories; the foundation and heart of this book are the magical and transformative experiences that they described. Kristina Bezanson, Clarisse Hart, and Anne Tenholder kindly let me interview them several times; arborists Patrick O'Meara and Devin Austin spoke with me about their work and experiences. Bear LeVangie, Melissa Levangie Ingersoll, Kali Alcorn, Tana Byrd, Alex Julius, Wenda Li, Kate Odell, Roxy Seibel, and Nicole Benjamin-Harden, who are mentioned throughout the book, taught me to climb and answered endless questions on many occasions. Several other instructors worked closely with me and shared their kindness and deep knowledge: Cassandra Bryant, Melissa Duffy, Maria Tranguch, Krista Strating, and Amanda Whitton.

I talked with and observed arborists on several job sites—including Tom Ingersoll and his team, Brian Carpenter, and Steve Adams—and at the New England chapter of the International Society of Arboriculture's June 2022 competition in Framingham, Massachusetts.

Selected Bibliography

"7 Facts about the Hemlock Woolly Adelgid." Cary Institute of Ecosystem Studies, June 16, 2022.

"2020 Drought in New England." US Department of the Interior Open-File Report 2020–1148 U.S. Geological Survey ver. 1.1, February 2021

"About 75 Years of Synthetic Fiber Rope History." *IEEE Xplore*, 2015.

Abrams, Marc D. "Don't Downplay the Role of Indigenous People in Molding the Ecological Landscape." *Scientific American*. August 5, 2020.

Abrams, Marc D., Gregory J. Nowacki, and Brice B. Hanberry. "Oak Forests and Woodlands as Indigenous Landscapes in the Eastern United States." *Torrey Botanical Society* 149, no. 2 (2021): 1–10. https://doi.org/10.3159/torrey-d-21-00024.1.

Adams, Mark. "Climbing Hitches: Addenda and Corrigenda." *Arborist News*, April 2007.

Ajasa, Amudalat. "California's Trees Are Dying by the Millions. Here's Why." *Washington Post*, February 9, 2023.

Albro, Sandra L. *Vacant to Vibrant: Creating Successful Green Infrastructure Networks.* Washington, DC: Island Press, 2019.

"Allegheny National Forest"—News & Events. US Department of Agriculture, November 20, 2023.

Allen, Craig D., David D. Breshears, and Nate G. McDowell. "On Underestimation of Global Vulnerability to Tree Mortality and Forest Die-Off from Hotter Drought in the Anthropocene." *Ecosphere* 6, no. 8 (2015): art129. https://doi.org/10.1890/es15-00203.1.

Allen, Craig D., Alison K. Macalady, Haroun Chenchouni, Dominique Bachelet, Nate McDowell, Michel Vennetier, Thomas Kitzberger, et al. "A Global Overview of Drought and Heat-Induced Tree Mortality Reveals Emerging Climate Change Risks for Forests." *Forest Ecology and*

Management 259, no. 4 (2010): 660–84. https://doi.org/10.1016/j.foreco.2009.09.001.

"American Beech (*Fagus grandifolia*)." *Adirondacks Forever Wild.*

Anchukaitis, Kevin J. "Tree Rings Reveal Climate Change Past, Present, and Future." *Proceedings of the American Philosophical Society* 161, no. 3 (2017): 244–63. http://www.jstor.org/stable/45211559.

Anderegg, William R. L., Joseph A. Berry, Duncan D. Smith, John S. Sperry, Leander D. L. Anderegg, and Christopher B. Field. "The Roles of Hydraulic and Carbon Stress in a Widespread Climate-Induced Forest Die-Off." *Proceedings of the National Academy of Sciences* 109, no. 1 (2011): 233–37. https://doi.org/10.1073/pnas.1107891109.

Anderegg, William R. L., Oriana S. Chegwidden, Grayson Badgley, Anna T. Trugman, Danny Cullenward, John T. Abatzoglou, Jeffrey A. Hicke, et al. "Future Climate Risks from Stress, Insects and Fire across US Forests." *Ecology Letters*, May 2022. https://doi.org/10.1111/ele.14018.

Anderegg, William R. L., Anna T. Trugman, Grayson Badgley, Christa M. Anderson, Ann Bartuska, Philippe Ciais, Danny Cullenward, et al. "Climate-Driven Risks to the Climate Mitigation Potential of Forests." *Science* 368, no. 6497 (2020): eaaz7005. https://doi.org/10.1126/science.aaz7005. PMID: 32554569.

Anderegg, William R. L., Chao Wu, Nezha Acil, Nuno Carvalhais, Thomas A. M. Pugh, Jon P. Sadler, and Rupert Seidl. "A Climate Risk Analysis of Earth's Forests in the 21st Century." *Science* 377, no. 6610 (2022): 1099–1103. https://doi.org/10.1126/science.abp9723.

Anderson, Kathleen S. "Cumberland Farms Fields." *Bird Observer* 24, no. 1 (1996).

"Annual Survey of State Winter Maintenance Data." *Clear Roads.*

"Areas with Tree Mortality from Bark Beetles: Summary for 2000—2020." US Department of Agriculture.

Armstrong, Joseph E. *How the Earth Turned Green.* Chicago: University of Chicago Press, 2014.

Asbjornsen, Heidi, Cameron D. McIntire, Matthew A. Vadeboncoeur, Katie A. Jennings, Adam P. Coble, and Z. Carter Berry. "Sensitivity and Threshold Dynamics of *Pinus strobus* and *Quercus* spp. in Response to Experimental and Naturally Occurring Severe Droughts." *Tree Physiology.* October 2021. https://doi.org/10.1093/treephys/tpab056.

Ashley, Clifford W. *The Ashley Book of Knots.* New York: Doubleday, 1944.

"Asian Longhorned Beetle." *Don't Move Firewood.*

Åström, Alexander, and Christoffer Åström. "Art and Science of Rope." *Handbook of the Mathematics of the Arts and Sciences.* August 15, 2021. https://doi.org/10.1007/978-3-319-57072-3_15.

Aukema, Juliann E., Deborah G. McCullough, Betsy Von Holle, Andrew M. Liebhold, Kerry Britton, and Susan J. Frankel. "Historical Accumulation of Nonindigenous Forest Pests in the Continental United States." *BioScience* 60, no. 11 (2010): 886–97. https://doi.org/10.1525/bio.2010.60.11.5.

Bagenstose, Kyle. "Heavy Road Salt Use in Winter Is a Growing Problem, Scientists Say." *USA Today.* December 24, 2019.

Ball, John. "Tree Worker Safety Update by the Numbers: Another Us vs. Them." *Tree Care Industry Magazine,* February 1, 2022.

Ball, John. "Tree-Work Safety by the Numbers." *Tree Care Industry Magazine,* April 1, 2023.

Bardekjian, Adrina C., Lorien Nesbitt, Cecil C. Konijnendijk, and Barend T. Lötter. "Women in Urban Forestry and Arboriculture: Experiences, Barriers and Strategies for Leadership." *Urban Forestry & Urban Greening.* December 2019. https://doi.org/10.1016/j.ufug.2019.126442.

Barkhordarian, Armineh, Sassan S. Saatchi, Ali Behrangi, Paul C. Loikith, and Carlos R. Mechoso. "A Recent Systematic Increase in Vapor Pressure Deficit over Tropical South America." *Scientific Reports* 9, no. 1 (2019). https://doi.org/10.1038/s41598-019-51857-8.

Barndollar, Hadley. "NOAA Says New England's Temps Are Warming, Sea Levels Rising Faster than the Global Rate." *Providence Journal,* February 18, 2022.

Barnes, Mallory L., Quan Zhang, Scott M. Robeson, Lily Young, Elizabeth A. Burakowski, A. Christopher Oishi, Paul C. Stoy, et al. "A Century of Reforestation Reduced Anthropogenic Warming in the Eastern United States." *Earth's Future* 12, no. 2 (2024). https://doi.org/10.1029/2023ef003663.

Barton, Andrew M., William S. Keeton, and Thomas A. Spies, eds. *Ecology and Recovery of Eastern Old-Growth Forests.* Washington, DC: Island Press, 2018.

Barton, Andrew M., Alan S. White, and Charles V. Cogbill. *The Changing Nature of the Maine Woods.* Durham, N.H: University of New Hampshire Press, 2012.

Basso, Keith H. *Wisdom Sits in Places: Landscape and Language among the Western Apache.* Albuquerque: University of New Mexico Press, 1996.

Baumflek, M., T. Cabe, J. Schelhas, and M. Dunlavey. "Managing Forests for Culturally Significant Plants in Traditional Cherokee Homelands: Emerging Platforms." *International Forestry Review* 24, no. 3 (2022): 298–314. https://doi.org/10.1505/146554822835941841.

Baumgarten, Frederik, Arthur Gessler, and Yann Vitasse. "No Risk—No Fun: Penalty and Recovery from Spring Frost Damage in Deciduous Temperate Trees." *Functional Ecology* 37, no. 3 (2022): 648–63. https://doi.org/10.1111/1365-2435.14243.

Bayer, Mandy, and Geoffrey Njue. "The Impact of Salts on Plants and How to Reduce Plant Injury from Winter Salt Applications." *Center for Agriculture, Food and the Environment,* January 15, 2016.

Beckman, Emily, Abby Meyer, David Pivorunas, Sean Hoban, and Murphy Westwood. *Conservation Gap Analysis of American Beech.* Lisle, IL: The Morton Arboretum, 2021.

"Beech Bark Disease." Cary Institute of Ecosystem Studies.

Bemelmans, Ludwig. *Parsley.* New York: Harper, 1955.

Benton, Michael J., Peter Wilf, and Hervé Sauquet. "The Angiosperm Terrestrial Revolution and the Origins of Modern Biodiversity." *New Phytologist*. October 26, 2021. https://doi.org/10.1111/nph.17822.

Bentz, Barbara, and Kier Klepzig. "Bark Beetles and Climate Change in the United States | Climate Change Resource Center." US Department of Agriculture, 2010.

Bentz, Barbara J., Constance I. Millar, James C. Vandygriff, and Earl M. Hansen. "Great Basin Bristlecone Pine Mortality: Causal Factors and Management Implications." *Forest Ecology and Management*. April 1, 2022. https://doi.org/10.1016/j.foreco.2022.120099.

Beresford-Kroeger, Diana. *To Speak for the Trees: My Life's Journey from Ancient Celtic Wisdom to a Healing Vision of the Forest*. Toronto: Random House Canada, 2019.

Berwyn, Bob. " 'We Need to Hear These Poor Trees Scream': Unchecked Global Warming Means Big Trouble for Forests." *Inside Climate News*, April 25, 2020.

"Between the Devil and the Deep Blue Sea: Deer Browsing May Constrain Climate-Smart Reforestation." USDA Climate Change Resource Center, 2022.

Biedermann, Peter H.W., Jörg Müller, Jean-Claude Grégoire, Axel Gruppe, Jonas Hagge, Almuth Hammerbacher, Richard W. Hofstetter, et al. "Bark Beetle Population Dynamics in the Anthropocene: Challenges and Solutions." *Trends in Ecology & Evolution*. October 2019. https://doi.org/10.1016/j.tree.2019.06.002.

Boczoń, Andrzej, Dorota Hilszczańska, Marta Wrzosek, Andrzej Szczepkowski, and Zbigniew Sierota. "Drought in the Forest Breaks Plant–Fungi Interactions." *European Journal of Forest Research* 140 (2021): 1301–21. https://doi.org/10.1007/s10342-021-01409-5.

"Bois Forte Band Regains Historic Tribal Land." *The Conservation Fund*.

Bond, William J. *Open Ecosystems*. New York: Oxford University Press, 2019.

Bonello, Pierluigi, Faith T. Campbell, Don Cipollini, Anna O. Conrad, Coralie Farinas, Kamal J. K. Gandhi, Fred P. Hain, et al. "Invasive Tree Pests Devastate Ecosystems—A Proposed New Response Framework." *Frontiers in Forests and Global Change* 3 (2020): 00002. https://doi.org/10.3389/ffgc.2020.00002.

Bonfante, Paola. "The Future Has Roots in the Past: The Ideas and Scientists That Shaped Mycorrhizal Research." *New Phytologist* 220, no. 4 (2018): 982–95. https://doi.org/10.1111/nph.15397.

Borges, Renee M. "Plasticity Comparisons between Plants and Animals." *Plant Signaling & Behavior* 3, no. 6 (2008): 367–75. https://doi.org/10.4161/psb.3.6.5823.

Botanical Gardens Conservation International. State of the World's Trees. 2021. BGCI, Richmond, UK.

Boulton, Chris A., Timothy M. Lenton, and Niklas Boers. "Pronounced Loss of Amazon Rainforest Resilience since the Early 2000s." *Nature*

Climate Change 12, no. 12 (2022): 271–78. https://doi.org/10.1038/s41558 -022-01287-8.

Bourbia, Ibrahim, and Timothy J Brodribb. "A New Technique for Monitoring Plant Transpiration under Field Conditions Using Leaf Optical Dendrometry." *Agricultural and Forest Meteorology*. March 15, 2023. https://doi.org/10.1016/j.agrformet.2023.109328.

Bourgon, Lyndsie. *Tree Thieves: Crime and Survival in North America's Woods*. New York: Little, Brown, 2022.

Bowcutt, Frederica. *The Tanoak Tree: An Environmental History of a Pacific Coast Hardwood*. Seattle: University of Washington Press, 2015.

Brack, Duncan. "Background Analytical Study: Forests and Climate Change." March 2019.

Bradley, Raymond S. *Paleoclimatology: Reconstructing Climates of the Quaternary*. Amsterdam: Elsevier. 2014.

Brodribb, Timothy J. "Learning from a Century of Droughts." *Nature Ecology & Evolution* 4, no. 8 (2020): 1007–8. https://doi.org/10.1038/s41559-020 -1226-2.

Brodribb, Timothy J. "Progressing from 'Functional' to Mechanistic Traits." *New Phytologist* 215, no. 1 (2017): 9–11. https://doi.org/10.1111/nph.14620.

Brodribb, Timothy J., Diane Bienaimé, and Philippe Marmottant. "Revealing Catastrophic Failure of Leaf Networks under Stress." *Proceedings of the National Academy of Sciences* 113, no. 17 (2016): 4865–69. https://doi .org/10.1073/pnas.1522569113.

Brodribb, Timothy J., Marc Carriqui, Sylvain Delzon, and Christopher Lucani. 2017. "Optical Measurement of Stem Xylem Vulnerability." *Plant Physiology*, August 2017. https://doi.org/10.1104/pp.17.00552.

Brodribb, Timothy J., Jennifer Powers, Hervé Cochard, and Brendan Choat. "Hanging by a Thread? Forests and Drought." *Science* 368, no. 6488 (2020): 261–66. https://doi.org/10.1126/science.aat7631.

Bruchac, Joseph, and Michael J. Caduto. *Native Plant Stories*. Golden, CO: Fulcrum, 1995.

Brunelle, Andrea, Gerald E. Rehfeldt, Barbara Bentz, and A. Steven Munson. "Holocene Records of *Dendroctonus* Bark Beetles in High Elevation Pine Forests of Idaho and Montana, USA." *Forest Ecology and Management* 255, no. 3–4 (2008): 836–46. https://doi.org/10.1016/j.foreco.2007.10.008.

Buckley, Cara, and Jamie Kelter Davis. "The Giving Forest." *New York Times*, April 22, 2023.

Buggs, Richard J. A. "Changing Perceptions of Tree Resistance Research." *Plants, People, Planet* 2, no. 1 (2019): 2–4. https://doi.org/10.1002/ppp3 .10089.

Bull, Brian. "Native American Tribes Gaining Recognition for Timber and Forestry Practices." *KLCC | NPR for Oregonians*, January 30, 2019.

Burakowski, Elizabeth A., Alexandra R. Contosta, Danielle Grogan, Sarah J. Nelson, Sarah Garlick, and Nora Casson. "Future of Winter in Northeastern North America: Climate Indicators Portray Warming and Snow

Loss That Will Impact Ecosystems and Communities." *Northeastern Naturalist* 28, no. sp11 (2022). https://doi.org/10.1656/045.028.s1112.

Calma, Justine. "Instead of Planting Trees, Give Forests Back to People." *The Verge*, February 10, 2023.

Campana, Richard J. *Arboriculture: History and Development in North America.* East Lansing: Michigan State University Press, 1999.

Campanella, Thomas J. *Republic of Shade: New England and the American Elm.* New Haven: Yale University Press, 2011.

Canada Report 2018. Canadian Interagency Forest Fire Centre Inc.

Canadell, Josep G., Pedro M. S. Monteiro, Macros H. Costa, Leticia Cotrim da Cunha, Peter M. Cox, Alexey V. Eliseev, Stephanie Henson, et al. "Global Carbon and other Biogeochemical Cycles and Feedbacks." In *Climate Change 2021: The Physical Science Basis. Contribution of Working Group I to the Sixth Assessment Report of the Intergovernmental Panel on Climate Change*, edited by V. Masson-Delmotte, P. Zhai, A. Pirani, S. L. Connors, C. Péan, S. Berger, N. Caud, et al., 673–816. Cambridge: Cambridge University Press, 2021. https://doi.org/10.1017/9781009157896.007.

Candeias, Matt. *In Defense of Plants*, podcast.

Candeias, Matt. *In Defense of Plants: An Exploration into the Wonder of Plants.* Coral Gables: Mango, 2021.

Canham, Charles D. *Forests Adrift: Currents Shaping the Future of Northeastern Trees.* New Haven: Yale University Press, 2020.

Canham, Hugh O. "Hemlock and Hide: The Tanbark Industry in Old New York." *Northern Woodlands*, Summer 2011.

Carrero, Christina, Emily Beckman Bruns, Anne Frances, Diana Jerome, Wesley Knapp, Abby Meyer, Ray Mims, et al. "Data Sharing for Conservation: A Standardized Checklist of US Native Tree Species and Threat Assessments to Prioritize and Coordinate Action." *Plants, People, Planet*, August 2022. https://doi.org/10.1002/ppp3.10305.

Carrero, Christina, Diana Jerome, Emily Beckman, Amy Byrne, Allen J. Coombes, Min Deng, Antonio González-Rodríguez, et al. *The Red List of Oaks 2020.* Lisle, IL: The Morton Arboretum, 2020.

Carswell, Cally. "The Tree Coroners." *High Country News*, December 16, 2013.

Carta, Lynn Kay, Zafar A. Handoo, Shiguang Li, Mihail Kantor, Gary Bauchan, David McCann, Colette K. Gabriel, et al. "Beech Leaf Disease Symptoms Caused by Newly Recognized Nematode Subspecies *Litylenchus crenatae · mccannii* (Anguinata) Described from *Fagus grandifolia* in North America." *Forest Pathology* 50, no. 2 (2020): e12580. https://doi.org/10.1111/efp.12580.

Casson, N. J., A. R. Contosta, E. A. Burakowski, J. L. Campbell, M. S. Crandall, I. F. Creed, M. C. Eimers, et al. "Winter Weather Whiplash: Impacts of Meteorological Events Misaligned with Natural and Human Systems in Seasonally Snow-Covered Regions." *Earth's Future* 7, no. 12 (2019): 1434–50. https://doi.org/10.1029/2019ef001224.

Catton, Theodore. *American Indians and National Forests*. Tucson: University of Arizona Press, 2016.

Cavender-Bares, Jeannine, John A. Gamon, and Philip A. Townsend. *Remote Sensing of Plant Biodiversity*. Cham, Switzerland: Springer Nature, 2020.

Cavender-Bares, Jeannine, Fabian D. Schneider, Maria J. Santos, Amanda Armstrong, Ana Carnaval, Kyla M. Dahlin, Lola Fatoyinbo, et al. "Integrating Remote Sensing with Ecology and Evolution to Advance Biodiversity Conservation." *Nature Ecology & Evolution* 6 (March 2022): 506–19. https://doi.org/10.1038/s41559-022-01702-5.

Cazzolla Gatti, Roberto, et al. "The Number of Tree Species on Earth." *Proceedings of the National Academy of Sciences*. January 31, 2022. https://www.pnas.org/doi/epub/10.1073/pnas.2115329119.

Chamovitz, Daniel. *What a Plant Knows: A Field Guide to the Senses*. New York: Scientific American/Farrar, Straus and Giroux, 2017.

Champagne, Emilie, Patricia Raymond, Alejandro A. Royo, James D. M. Speed, Jean-Pierre Tremblay, and Steeve D. Côté. "A Review of Ungulate Impacts on the Success of Climate-Adapted Forest Management Strategies." *Current Forestry Reports* 7 (2021): 305–20. https://doi.org/10.1007/s40725-021-00148-5.

Chandler, Jennifer L., Joseph S. Elkinton, and David A. Orwig. "High Rainfall May Induce Fungal Attack of Hemlock Woolly Adelgid (Hemiptera: Adelgidae) Leading to Regional Decline." *Environmental Entomology*, November 2021. https://doi.org/10.1093/ee/nvab125.

Chaudoin, Patricia. "Solving the Challenges of Outfitting Female Arborists with PPE." *Tree Care Industry*, March 2019.

Chávez, Karen. "Great Smokies Approves Historic Sochan Collecting Agreement with Eastern Band of Cherokee." *Asheville Citizen Times*, March 25, 2019.

Chiodi, Andrew M., Brian E. Potter, and Narasimhan K. Larkin. 2021. "Multi-Decadal Change in Western US Nighttime Vapor Pressure Deficit." *Geophysical Research Letters*, July 15, 2021. https://doi.org/10.1029/2021gl092830.

Choat, Brendan, Timothy J. Brodribb, Craig R. Brodersen, Remko A. Duursma, Rosana López, and Belinda E. Medlyn. "Triggers of Tree Mortality under Drought." *Nature* 558, no. 7711 (2018): 531–39. https://doi.org/10.1038/s41586-018-0240-x.

Clapp, Casey, and Alex Crowson. *Completely Arbortrary*, podcast.

Clark, Peter W., Anthony W. D'Amato, Brian J. Palik, Christopher W. Woodall, Paul A. Dubuque, Gregory J. Edge, Jason P. Hartman, et al. "A Lack of Ecological Diversity in Forest Nurseries Limits the Achievement of Tree-Planting Objectives in Response to Global Change." *BioScience* 73, no. 8 (2023): 575–86. https://doi.org/10.1093/biosci/biad049.

Clarke, Stephen R., and J. T. Nowak. "USDA Forest Service, Forest Health Protection, Southern Region, Lufkin, TX. 2 SPB Prevention Program Coordinator." US Department of Agriculture Forest Service, 2009.

Coffin, Alisa W., Douglas S. Ouren, Neil D. Bettez, Luís Borda-de-Água, Amy E. Daniels, Clara Grilo, Jochen A.G. Jaeger, et al. "The Ecology of Rural Roads: Effects, Management, and Research." *Issues in Ecology*, Summer 2021, 1–30.

Cohen, Jocelyn. "Women Who Climb." *Western Arborist*, 2019.

"Conservation Gap Analysis of Native Magnolias of the U.S. and Canada." *Botanic Gardens Conservation International*, 2022.

Contosta, Alexandra R., Alden Adolph, Denise Burchsted, Elizabeth Burakowski, Mark Green, David Guerra, Mary Albert, et al. "A Longer Vernal Window: The Role of Winter Coldness and Snowpack in Driving Spring Transitions and Lags." *Global Change Biology* 23, no. 4 (2016): 1610–25. https://doi.org/10.1111/gcb.13517.

Contosta, Alexandra R., John J. Battles, John L. Campbell, Charles T. Driscoll, Sarah R. Garlick, Richard T. Holmes, Gene E. Likens, et al. "Early Warning Signals of Changing Resilience in the Biogeochemistry and Biology of a Northern Hardwood Forest." *Environmental Research Letters* 18, no. 9 (2023): 094052. https://doi.org/10.1088/1748-9326/acf3fe.

Contosta, Alexandra R., Nora J. Casson, Sarah Garlick, Sarah J. Nelson, Matthew P. Ayres, Elizabeth A. Burakowski, John Campbell, et al. "Northern Forest Winters Have Lost Cold, Snowy Conditions That Are Important for Ecosystems and Human Communities." *Ecological Applications* 29, no. 7 (2019). https://doi.org/10.1002/eap.1974.

Cook, Benjamin I., Edward R. Cook, Paul C. Huth, John E. Thompson, Anna Forster, and Daniel Smiley. "A Cross-Taxa Phenological Dataset from Mohonk Lake, NY and Its Relationship to Climate." *International Journal of Climatology* 28, no. 10 (2007): 1369–83. https://doi.org/10.1002/joc.1629.

Cook, Edward R. "Early Days of Dendrochronology in the Hudson Valley of New York: Some Reminiscences and Reflections." *Tree-Ring Research*. July 2014. https://doi.org/10.3959/1536-1098-70.2.113.

Cook, Edward R., W. Stahle, and M. K. Cleaveland. "Dendroclimatic Evidence from Eastern North America." In *Climate Since AD 1500*, edited by R. S. Bradley and P. D. Jones, 331–348. New York: Routledge, 1995.

Cook, Edward R., Richard Seager, Richard R. Heim Jr., Russell S. Vose, Celine Herweijer, and Connie Woodhouse. "Megadroughts in North America: Placing IPCC Projections of Hydroclimatic Change in a Long-Term Palaeoclimate Context." *Journal of Quaternary Science* 25, no. 1 (2009): 48–61. https://doi.org/10.1002/jqs.1303.

Cordell, Susan, Celia Bardwell-Jones, Rebecca Ostertag, Amanda Uowolo, and Nicole DiManno. "Species Home-Making in Ecosystems: Toward Place-Based Ecological Metrics of Belonging." *Frontiers in Ecology and Evolution* 9 (November 2021). https://doi.org/10.3389/fevo.2021.726571.

Cortés, Andrés J., Manuela Restrepo-Montoya, and Larry E. Bedoya-Canas. "Modern Strategies to Assess and Breed Forest Tree Adaptation to Changing Climate." *Frontiers in Plant Science* 11 (October 2020). https://doi.org/10.3389/fpls.2020.583323.

Costanza, Kara K. L., Thomas D. Whitney, Cameron D. McIntire, William H. Livingston, and Kamal J. K. Gandhi. "A Synthesis of Emerging Health Issues of Eastern White Pine (*Pinus strobus*) in Eastern North America." *Forest Ecology and Management* 423 (September 2018): 3–17. https://doi.org/10.1016/j.foreco.2018.02.049.

Coulthard, B. L., and D. J. Smith. "Dendrochronology." In *Encyclopedia of Quaternary Science*, edited by Scott A. Elias and Cary J. Mack, 453–58. Amsterdam: Elsevier, 2014.

Cranage, Alison. "Genomes Great and Small: The Diversity of Plants." *Darwin Tree of Life*, February 17, 2022.

Crane, Peter. *Ginkgo: The Tree that Time Forgot*. New Haven: Yale University Press, 2013

Crimmins, Theresa. *Phenology*. Cambridge: MIT Press, 2025.

Cronon, William. *Changes in the Land: Indians, Colonists, and the Ecology of New England*. New York: Hill and Wang. 2003.

Cronon, William. *Uncommon Ground: Toward Reinventing Nature*. New York: Norton, 1995.

Crouch, Connor D., Nicholas P. Wilhelmi, Paul C. Rogers, Margaret M. Moore, and Kristen M. Waring. "Sustainability and Drivers of *Populus tremuloides* Regeneration and Recruitment near the Southwestern Edge of Its Range." *Forestry*, April 2024. https://doi.org/10.1093/forestry/cpae018.

Crowther, T. W., H. B. Glick, K. R. Covey, C. Bettigole, D. S. Maynard, S. M. Thomas, J. R. Smith, et al. "Mapping Tree Density at a Global Scale." *Nature*, September 2, 2015. https://doi.org/10.1038/nature14967.

Cruaud, Astrid, Nina Rønsted, Bhanumas Chantarasuwan, Lien Siang Chou, Wendy L. Clement, Arnaud Couloux, Benjamin Cousins, et al. "An Extreme Case of Plant–Insect Codiversification: Figs and Fig-Pollinating Wasps." *Systematic Biology* 61, No. 6 (2011): 1029–47. https://doi.org/10.1093/sysbio/sys068.

Culin, Joseph. "Asian Longhorned Beetle." Chicago: Encyclopædia Britannica. 2017.

Dahl, Kristy. "With Climate Change, Nights Are Warming Faster than Days. Why?" *The Equation*, July 12, 2022.

Dahl, Tais W., and Susanne K.M. Arens. "The Impacts of Land Plant Evolution on Earth's Climate and Oxygenation State—An Interdisciplinary Review." *Chemical Geology*, August 5, 2020. https://doi.org/10.1016/j.chemgeo.2020.119665.

Dale, Adam G., Travis Birdsell, and Jill Sidebottom. "Evaluating the Invasive Potential of an Exotic Scale Insect Associated with Annual Christmas Tree Harvest and Distribution in the Southeastern U.S." *Trees, Forests and People* 2 (December 2020): 100013. https://doi.org/10.1016/j.tfp.2020.100013.

D'Amato, Anthony, Benjamin Baiser, Aaron M. Ellison, David Orwig, Wyatt Oswald, Audrey Barker Plotkin, and Jonathan Thompson. In *Hemlock: A Forest Giant on the Edge*, edited by David R. Foster. New Haven: Yale University Press, 2014.

Das, Ripan, Rajiv K. Chaturvedi, Adrija Roy, et al. "Warming Inhibits Increases in Vegetation Net Primary Productivity Despite Greening in India." *Scientific Reports* 13 (2023): 21309. https://doi.org/10.1038/s41598 -023-48614-3.

"DATCP Home Check Out-of-State Christmas Trees and Décor for Elongate Hemlock Scale and Other Invasive Pests." Department of Agriculture, Trade and Consumer Protection, Wisconsin.

Davis, Kimberley T., Marcos D. Robles, Kerry B. Kemp, Philip E. Higuera, Teresa Chapman, Kerry L. Metlen, Jamie L. Peeler, et al. "Reduced Fire Severity Offers Near-Term Buffer to Climate-Driven Declines in Conifer Resilience across the Western United States." *Proceedings of the National Academy of Sciences.* March 6, 2023. https://doi.org/10.1073/pnas.2208120120.

De Manincor, Natasha, Alessandro Fisogni, and Nicole E. Rafferty. "Warming of Experimental Plant–Pollinator Communities Advances Phenologies, Alters Traits, Reduces Interactions and Depresses Reproduction." *Ecology Letters* 26 (2023): 323–34.

Debuys, William. *A Great Aridness: Climate Change and the Future of the American Southwest.* New York: Oxford University Press. 2013

Del Tredici, Peter. "Layering and Rejuvenation in *Tsuga canadensis* (Pinaceae) on Wachusett Mountain, Massachusetts." *Rhodora*, January 2017. https://doi.org/10.3119/16-12.

Delgado, Anton L. "Juniper Trees Usually Thrive in Arizona's Arid Climate. The Drought Is Killing Them." *Arizona Republic*, July 13, 2021.

Denevan, William M. "'The Pristine Myth' Revisited." *Geographical Review* 101, no. 4 (2011): 576–91. https://doi.org/10.1111/j.1931-0846.2011.00118.x.

Department of State, Office of Electronic Information, Bureau of Public Affairs. "Case Study: Pine Wood Nematode." 2001–2009.

Diamond, Jared. *Collapse: How Societies Choose to Fail or Succeed.* New York: Viking Penguin, 2005.

Dickinson, H. W. "A Condensed History of Rope-Making." *Transactions of the Newcomen Society*, February 1, 2014. https://doi.org/10.1179/tns.1942.007.

DK. *The Tree Book.* Penguin. 2022.

Dockry, Michael. "Menominee Oral History: Using Historical Perspectives to Inform Contemporary Sustainable Forest Management Introduction," Chapter 4.

Dockry, Michael J., and Serra J. Hoagland. "A Special Issue of the Journal of Forestry—Tribal Forest Management: Innovations for Sustainable Forest Management." *Journal of Forestry* 115, no. 5 (2017): 339–40. https://doi.org/10.5849/jof-2017-040.

Dodds, Kevin J., Carissa F. Aoki, Adriana Arango-Velez, Jessica Cancelliere, Anthony W. D'Amato, Marc F. DiGirolomo, and Robert J. Rabaglia. "Expansion of Southern Pine Beetle into Northeastern Forests: Management and Impact of a Primary Bark Beetle in a New Region." *Journal of Forestry*, March 12, 2018. https://doi.org/10.1093/jofore/fvx009.

Donovan, Geoffrey H., David T. Butry, Yvonne L. Michael, Jeffrey P. Prestemon, Andrew M. Liebhold, Demetrios Gatziolis, and Megan Y. Mao. "The Relationship between Trees and Human Health." *American Journal of Preventive Medicine* 44, no. 2 (2013): 139–45. https://doi.org/10.1016/j.amepre.2012.09.066.

Donovan, Victoria M., Raelene Crandall, Jennifer Fill, and Carissa L. Wonkka. "Increasing Large Wildfire in the Eastern United States." *Geophysical Research Letters* 50. No. 24 (2023). https://doi.org/10.1029/2023gl107051.

Doughty, Christopher E., Jenna M. Keany, Benjamin C. Wiebe, Camilo Rey-Sanchez, Kelsey R. Carter, Kali B. Middleby, Alexander W. Cheesman, et al. "Tropical Forests Are Approaching Critical Temperature Thresholds." *Nature* 621 (2023): 105–11. https://doi.org/10.1038/s41586-023-06391-z.

Douville, Hervé, Krishnan Raghavan, James Renwick, Richard P. Allan, Poala A. Arias, Mathew Barlow, Ruth Cerezo-Mota, et al. "Water Cycle Changes." In *Climate Change 2021: The Physical Science Basis. Contribution of Working Group I to the Sixth Assessment Report of the Intergovernmental Panel on Climate Change*, edited by V. Masson-Delmotte, P. Zhai, A. Pirani, S. L. Connors, C. Péan, S. Berger, N. Caud, et al., 1055–1210. Cambridge: Cambridge University Press, 2021. https://doi.org/10.1017/9781009157896.010.

Doyle, James M., Kendal E. Earley, and Robert B. Atkinson. "An Analysis of Atlantic White Cedar (*Chamaecyparis thyoides* (L.) B.S.P.) Tree Rings as Indicators of Ghost Forest Development in a Globally Threatened Ecosystem." *Forests* 12, no. 8 (2021): 973. https://doi.org/10.3390/f12080973.

Drori, Jonathan, and Lucille Clerc. *Around the World in 80 Trees*. London: Laurence King Publishing, 2018.

Duberman, Amanda. "Women with Chainsaws: Confessions of a Lady Lumberjack." *HuffPost*. August 28, 2014.

Dümpelmann, Sonja. *Seeing Trees: A History of Street Trees in New York City and Berlin*. New Haven: Yale University Press, 2019.

Dunlap, Tom. "The Single Rope Technique." *Tree Care Industry*, 2002.

Early, Regan, Bethany A. Bradley, Jeffrey S. Dukes, et al. "Global Threats from Invasive Alien Species in the Twenty-First Century and National Response Capacities." *Nature Communications* 7 (2016): 12485. https://doi.org/10.1038/ncomms12485.

Egan, Timothy. *The Big Burn: Teddy Roosevelt and the Fire That Saved America*. Boston: Houghton Mifflin Harcourt, 2009.

Ellender, Lulah. "The Knotty Story of Women in Trees." *Caught by the River*. April 20, 2019.

Ellis, Erle C., Nicolas Gauthier, Kees Klein Goldewijk, Rebecca Bliege Bird, Nicole Boivin, Sandra Díaz, Dorian Q. Fuller, et al. "People Have Shaped Most of Terrestrial Nature for at Least 12,000 Years." *Proceedings of the National Academy of Sciences* 118, no. 17 (2021). https://doi.org/10.1073/pnas.2023483118.

Ellwood, Elizabeth R., Amanda S. Gallinat, Caitlin McDonough MacKenzie,

Tara Miller, Abraham J. Miller-Rushing, Caroline Polgar, and Richard B. Primack. "Plant and Bird Phenology and Plant Occurrence from 1851 to 2020 (Non-Continuous) in Thoreau's Concord, Massachusetts." *Ecology* 103, no. 5 (2022). https://doi.org/10.1002/ecy.3646.

Elpel, Thomas J. *Botany in a Day: The Patterns Method of Plant Identification: An Herbal Field Guide to Plant Families of North America*, edition 6.2. Pony, MT: HOPS Press, 2021.

"Endangered and Threatened Wildlife and Plants; Threatened Species Status with Section 4(D) Rule for Whitebark Pine (*Pinus albicaulis*)." *Federal Register*, December 15, 2022.

Esper, Jan, Paolo Cherubini, David Kaltenbach, and Ulf Büntgen. "London Plane Bark Exfoliation and Tree-Ring Growth in Urban Environments." *Arboriculture & Urban Forestry*, November 2023. https://doi.org/10.48044/jauf.2023.021.

Fa, Julia E., James E. M. Watson, Ian Leiper, Peter Potapov, Tom D. Evans, Neil D. Burgess, Zsolt Molnár, et al. "Importance of Indigenous Peoples' Lands for the Conservation of Intact Forest Landscapes." *Frontiers in Ecology and the Environment* 18, no. 3 (2020): 135–40. https://doi.org/10.1002/fee.2148.

Fady, Bruno, Filippos Aravanopoulos, Raquel Benavides, Santiago González-Martínez, Delphine Grivet, et al. "Genetics to the Rescue: Managing Forests Sustainably in a Changing World." *Tree Genetics and Genomes* 16, 80 (2020). https://doi.org/10.1007/s11295-020-01474-8.

Farmer, Jared. *Elderflora: A Modern History of Ancient Trees*. New York: Basic Books, 2022.

Farrell, Justin, Paul Berne Burow, Kathryn McConnell, Jude Bayham, Kyle Whyte, and Gal Koss. "Effects of Land Dispossession and Forced Migration on Indigenous Peoples in North America." *Science* 374, no. 6567 (2021). https://doi.org/10.1126/science.abe4943.

Faulkenberry, Mark, Donald Eggen, and Ellen Shultzbarger. *Eastern Hemlock Conservation Plan*. Pennsylvania Department of Conservation and Natural Resources; Bureau of Forestry, 2019.

Feild, Taylor S., Nan Crystal Arens, James A. Doyle, Todd E. Dawson, and Michael J. Donoghue. "Dark and Disturbed: A New Image of Early Angiosperm Ecology." *Paleobiology*, Winter 2004. https://www.jstor.org/stable/4096922.

Fettig, Christopher J., Sharon M. Hood, Justin B. Runyon, Chris M. Stalling. "Bark Beetle and Fire Interactions in Western Coniferous Forests: Research Findings." *Fire Management Today*, 2021.

"Fighting Fire with Fire." *Plant People*, podcast, episode 3. New York Botanical Garden. 2024.

"Fire-Dependent Ecosystem Restoration Project." US Department of Agriculture, Forest Service, 2022.

Fletcher, Michael-Shawn, Rebecca Hamilton, Wolfram Dressler, and Lisa Palmer. "Indigenous Knowledge and the Shackles of

Wilderness." *Proceedings of the National Academy of Sciences* 118, no. 40 (2021). https://doi.org/10.1073/pnas.2022218118.

"Forest Atlas of the United States." Northern Research Station: United States Forest Service, 2022.

Forzieri, Giovanni, Vasilis Dakos, Nate G. McDowell, Alkama Ramdane, and Alessandro Cescatti. "Emerging Signals of Declining Forest Resilience under Climate Change." *Nature* 608, No. 7923 (2022): 534–39. https://doi.org/10.1038/s41586-022-04959-9.

Franklin, Jerry F., L. J. Dempster, and Richard H. Waring, eds. *Research on Coniferous Forest Ecosystems: First Year Progress in the Coniferous Forest Biome, US/IBP*: Proceedings of a Symposium. Forest Service, US Department of Agriculture, 1972.

Freinkel, Susan. *American Chestnut: The Life, Death, and Rebirth of a Perfect Tree.* Berkeley: University of California Press, 2007.

Funk, Jason, Stephen Saunders, Todd Sanford, Tom Easley, and Adam Markham. *Rocky Mountain Forests at Risk: Confronting Climate-Driven Impacts from Insects, Wildfires, Heat, and Drought.* Report from the Union of Concerned Scientists and the Rocky Mountain Climate Organization. Cambridge, MA: Union of Concerned Scientists, September 2014.

Fusco, Emily J., John T. Finn, Jennifer K. Balch, R. Chelsea Nagy, and Bethany A. Bradley. "Invasive Grasses Increase Fire Occurrence and Frequency across US Ecoregions." *Proceedings of the National Academy of Sciences* 116, no. 47 (2019): 23594–99. https://doi.org/10.1073/pnas.1908253116.

Gabbert, Bill. "Moose Fire Burns Tens of Thousands of Acres North of Salmon, Idaho." *Wildfire Today*, July 21, 2022.

Gagliano, Monica. *Thus Spoke the Plant: A Remarkable Journey of Groundbreaking Scientific Discoveries and Personal Encounters with Plants.* Berkeley: North Atlantic Books, 2018.

Gallinat, Amanda S., Richard B. Primack, and David L. Wagner. "Autumn, the Neglected Season in Climate Change Research." *Trends in Ecology & Evolution* 30, no. 3 (2015): 169–76. https://doi.org/10.1016/j.tree.2015.01.004.

Garbelotto, Matteo, and Paolo Gonthier. "Ecological, Evolutionary, and Societal Impacts of Invasions by Emergent Forest Pathogens." In *Forest Microbiology.* Amsterdam: Academic Press, 2022.

Geils, Brian W., Kim E. Hummer, and Richard S. Hunt. "White Pines, Ribes, and Blister Rust: A Review and Synthesis." *Forest Pathology*, August 16, 2010. https://doi.org/10.1111/j.1439-0329.2010.00654.x.

Gérard, Maxence, Maryse Vanderplanck, Thomas Wood, and Denis Michez. "Global Warming and Plant–Pollinator Mismatches." *Emerging Topics in Life Sciences* 4, no. 1 (2020): 77–86. https://doi.org/10.1042/etls20190139.

Gerst, Katharine L., Natalie L. Rossington, and Susan J. Mazer. "Phenological Responsiveness to Climate Differs among Four Species of *Quercus* in North America." *Journal of Ecology* 105, no. 6 (2017): 1610–22. https://doi.org/10.1111/1365-2745.12774.

Giardina, Christian P., Erika S. Svendsen, Heather L. McMillen, Kainana

S. Francisco, Kekuhi Kealiikanakaoleohaililani, and Lindsay K. Campell. "Biocultural Stewardship, Indigenous and Local Ecological Knowledge, and the Urban Crucible." *Ecology and Society* 25, no. 2 (2020). https://doi.org/10.5751/es-11386-250209.

Gillerot, Loïc, Dries Landuyt, Pieter De Frenne, Bart Muys, and Kris Verheyen. "Urban Tree Canopies Drive Human Heat Stress Mitigation." *Urban Forestry & Urban Greening* 92 (2024): 128192. https://doi.org/10.1016/j.ufug.2023.128192.

Gilles, Nathan. "Climate Change Is Hastening the Demise of Pacific Northwest Forests." *Phys Org*, November 16, 2023.

Gillis, Justin. "Climate Change Threatens to Kill off More Aspen Forests by 2050s, Scientists Say." *New York Times*, March 31, 2015.

Goldfarb, Ben. *Crossings: How Road Ecology Is Shaping the Future of Our Planet.* New York: Norton, 2023.

Gollan, Jennifer. "Tree Trimming Deaths Alarm Federal Officials and Industry Insiders." *Reveal*, January 27, 2016.

Gooley, Tristan. *How to Read a Tree: Clues and Patterns from Bark to Leaves.* New York: The Experiment, 2023.

Gotsch, Sybil G., Nalini Nadkarni, Alexander Darby, Andrew Glunk, Mackenzie Dix, Kenneth Davidson, and Todd E. Dawson. "Life in the Treetops: Ecophysiological Strategies of Canopy Epiphytes in a Tropical Montane Cloud Forest." *Ecological Monographs* 85, no. 3 (2015): 393–412. https://doi.org/10.1890/14-1076.1.

Grandoni, Dino. "Genetic Engineering Was Meant to Save Chestnut Trees. Then There Was a Mistake." *Washington Post*, December 24, 2023.

Graziosi, Ignazio, Mathias Tembo, Jean Kuate, and Alice Muchugi. "Pests and Diseases of Trees in Africa: A Growing Continental Emergency." *Plants, People, Planet*, June 2019. https://doi.org/10.1002/ppp3.31.

Greenfield, Patrick, and Mette Lampcov. "Beetles and Fire Kill Dozens of 'Indestructible' Giant Sequoia Trees." *The Guardian*, January 18, 2020.

Greenwood, Leigh, David R. Coyle, María E. Guerrero, Gustavo Hernández, Chris J. K. MacQuarrie, Oscar Trejo, and Meghan K. Noseworthy. "Exploring Pest Mitigation Research and Management Associated with the Global Wood Packaging Supply Chain: What and Where Are the Weak Links?" *Biological Invasions* 25 (2023): 2395–2421. https://doi.org/10.1007/s10530-023-03058-8.

Greer, Burke T., Christopher Still, Grace L. Cullinan, J. Renée Brooks, and Frederick C. Meinzer. "Polyploidy Influences Plant–Environment Interactions in Quaking Aspen (Populus Tremuloides Michx.)." *Tree Physiology* 38, no. 4 (2018): 630–40. https://doi.org/10.1093/treephys/tpx120.

Grossiord, Charlotte, Thomas N. Buckley, Lucas A. Cernusak, Kimberly A. Novick, Benjamin Poulter, Rolf T. W. Siegwolf, John S. Sperry, et al. "Plant Responses to Rising Vapor Pressure Deficit." *New Phytologist* 226, no. 6 (2020): 1550–66. https://doi.org/10.1111/nph.16485.

Grossman, Daniel. "What Ballooning Carbon Emissions Will Do to Trees." *Atlantic*, October 18, 2019.

Haack, Robert A., Yuri Baranchikov, Leah S. Bauer, and Therese M. Poland. "Emerald Ash Borer Biology and Invasion History." In *Biology and Control of Emerald Ash Borer*, edited by R.G. Van Driesche and R.C. Reardon, 1–13, FHTET-2014-09. Morgantown, WV: US Department of Agriculture, Forest Service, Forest Health Technology Enterprise Team.

Haase, Diane L., and Anthony S. Davis. "Developing and Supporting Quality Nursery Facilities and Staff Are Necessary to Meet Global Forest and Landscape Restoration Needs." *Reforesta* 4 (2017): 69–93.

Hadley, Debbie. "How the Invasive Gypsy Moth Came to America." *ThoughtCo.*, 2018.

Hageneder, Fred. *The Spirit of Trees: Science, Symbiosis and Inspiration*. Edinburgh: Floris Books, 2017.

Hain, Fred P., Adrian J. Duehl, Micah J. Gardner, and Thomas L. Payne. "Natural History of the Southern Pine Beetle." In Southern Pine Beetle II. Gen. Tech. Rep. SRS-140, edited by R. N. Coulson and K. D. Klepzig, 13–24. Asheville, NC: US Department of Agriculture Forest Service, Southern Research Station, 2011.

Halik, Shari. "Will Red Oak Dominate Vermont Forests in a Warmer Future?" *University of Vermont*. October 30, 2020.

Hallett, Richard, Michelle L. Johnson, and Nancy F. Sonti. "Assessing the Tree Health Impacts of Salt Water Flooding in Coastal Cities: A Case Study in New York City." *Landscape and Urban Planning* 177 (September 2018): 171–77. https://doi.org/10.1016/j.landurbplan.2018.05.004.

Hammond, William M., A. Park Williams, John T. Abatzoglou, Henry D. Adams, Tamir Klein, Rosana López, Cuauhtémoc Sáenz-Romero, et al. "Global Field Observations of Tree Die-Off Reveal Hotter-Drought Fingerprint for Earth's Forests." *Nature Communications* 13, no. 1 (2022): 1761. https://doi.org/10.1038/s41467-022-29289-2.

Hanberry, Brice B., and Gregory J. Nowacki. "Oaks Were the Historical Foundation Genus of the East-Central United States." *Quaternary Science Reviews* 145 (2016): 94–103. https://doi.org/10.1016/j.quascirev.2016.05.037.

Hancock, Elaina. "Palms at the Poles: Fossil Plants Reveal Lush Southern Hemisphere Forests in Ancient Hothouse Climate." *Uconn Today*, May 31, 2022.

Hansson, Amanda, Paul Dargusch, and Jamie Shulmeister. "A Review of Modern Treeline Migration, the Factors Controlling It and the Implications for Carbon Storage." *Journal of Mountain Science* 18, no. 2 (2021). https://doi.org/10.1007/s11629-020-6221-1.

Hararuk, Oleksandra, Elizabeth M. Campbell, Joseph A. Antos, and Roberta Parish. "Tree Rings Provide No Evidence of a CO_2 Fertilization Effect in Old-Growth Subalpine Forests of Western Canada." *Global Change Biology* 25, no. 4 (2018): 1222–34. https://doi.org/10.1111/gcb.14561.

Harrison, Robert Pogue. *Forests: The Shadow of Civilization*. Chicago: University of Chicago Press, 1993.

Harrison, Robert Pogue. *Gardens: An Essay on the Human Condition*. Chicago: University of Chicago Press, 2009.

Hartmann, Henrik, Ana Bastos, Adrian J. Das, Adriane Esquivel-Muelbert, William M. Hammond, Jordi Martínez-Vilalta, Nate G. McDowell, et al. "Climate Change Risks to Global Forest Health: Emergence of Unexpected Events of Elevated Tree Mortality Worldwide." *Annual Review of Plant Biology*, May 2022. https://doi.org/10.1146/annurev-arplant-102820-012804.

Haupt, Erik H. "The Private Tree Worker and Energized Lines." *Arboriculture & Urban Forestry* 6, no. 4 (1980): 93–95. https://doi.org/10.48044/jauf.1980.025.

Hayden, Katherine J., Giles E. St. J. Hardy, and Matteo Garbelotto. "Oomycete Diseases." In *Infectious Forest Diseases*, edited by P. Gonthier and G. Nicolotti, CABI, Wallingford, UK, 2013.

Heberling, J. Mason, Caitlin McDonough MacKenzie, Jason D. Fridley, Susan Kalisz, and Richard B. Primack. "Phenological Mismatch with Trees Reduces Wildflower Carbon Budgets." *Ecology Letters* 22, no. 4 (2019): 616–23. https://doi.org/10.1111/ele.13224.

Heberling, J. Mason, and Rose-Marie Muzika. "Not All Temperate Deciduous Trees Are Leafless in Winter: The Curious Case of Marcescence." *Ecosphere* 14, no. 3 (2023). https://doi.org/10.1002/ecs2.4410.

Heeter, Karen J., Grant L. Harley, John T. Abatzoglou, et al. Unprecedented 21st Century Heat across the Pacific Northwest of North America. *NPJ Climate Atmospheric Science* 6, 5 (2023). https://doi.org/10.1038/s41612-023-00340-3

Hemery, Gabriel, and Sarah Simblet. *The New Sylva: A Discourse of Forest and Orchard Trees for the Twenty-First Century*. New York: Bloomsbury, 2021.

"Hemlock Cones: A Sign of Good Health or Something Else?" Hemlock Restoration Initiative, October 15, 2021.

Henry, Augustine, and Margaret G. Flood. "The History of the London Plane, *Platanus acerifolia*, with Notes on the Genus *Platanus*." *Proceedings of the Royal Irish Academy. Section B: Biological, Geological, and Chemical Science* 35 (1919): 9–28. http://www.jstor.org/stable/20517052.

Hepting, George H. "Climate and Forest Diseases." *Annual Review of Phytopathology* 1, no. 1 (1963): 31–50. https://doi.org/10.1146/annurev.py.01.090163.000335.

Herms, Daniel A., and Deborah G. McCullough. "Emerald Ash Borer Invasion of North America: History, Biology, Ecology, Impacts, and Management." *Annual Review of Entomology*, January 2014. https://www.annualreviews.org/content/journals/10.1146/annurev-ento-011613-162051.

Hicke, Jeffrey A., Arjan J. H. Meddens, Craig D. Allen, and Crystal A. Kolden. "Carbon Stocks of Trees Killed by Bark Beetles and Wildfire in the Western United States." *Environmental Research Letters*, August 29, 2013. https://doi.org/10.1088/1748-9326/8/3/035032.

Hipp, Andrew L., Paul S. Manos, and Jeannine Cavdender-Bares. "How Oak Trees Evolved to Rule the Forests of the Northern Hemisphere." *Scientific American*, August 1, 2020.

Hirata, Akiko, Katsunori Nakamura, Katsuhiro Nakao, Yuji Kominami, Nobuyuki Tanaka, Haruka Ohashi, Kohei Takenaka Takano, et al. "Potential Distribution of Pine Wilt Disease under Future Climate Change Scenarios." *PLOS ONE* 12, no. 8 (2017): e0182837. https://doi.org/10.1371/journal.pone.0182837.

Holloway, Marguerite, and George Etheredge. "New England's Forests Are Sick. They Need More Tree Doctors." *New York Times*, October 7, 2020.

Holloway, Marguerite, and George Etheredge. "When There's No Heat: 'You Need Wood, You Get Wood.'" *New York Times*, February 19, 2021.

Horton, Helena. 2023. "Government Should Target Tree Aftercare Rather than Planting, Say UK Experts." *The Guardian*, November 2, 2023.

Hubbart, Jason A., Richard Guyette, and Rose-Marie Muzika. "More than Drought: Precipitation Variance, Excessive Wetness, Pathogens and the Future of the Western Edge of the Eastern Deciduous Forest." *Science of the Total Environment*, October 2016. https://doi.org/10.1016/j.scitotenv.2016.05.108.

Hudgins, Emma J., Frank H. Koch, Mark J. Ambrose, and Brian Leung. "Hotspots of Pest-Induced US Urban Tree Death, 2020–2050." *Journal of Applied Ecology*, March 13, 2022. https://doi.org/10.1111/1365-2664.14141.

Hudiburg, Tara, Beverly Law, David P. Turner, John Campbell, Dan Donato, and Maureen Duane. "Carbon Dynamics of Oregon and Northern California Forests and Potential Land-Based Carbon Storage." *Ecological Applications* 19, no. 1 (2009): 163–80. https://doi.org/10.1890/07-2006.1.

Hughes, R. F., M. T. Johnson, and A. Uowolo. "The Invasive Alien Tree *Falcataria moluccana*: Its Impacts and Management." *XIII International Symposium on Biological Control of Weeds*. US Department of Agriculture, Forest Service, Forest Health Technology Enterprise Team, 2012-07: 218–23.

Hummer, Kim E. "History of the Origin and Dispersal of White Pine Blister Rust." *HortTechnology* 10, no. 3 (2000): 515–17. https://doi.org/10.21273/horttech.10.3.515.

IPCC. *Climate Change 2023: Synthesis Report. Contribution of Working Groups I, II and III to the Sixth Assessment Report of the Intergovernmental Panel on Climate Change*, edited by H. Lee and J. Romero. Geneva, Switzerland: IPCC, 2023. https://doi.org/10.59327/IPCC/AR6-9789291691647.

International Society for Arboriculture. "Women Climb New Heights in Arboriculture." *Tree Trust*. December 15, 2023.

Irwin, Aisling. "The Loneliest Trees: Can Science Save These Threatened Species from Extinction?" *Nature* 609 (2022): 24–27. https://doi.org/10.1038/d41586-022-02765-x.

Jacoby, Karl. *Crimes against Nature: Squatters, Poachers, Thieves, and the Hidden History of American Conservation*. Berkeley: University of California Press, 2014.

Jahren, Hope. *Lab Girl*. New York: Alfred A. Knopf, 2016.

Janowiak, Maria K., Anthony W. D'Amato, Christopher W. Swanston, Louis Iverson, Frank R. Thompson, William D. Dijak, Stephen Matthews, et al. *New England and Northern New York Forest Ecosystem Vulnerability Assessment and Synthesis: A Report from the New England Climate Change Response Framework Project*. Gen. Tech. Rep. NRS-173. Newtown Square, PA: US Department of Agriculture, Forest Service, Northern Research Station, 2018. https://doi.org/10.2737/nrs-gtr-173.

Janowiak, Maria K., Leslie A. Brandt, Kathleen L. Wolf, Mattison Brady, Lindsay Darling, Abigail Derby Lewis, Robert T. Fahey, et al. *Climate Adaptation Actions for Urban Forests and Human Health*. Gen. Tech. Rep. NRS-203. Madison, WI: US Department of Agriculture, Forest Service, Northern Research Station, 2021. https://doi.org/10.2737/NRS-GTR-203.

Jeon, Hee Won, Ae Ran Park, Minjeong Sung, Namgyu Kim, Mohamed Mannaa, Gil Han, Junheon Kim, Yeonjong Koo, et al. "Systemic Acquired Resistance-Mediated Control of Pine Wilt Disease by Foliar Application with Methyl Salicylate." *Frontiers in Plant Science* 12 (2021). https://doi.org/10.3389/fpls.2021.812414.

Jepson, Jeff. *The Tree Climber's Companion: A Reference and Training Manual for Professional Tree Climbers*, second edition. Longville, MN: Beaver Tree Pub, 2000.

Jet Propulsion Laboratory. "Watching Earth Breathe: The Seasonal Vegetation Cycle and Atmospheric Carbon Dioxide." AIRS.

Jetton, Robert M., W. Andrew Whittier, Barbara S. Crane, and Gary R. Hodge. "A Range-Wide Seed Collection to Support the Genetic Resource Conservation of Atlantic White Cedar." *Camcore* 62, nos. 1 & 2 (2019): 5. https://camcore.cnr.ncsu.edu/files/2020/04/A-Range-Wide-Seed-Collection-to-Support-the-Genetic-Resource-Conservation-of-Atlantic-White-Cedar-2.pdf.

Jia, Kang, Meng Lingxiao, and Cai Xuejiao. "In Depth: Combating the North American Pest That Has Reveled in Beijing's Wet Summer - Caixin Global." n.d. Caixin Global. Accessed July 28, 2024. https://www.caixinglobal.com/2021-11-03/in-depth-combating-the-north-american-pest-that-has-reveled-in-beijings-wet-summer-101795746.html.

Johnson, Daniel, and Raquel Partelli Feltrin. "Trees Are Dying of Thirst in the Western Drought—Here's What's Going on inside Their Veins." *The Conversation*, June 29, 2021.

Johnston, Mark. *Trees in Towns and Cities*. Oxford: Windgather Press, 2015.

Jones, Benji. "The Earth Is Getting Greener. Hurray?" *Vox*, February 7, 2024.

Jones, Benji. "Florida Has Become a Zoo. A Literal Zoo." *Vox*. September 18, 2023.

Jones, Benji. "Indigenous People Are the World's Biggest Conservationists, but They Rarely Get Credit for It." *Vox*, June 11, 2021.

Jones, Melanie, Jason Hoeksema, and Justine Karst. "Where the 'Wood-Wide Web' Narrative Went Wrong." *Undark Magazine*, May 25, 2023.

Kalm, Peter. *Travels into North America*. Wisconsin Historical Society Digital Library and Archives, 2003.

Kannenberg, Steven A., Christopher R. Schwalm, and William R. L. Anderegg. "Ghosts of the Past: How Drought Legacy Effects Shape Forest Functioning and Carbon Cycling." *Ecology Letters* 23 (2020): 891–901.

Kaplan, Sarah. "Scientists Tangle over 'Wood Wide Web' Connecting Forests and Fungi." *Washington Post*, February 14, 2023.

Kaplan, Stef. "With Forests in Peril, She's on a Mission to Save 'Mother Trees.'" *Washington Post*, December 22, 2022.

Kapoor, Maya L. 2017. "Why the Endangered Species Act Can't Save Whitebark Pines." *High Country News*, June 2, 2017.

Karmalkar, Ambarish V., and Radley M. Horton. "Drivers of Exceptional Coastal Warming in the Northeastern United States." *Nature Climate Change* 11 (2021): 854–60. https://doi.org/10.1038/s41558-021-01159-7.

Karst, Justine, Melanie D. Jones, and Jason D. Hoeksema. "Positive Citation Bias and Overinterpreted Results Lead to Misinformation on Common Mycorrhizal Networks in Forests." *Nature Ecology & Evolution* 7 (February 2023): 501–11. https://doi.org/10.1038/s41559-023-01986-1.

Katz, Brigit. "Pando, One of the World's Largest Organisms, Is Dying." *Smithsonian*, October 18, 2018.

Katz, Cheryl. "Small Pests, Big Problems: The Global Spread of Bark Beetles." *Yale E360*. 2017.

Kelly, Victoria R., Stuart E. G. Findlay, William H. Schlesinger, Kristen Menking, and Allison M. Chatrchyan. *Road Salt: Moving Toward the Solution*. The Cary Institute of Ecosystem Studies, 2010.

Kern, Christel C., Manfred Schoelch, Paul Crocker, Dean Fellman, Angela Marsh, David Mausel, Marshall Pecore, et al. "Group Opening Outcomes, Sustainable Forest Management, and the Menominee Nation Lands." *Journal of Forestry* 115, no. 5 (2017): 416–24. https://doi.org/10.5849/jof.2016-092.

Kimmerer, Robin Wall. *Gathering Moss: A Natural and Cultural History of Mosses*. Corvallis: Oregon State University Press, 2003.

Kimmerer, Robin Wall. *Braiding Sweetgrass: Indigenous Wisdom, Scientific Knowledge and the Teachings of Plants*. Minneapolis: Milkweed Editions, 2013.

Kinahan, Ian G., Gabrielle Grandstaff, Alana Russell, Chad M. Rigsby, Richard A. Casagrande, and Evan L. Preisser. "A Four-Year, Seven-State Reforestation Trial with Eastern Hemlocks (*Tsuga canadensis*) Resistant to Hemlock Woolly Adelgid (*Adelges tsugae*)." *Forests* 11, no. 3 (2020): 312. https://doi.org/10.3390/f11030312.

Kish, Rosalyn, James M. A. Patrick, Rachel O. Mariani, Jonathan S. Schurman, Sean C. Thomas, Emily N. Young, and Adam R. Martin. "Beech

Bark Disease in an Unmanaged Temperate Forest: Patterns, Predictors, and Impacts on Ecosystem Function." *Frontiers in Forests and Global Change* 5 (2022).

Klein, Naomi. *This Changes Everything: Capitalism vs. the Climate.* New York: Simon & Schuster, 2014.

Kliejunas, John T. "Sudden Oak Death and *Phytophthora ramorum*: A Summary of the Literature, 2010 Edition." US Department of Agriculture, Forest Service.

Kline, Rachel D. "Women's Legacy and Future in Forestry Paving the Way for Progress." *Forest History Today,* Spring/Fall 2022.

Kling, Matthew M., and David D. Ackerly. "Global Wind Patterns Shape Genetic Differentiation, Asymmetric Gene Flow, and Genetic Diversity in Trees." *Proceedings of the National Academy of Sciences* 118, no. 17 (2021): e2017317118. https://doi.org/10.1073/pnas.2017317118.

Kmitta, John. 2020. "Utility Arborist Labor Shortage Highest in Areas Most in Need." *OPE+,* March 2, 2020.

Knott, Jonathan A., Johanna M. Desprez, Christopher M. Oswalt, and Songlin Fei. "Shifts in Forest Composition in the Eastern United States." *Forest Ecology and Management* 433 (February 2019): 176–83. https://doi.org/10.1016/j.foreco.2018.10.061.

Knott, Jonathan A., Liang Liang, Jeffrey S. Dukes, Robert K. Swihart, and Songlin Fei. "Phenological Response to Climate Variation in a Northern Red Oak Plantation: Links to Survival and Productivity." *Ecology* 104, no. 3 (2022). https://doi.org/10.1002/ecy.3940.

Kopp, R. E., K. Hayhoe, D. R. Easterling, T. Hall, R. Horton, K. E. Kunkel, and A. N. LeGrande. "Potential Surprises—Compound Extremes and Tipping Elements." In *Climate Science Special Report: Fourth National Climate Assessment, Volume I,* edited by D. J. Wuebbles, D. W. Fahey, K. A. Hibbard, D. J. Dokken, B. C. Stewart, and T. K. Maycock, 411–29. Washington, DC: U.S. Global Change Research Program, 2017. https://doi.org/10.7930/J0GB227J.

Kornei, Katherine. "The USDA Updated Its Gardening Map, but Downplays Connection to Climate Change." *Civil Eats,* January 29, 2024.

Körner, Christian. "A Matter of Tree Longevity." *Science* 355, no. 6321 (2017): 130–31. https://doi.org/10.1126/science.aal2449.

Kremer, Antoine, and Andrew L. Hipp. "Oaks: An Evolutionary Success Story." *New Phytologist* 226, no. 4 (2019): 987–1011. https://doi.org/10.1111/nph.16274.

Kuhn, Tim J., Hugh D. Safford, Bobette E. Jones, and Ken W. Tate. "Aspen (*Populus tremuloides*) Stands and Their Contribution to Plant Diversity in a Semiarid Coniferous Landscape." *Plant Ecology* 212 (2011): 1451–63. https://doi.org/10.1007/s11258-011-9920-4.

Kummer, Frank. "N.J. on the Brink: Surviving 400 Years or More, but Climate Threatens." *Philadelphia Inquirer,* December 16, 2018.

Laderman, Aimlee D., Michael Brody, and Edward Pendleton. *The Ecology of Atlantic White Cedar Wetlands: A Community Profile*. AquaDocs. Washington, D.C.: US Department of Interior, Fish and Wildlife Service, National Wetlands Research Center, 1989.

Lake, Frank K., Vita Wright, Penelope Morgan, Mary McFadzen, Dave McWethy, and Camille Stevens-Rumann. "Returning Fire to the Land: Celebrating Traditional Knowledge and Fire." *Journal of Forestry* 115, no. 5 (2017): 343–53. https://doi.org/10.5849/jof.2016-043r2.

Lamb, Robert. *World Without Trees*. New York: Paddington Press, 1979.

Larter, Maximilian, Tim J. Brodribb, Sebastian Pfautsch, Régis Burlett, Hervé Cochard, and Sylvain Delzon. "Extreme Aridity Pushes Trees to Their Physical Limits." *Plant Physiology* 168, no. 3 (2015): 804–7. https://doi.org/10.1104/pp.15.00223.

Le Page, Michael. "Many US Cities Will Lose Nearly All Ash Trees by 2060." *New Scientist*, May 6, 2021.

Lenton, Timothy M., Tais W. Dahl, Stuart J. Daines, Benjamin J. W. Mills, Kazumi Ozaki, Matthew R. Saltzman, and Philipp Porada. "Earliest Land Plants Created Modern Levels of Atmospheric Oxygen." *Proceedings of the National Academy of Sciences*, August 15, 2016. https://doi.org/10.1073/pnas.1604787113.

Leonard, Josh. "OSHA Focusing on Regional Fatality and Injury Rates in Tree Care." *Tree Care Industry Magazine*, March 1, 2024.

Leonard, Josh. "OSHA Issues Regional Emphasis Programs to Address Fatality and Injury Rates in Tree Care Operations." *TCIA—Advancing Tree Care Businesses*, January 25, 2024.

Leonelli, Sabina, and Rachel A. Ankeny. "What Makes a Model Organism?" *Endeavour* 37, no. 4 (2013): 209–12. https://doi.org/10.1016/j.endeavour.2013.06.001.

Lesk, Corey, Ethan Coffel, Anthony W. D'Amato, Kevin Dodds, and Radley Horton. "Threats to North American Forests from Southern Pine Beetle with Warming Winters." *Nature Climate Change* 7 (2017): 713–17. https://doi.org/10.1038/nclimate3375.

Leverkus, Alexandro B., Lena Gustafsson, David B. Lindenmayer, Jorge Castro, José María Rey Benayas, Thomas Ranius, and Simon Thorn. "Salvage Logging Effects on Regulating Ecosystem Services and Fuel Loads." *Frontiers in Ecology and the Environment* 18, no. 7 (2020): 391–400. https://doi.org/10.1002/fee.2219.

Li, Xiangyi, Kai Wang, Chris Huntingford, Zaichun Zhu, Josep Peñuelas, Ranga B. Myneni, and Shilong Piao. "Vegetation Greenness in 2023." *Nature Reviews Earth & Environment* 5 (2024): 241–43. https://doi.org/10.1038/s43017-024-00543-z.

Li, Xiangyi, Shilong Piao, Kai Wang, Xuhui Wang, Tao Wang, Philippe Ciais, Anping Chen, Xu Lian, Shushi Peng, and Josep Peñuelas. "Temporal Trade-off between Gymnosperm Resistance and Resilience Increases Forest Sensitivity to Extreme Drought." *Nature Ecology & Evolution* 4, no. 8 (2020): 1075–83. https://doi.org/10.1038/s41559-020-1217-3.

Library & Archive. "Sudden Oak Death."

Lilly, Sharon J., and Alex K. Julius. *Tree Climbers' Guide*, 4th edition. Atlanta, GA: International Society of Arboriculture, 2021.

Lim, Jamie, Brian Kane, and David Bloniarz. "Arboriculture Safety Standards: Consistent Trends." *Urban Forestry & Urban Greening* 53 (August 2020): 126736. https://doi.org/10.1016/j.ufug.2020.126736.

Lindenmayer, David, and Reed Noss. "Salvage Logging, Ecosystem Processes, and Biodiversity Conservation." *Conservation Biology* 20, no. 4 (2006): 949–58. https://doi.org/10.1111/j.1523-1739.2006.00497.x.

Liu, Jiawei. "Effects of Climate Change on Interactions between a Forest Pest and Its Natural Enemies." *Knowledge UChicago*, 2022.

Logan, William Bryant. *Oak: The Frame of Civilization*. New York: Norton, 2005.

Lombard, Pamela J., Janet R. Barclay, and Dee-Ann E. McCarthy. "2020 Drought in New England." U.S. Geological Survey Open-File Report 2020–1148, 2020.

Long, Jonathan W., Ron W. Goode, and Frank K. Lake. "Recentering Ecological Restoration with Tribal Perspectives." *Fremontia* 48, no. 1 (2020): 14–19.

Lovett, Gary M., Marissa Weiss, Andrew M. Liebhold, Thomas P. Holmes, Brian Leung, Kathy Fallon Lambert, David A. Orwig, et al. "Nonnative Forest Insects and Pathogens in the United States: Impacts and Policy Options." *Ecological Applications* 26, no. 5 (2016): 1437–55. https://doi.org/10.1890/15-1176.

Lowman, Margaret. *The Arbornaut: A Life Discovering the Eighth Continent in the Trees above Us*. New York: Farrar, Straus and Giroux, 2021.

Lu, Ruiling, Ying Du, Huanfa Sun, Xiaoni Xu, Liming Yan, and Jianyang Xia. 2021. "Nocturnal Warming Accelerates Drought-Induced Seedling Mortality of Two Evergreen Tree Species." *Tree Physiology*, December 17, 2021. https://doi.org/10.1093/treephys/tpab168.

Luckman, B.H. "Dendroclimatology." In *Encyclopedia of Quaternary Science*, edited by Scott A. Elias, 459–470. Amsterdam: Elsevier, 2014.

Luoma, Jon R. *Hidden Forest: The Biography of an Ecosystem*. Corvallis: Oregon State University Press, 2006.

Macon, D., T. Schohr, D. Schmidt, and N. Garbelotto Benzon. "Recent Blue Oak Mortality on Sierra Nevada Foothill Rangelands May Be Linked to Drought, Climate Change." *California Agriculture* 74, no. 2 (2020): 71–72. https://doi.org/10.3733/ca.2020a0016.

Madhusoodanan, Jyoti. "Top US Scientist on Melting Glaciers: 'I've Gone from Being an Ecologist to a Coroner.'" *The Guardian*, July 21, 2021.

Maffly, Brian. "Turns Out, Southern Utah's Juniper Trees Aren't So Indestructible after All. But What Is Killing Them?" *Salt Lake Tribune*, June 25, 2019.

Mahamud, Faiza, and James Walsh. "Minneapolis and St. Paul Are Losing Thousands of Trees to Emerald Ash Borer." *Star Tribune*, May 9, 2017.

Maldonado, Julie Koppel, Benedict Colombi, and Rajul Pandya. *Climate Change and Indigenous Peoples in the United States: Impacts, Experiences and Actions*. Cham, Switzerland: Springer International Publishing, 2014.

Maloof, Joan. *Nature's Temples: A Natural History of Old-Growth Forests*. Expanded and Revised Edition. Princeton: Princeton University Press, 2023.

Maloof, Joan. *Teaching the Trees: Lessons from the Forest*. Athens: University of Georgia Press, 2005.

Maloy, Otis C. "White Pine Blister Rust Control in North America: A Case History." *Annual Review of Phytopathology* 35, no. 1 (1997): 87–109. https://doi.org/10.1146/annurev.phyto.35.1.87.

Mancuso, Stefano. *The Nation of Plants*. New York: Other Press, 2021.

Mancuso, Stefano, and Alessandra Viola. *Brilliant Green: The Surprising History and Science of Plant Intelligence*. Island Press, 2016.

Mann, Charles C. *1491: New Revelations of the Americas before Columbus*. New York: Knopf, 2005.

Mann, Charles C. "'There's Good Fire and Bad Fire.' An Indigenous Practice May Be Key to Preventing Wildfires." *National Geographic*, December 17, 2020.

Mapes, Lynda V. *Witness Tree: Seasons of Change with a Century-Old Oak*. New York: Bloomsbury, 2017.

Marché, Jordan D. II. *The Green Menace: Emerald Ash Borer and the Invasive Species Problem*. New York: Oxford University Press, 2017.

Marder, Michael. *The Philosopher's Plant: An Intellectual Herbarium*. New York: Columbia University Press, 2014.

Marino, Paul. "Maine Forests at Risk after Discovery of Southern Pine Beetle in York County." *Maine Public*. January 10, 2022.

Markham, Lauren. "Can We Move Our Forests in Time to Save Them?" *Mother Jones*, November-December 2021.

Marris, Emma. "The Myth of the Wild." *New Scientist*, December 4, 2021.

Marris, Emma. *Wild Souls: Freedom and Flourishing in the Non-Human World*. New York: Bloomsbury, 2021.

Martin, Thomas E., and John L. Maron. "Climate Impacts on Bird and Plant Communities from Altered Animal–Plant Interactions." *Nature Climate Change* 2 (2012): 195–200. https://doi.org/10.1038/nclimate1348.

Marvel, Kate, Benjamin I. Cook, Céline J. W. Bonfils, Paul J. Durack, Jason E. Smerdon, and A. Park Williams. "Twentieth-Century Hydroclimate Changes Consistent with Human Influence." *Nature* 569 (2019): 59–65. https://doi.org/10.1038/s41586-019-1149-8.

Mathews, Daniel. *Trees in Trouble: Wildfires, Infestations, and Climate Change*. Berkeley: Counterpoint, 2020.

Mausel, David L., Anthony Waupochick, Jr., and Marshall Pecore. "Menominee Forestry: Past, Present, Future." *Journal of Forestry* 115, no. 5 (2017): 366–69. https://doi.org/10.5849/jof.16-046.

McCarty, Elizabeth P., and Karla M. Addesso. "Hemlock Woolly Adelgid

(Hemiptera: Adelgidae) Management in Forest, Landscape, and Nursery Production." *Journal of Insect Science* 19, no. 2 (2019). https://doi.org/10.1093/jisesa/iez031.

McCarty, James F. "Newly Discovered Microscopic Worm Species Eyed as Potential Cause of Beech Leaf Disease." *Cleveland*, May 3, 2018.

McCullough, Deborah G. "Challenges, Tactics and Integrated Management of Emerald Ash Borer in North America." *Forestry,* August 14, 2019. https://doi.org/10.1093/forestry/cpz049.

McDowell, Nate G., Gerard Sapes, Alexandria Pivovaroff, et al. "Mechanisms of Woody-Plant Mortality under Rising Drought, CO_2 and Vapour Pressure Deficit." *Nature Reviews Earth & Environment* 3 (2022): 294–308. https://doi.org/10.1038/s43017-022-00272-1.

McDowell, Nate G., Timothy J. Brodribb, and Andrea Nardini. "Hydraulics in the 21st Century." *New Phytologist* 224, no. 2 (2019): 537–42. https://doi.org/10.1111/nph.16151.

McGowan, Kat. "The Secret Language of Plants." *Quanta Magazine*, December 16, 2013.

McGregor, Deborah. "Traditional Ecological Knowledge: An Anishnabe Woman's Perspective." *Atlantis* 29, no. 2 (Spring/Summer 2005).

McKay, Jeff (director). "Call of the Forest: The Forgotten Wisdom of Trees." *Vimeo*, 2018.

McLeish, Todd. "Climate Change and Red Oak Expansion." *Northern Woodlands*, Autumn 2021.

Mech, Angela M., Kathryn A. Thomas, Travis D. Marsico, Daniel A. Herms, Craig R. Allen, Matthew P. Ayres, Kamal J. K. Gandhi, et al. "Evolutionary History Predicts High Impact Invasions by Herbivorous Insects." *Ecology and Evolution* 9, no. 21 (2019): 12216–30. https://doi.org/10.1002/ece3.5709.

Meddens, Arjan J. H., Jeffrey A. Hicke, Alison K. Macalady, Polly C. Buotte, Travis R. Cowles, and Craig D. Allen. "Patterns and Causes of Observed Piñon Pine Mortality in the Southwestern United States." *New Phytologist* 206, no. 1 (2014): 91–97.

Mei, Wenbin, Markus G. Stetter, Daniel J. Gates, Michelle C. Stitzer, and Jeffrey Ross-Ibarra. "Adaptation in Plant Genomes: Bigger Is Different." *American Journal of Botany* 105, no. 1 (2018): 16–19. https://doi.org/10.1002/ajb2.1002.

Meneely, Philip M., Caroline L. Dahlberg, and Jacqueline K. Rose. "Working with Worms: *Caenorhabditis elegans* as a Model Organism." *Current Protocols Essential Laboratory Techniques* 19, no. 1 (2019). https://doi.org/10.1002/cpet.35.

Mikolas, Mark. *A Beginner's Guide to Recognizing Trees of the Northeast*. New York: Countryman Press, 2017.

Mills, Maria B., Yadvinder Malhi, Robert M. Ewers, Lip Khoon Kho, Yit Arn Teh, Sabine Both, David F. R. P. Burslem, et al. "Tropical Forests Post-Logging Are a Persistent Net Carbon Source to the

Atmosphere." *Proceedings of the National Academy of Sciences* 120, no. 3 (2023). https://doi.org/10.1073/pnas.2214462120.

Milman, Oliver. "Global Heating Has Caused 'Shocking' Changes in Forests across the Americas, Studies Find." *The Guardian*, August 10, 2022.

Minorsky, Peter V. "American Racism and the Lost Legacy of Sir Jagadis Chandra Bose, the Father of Plant Neurobiology." *Plant Signaling & Behavior*, December 2020. https://doi.org/10.1080/15592324.2020.1818030.

More, David, and John White. *The Illustrated Encyclopedia of Trees*. Portland, OR: Timber Press, 2002.

Morris, Jennifer L., Mark N. Puttick, James W. Clark, Dianne Edwards, Paul Kenrick, Silvia Pressel, Charles H. Wellman, et al. "The Timescale of Early Land Plant Evolution." *Proceedings of the National Academy of Sciences* 115, no. 10 (2018): E2274–83. https://doi.org/10.1073/pnas.1719588115.

Mountain Research Initiative EDW Working Group. "Elevation-Dependent Warming in Mountain Regions of the World." *Nature Climate Change* 5 (2015): 424–30. https://doi.org/10.1038/nclimate2563.

Muldavin, Esteban, and F. Jack Triepke. "North American Pinyon–Juniper Woodlands: Ecological Composition, Dynamics, and Future Trends." In *Encyclopedia of the World's Biomes* 516–31. Amsterdam: Elsevier, 2020.

Mulhern, Owen. "A Graphical History of Atmospheric CO_2 Levels over Time." *Earth.org*, August 12, 2020.

Mulhollem, Jeff. "If Some Hemlock Trees Can Just Hang On, Birds That Need Them May Be OK." Penn State University.

Nadkarni, Andrew, director. *Between Earth and Sky*. By the Creek Productions, LLC., 2024.

Nadkarni, N. M. "Good-Bye, Tarzan: The Science of Life in the Treetops Gets Down to Business." *The Sciences* 35 (1995): 28–33.

Nadkarni, Nalini M., and Nathaniel T. Wheelwright, eds. *Monteverde: Ecology and Conservation of a Tropical Cloud Forest*. New York: Oxford University Press, 2000.

Nadkarni, Nalini M., Geoffrey Parker, and Margaret D. Lowman. "Forest Canopy Studies as an Emerging Field of Science." *Annals of Forest Science* 68 (2011): 217–24. https://doi.org/10.1007/s13595-011-0046-6.

Nandy, Ashis. *Alternative Sciences: Creativity and Authenticity in Two Indian Scientists*. Delhi: Oxford University Press, 1995.

National Academies of Sciences, Engineering, and Medicine. *Forest Health and Biotechnology: Possibilities and Considerations*. Washington, DC: The National Academies Press, 2019. https://doi.org/10.17226/25221.

"National Forests in North Carolina"—News & Events. US Department of Agriculture.

National Integrated Drought Information System. NOAA.

National Park Service. "Headwaters: Whitebark Pine." *Headwaters*, podcast, season 2, episode 1.

"National Recovery Plan for the Wollemi Pine." Department of Climate Change, Energy, the Environment and Water, 2024.

"Native American History, Life and Culture." *Native Hope.*

Nelson, Rett. "Moose Fire near Salmon 100% Contained." *East Idaho News,* November 14, 2022.

Nematode Collection Database. US Department of Agriculture.

Nijhuis, Michelle. "What's Killing the Aspen?" *Smithsonian Magazine,* December 2008.

Nikiforuk, Andrew. *Empire of the Beetle: How Human Folly and a Tiny Bug Are Killing North America's Great Forests.* Vancouver: Greystone Books, 2011.

Norton-Smith, Kathryn, Kathy Lynn, Karletta Chief, Karen Cozzetto, Jamie Donatuto, Margaret Hiza Redsteer, Linda E. Kruger, et al. *Climate Change and Indigenous Peoples: A Synthesis of Current Impacts and Experiences.* Gen. Tech. Rep. PNW-GTR-944. Portland, OR: US Department of Agriculture, Forest Service, Pacific Northwest Research Station, 2016.

Novey, Idra. "Women in Trees." *Paris Review,* March 22, 2018.

Novick, Kimberly A., Darren L. Ficklin, Paul C. Stoy, Christopher A. Williams, Gil Bohrer, A. Christopher Oishi, Shirley A. Papuga, et al. "The Increasing Importance of Atmospheric Demand for Ecosystem Water and Carbon Fluxes." *Nature Climate Change* 6 (2016): 1023–27. https://doi.org/10.1038/nclimate3114.

Novick, Kimberly, Insu Jo, Loïc D'Orangeville, Michael Benson, Tsun Fung Au, Mallory Barnes, Sanders Denham, et al. "The Drought Response of Eastern US Oaks in the Context of Their Declining Abundance." *BioScience,* April 2022. https://doi.org/10.1093/biosci/biab135.

Nowak, David J., Alexis Ellis, and Eric J. Greenfield. "The Disparity in Tree Cover and Ecosystem Service Values among Redlining Classes in the United States." *Landscape and Urban Planning* 221 (May 2022): 104370. https://doi.org/10.1016/j.landurbplan.2022.104370.

Nuccitelli, Dana. "The Little-Known Physical and Mental Health Benefits of Urban Trees." *Yale Climate Connections,* February 28, 2023.

Nuwer, Rachel. "What Would Happen If All the World's Trees Disappeared?" *BBC,* September 11, 2019.

"Oak Wilt." *Invasive Species Centre.*

Ohenhen, Leonard O., Manoochehr Shirzaei, Chandrakanta Ojha, and Matthew L. Kirwan. "Hidden Vulnerability of US Atlantic Coast to Sea-Level Rise Due to Vertical Land Motion." *Nature Communications* 14 (2023). https://doi.org/10.1038/s41467-023-37853-7.

Oliver, Mary. *Devotions: The Selected Poems of Mary Oliver.* New York: Penguin Press, 2017.

"On the Origin of Flowering Plants." *In Defense of Plants,* podcast, November 25, 2018.

Ourada, Patricia K. *The Menominee.* New York: Chelsea House Publishers, 1990.

Overton, Patrick. *The Leaning Tree.* Bloomington, MN: Bethany Press, 1975

Padgett, Allen, and Bruce Smith. *On Rope: North American Vertical Rope*

Techniques for Caving, Search and Rescue, Mountaineering. Huntsville, AL: Vertical Section, National Speleological Society, 1987.

Palomares-Rius, Juan E., Koichi Hasegawa, Shahid Siddique, and Claudia S. L. Vicente. "Protecting Our Crops—Approaches for Plant Parasitic Nematode Control." *Frontiers in Plant Science* 12 (2021). https://doi.org/10.3389/fpls.2021.726057.

Park Williams, A., Craig D. Allen, Alison K. Macalady, Daniel Griffin, Connie A. Woodhouse, David M. Meko, Thomas W. Swetnam, et al. "Temperature as a Potent Driver of Regional Forest Drought Stress and Tree Mortality." *Nature Climate Change* 3, no. 3 (2012): 292–97. https://doi.org/10.1038/nclimate1693.

Partida, José Pablo Ortiz. "California's Thirsty Future: The Role of Vapor Pressure Deficit in Our Changing Climate and Drought." *The Equation*, April 5, 2023.

Pastor, John. *White Pine: The Natural and Human History of a Foundational American Tree.* Washington: Island Press, 2023.

Patel, Kasha. "How Plants Communicate with Each Other When in Danger." *Washington Post*, October 24, 2023.

Pauls, Elizabeth Prine. "Native American." Chicago: Encyclopedia Britannica, July 2, 2024.

Pautasso, Marco, Thomas F. Döring, Matteo Garbelotto, Lorenzo Pellis, and Mike J. Jeger. "Impacts of Climate Change on Plant Diseases—Opinions and Trends." *European Journal of Plant Pathology* 133 (2012): 295–313. https://doi.org/10.1007/s10658-012-9936-1.

Pearl, Jessie K., Kevin J. Anchukaitis, Jeffrey P. Donnelly, Charlotte Pearson, Neil Pederson, Mary C. Lardie Gaylord, Ann P. McNichol, et al. "A Late Holocene Subfossil Atlantic White Cedar Tree-Ring Chronology from the Northeastern United States." *Quaternary Science Reviews* 228 (January 2020): 106104. https://doi.org/10.1016/j.quascirev.2019.106104.

Pearl, Jessie K., Kevin J. Anchukaitis, Neil Pederson, and Jeffrey P. Donnelly. "Multivariate Climate Field Reconstructions Using Tree Rings for the Northeastern United States." *Journal of Geophysical Research Atmospheres* 125, no. 1 (2019). https://doi.org/10.1029/2019jd031619.

Pearl, Jessie K., Kevin J. Anchukaitis, Neil Pederson, and Jeffrey P. Donnelly. "Reconstructing Northeastern United States Temperatures Using Atlantic White Cedar Tree Rings." *Environmental Research Letters* 12, no. 11 (2017): 114012. https://doi.org/10.1088/1748-9326/aa8f1b.

Pearsall, Susan. "Chestnut Trees Find a Friend." *The New York Times*, October 8, 1995.

Peattie, Donald C. "The Beech and the Pigeon." *The Atlantic*, August 1848.

Peattie, Donald Culross. *A Natural History of North American Trees.* Donald Culross Peattie Library. San Antonio, Texas: Trinity University Press, 2013.

Pederson, Neil. "External Characteristics of Old Trees in the Eastern Deciduous Forest." *Natural Areas Journal.* October 1, 2010. https://doi.org/10.3375/043.030.0405.

Pederson, Neil, James S. Dyer, Ryan W. McEwan, Amy E. Hessl, Cary J. Mock, David A. Orwig, Harald E. Rieder, et al. "The Legacy of Episodic Climatic Events in Shaping Temperate, Broadleaf Forests." *Ecological Monographs* 84, no. 4 (2014): 599–620. https://doi.org/10.1890/13-1025.1.

Pennisi, Elizabeth. "Earth Home to 3 Trillion Trees, Half as Many as When Human Civilization Arose." *Science*, September 2, 2015.

Perkins, Dana L., and Thomas W. Swetnam. "A Dendroecological Assessment of Whitebark Pine in the Sawtooth–Salmon River Region, Idaho." *Canadian Journal of Forest Research* 26, no. 12 (1996): 2123–33. https://doi.org/10.1139/x26-241.

Perry, Charles H., Mark V. Finco, and Barry T. Wilson, eds. *Forest Atlas of the United States.* FS-1172. Washington, D.C.: US Department of Agriculture, Forest Service, 2022.

Pinkwater, Daniel Manus. *The Big Orange Splot.* New York: Turtleback Books, 1993.

"Pinosaur Conservation: An Introduction to the Wollemi Pine." *In Defense of Plants,* podcast, August 5, 2018.

Plumer, Brad. "How America Got Addicted to Road Salt—and Why It's Become a Problem." *Vox,* January 13, 2015.

Plumwood, Val. *Feminism and the Mastery of Nature (Opening Out Feminism for Today).* London: Routledge, 2003.

Popkin, Gabriel. "To Save the Hemlock, Scientists Turn to Genetics and Natural Predators." *Washington Post,* August 1, 2020.

Poland, Therese M., Toral Patel-Weynand, Deborah M. Finch, Chelcy Ford Miniat, Deborah C. Hayes, and Vanessa M. Lopez. *Invasive Species in Forests and Rangelands of the United States: A Comprehensive Science Synthesis for the United States Forest Sector.* Heidelberg, Germany: Springer International Publishing, 2021. https://doi.org/10.1007/978-3-030-45367-1.

Potter, Kevin M., Robert M. Jetton, Andrew Bower, Douglass F. Jacobs, Gary Man, Valerie D. Hipkins, and Murphy Westwood. "Banking on the Future: Progress, Challenges and Opportunities for the Genetic Conservation of Forest Trees." *New Forests* 48 (2017): 153–80. https://doi.org/10.1007/s11056-017-9582-8.

Potter, Kevin M., Robert M. Jetton, William S. Dvorak, Valerie D. Hipkins, Rusty Rhea, and W. Andrew Whittier. "Widespread Inbreeding and Unexpected Geographic Patterns of Genetic Variation in Eastern Hemlock (Tsuga Canadensis), an Imperiled North American Conifer." *Conservation Genetics* 13, No. 2 (2011): 475–98. https://doi.org/10.1007/s10592-011-0301-2.

Powers, Richard. *The Overstory.* New York: Norton, 2018.

Preisser, Evan L., Joseph S. Elkinton, and Kristopher Abell. "Evolution of Increased Cold Tolerance during Range Expansion of the Elongate Hemlock Scale Fiorinia externa Ferris (Hemiptera: Diaspididae)." *Ecological Entomology,* October 2008. https://doi.org/10.1111/j.1365-2311.2008.01021.x.

Preston, Richard. *The Wild Trees: A Story of Passion and Daring.* New York: Random House, 2008.

Primack, Richard B. "The Sex Life of the Red Maple." *Arnoldia* 63, no. 1 (2004): 28–31.

Primack, Richard B., and Amanda S. Gallinat. "Spring Budburst in a Changing Climate." *American Scientist* 104, no. 2 (2016): 102. https://doi.org/10.1511/2016.119.102.

Proença, Diogo N., Gregor Grass, and Paula V. Morais. "Understanding Pine Wilt Disease: Roles of the Pine Endophytic Bacteria and of the Bacteria Carried by the Disease-Causing Pinewood Nematode." *MicrobiologyOpen* 6, no. 2 (2017): e00415. https://doi.org/10.1002/mbo3.415.

Proulx, Annie. *Barkskins.* New York: Scribner, 2016.

Pyšek, Petr, Philip E. Hulme, Dan Simberloff, Sven Bacher, Tim M. Blackburn, James T. Carlton, Wayne Dawson, et al. "Scientists' Warning on Invasive Alien Species." *Biological Reviews* 95, no. 6 (2020): 1511–34. https://doi.org/10.1111/brv.12627.

Raiho, A. M., C. J. Paciorek, A. Dawson, S. T. Jackson, D. J. Mladenoff, J. W. Williams, and J. S. McLachlan. "8000-Year Doubling of Midwestern Forest Biomass Driven by Population- and Biome-Scale Processes." *Science* 376, no. 6600 (2022): 1491–95. https://doi.org/10.1126/science.abk3126.

Rammer, Werner, Kristin H. Braziunas, Winslow D. Hansen, Zak Ratajczak, Anthony L. Westerling, Monica G. Turner, and Rupert Seidl. "Widespread Regeneration Failure in Forests of Greater Yellowstone under Scenarios of Future Climate and Fire." *Global Change Biology*, July 2, 2021. https://doi.org/10.1111/gcb.15726.

Ramsfield, T.D., B. J. Bentz, M. Faccoli, H. Jactel, and E. G. Brockerhoff. "Forest Health in a Changing World: Effects of Globalization and Climate Change on Forest Insect and Pathogen Impacts." *Forestry* 89, no. 3 (2016): 245–52. https://doi.org/10.1093/forestry/cpw018.

Raupp, Michael J., John J. Holmes, Clifford Sadof, Paula Shrewsbury, and John A. Davidson. "Effects of Cover Sprays and Residual Pesticides on Scale Insects and Natural Enemies in Urban Forests."*Arboriculture and Urban Forestry* 27, no. 4 (2001): 203–14. https://doi.org/10.48044/jauf.2001.022.

Rauschendorfer, James, Rebecca Rooney, and Carsten Külheim. "Strategies to Mitigate Shifts in Red Oak (*Quercus* sect. *Lobatae*) Distribution under a Changing Climate." *Tree Physiology*, July 22, 2022. https://doi.org/10.1093/treephys/tpac090.

Reed, Samuel P., Alejandro A. Royo, Alexander T. Fotis, Kathleen S. Knight, Charles E. Flower, and Peter S. Curtis. "The Long-Term Impacts of Deer Herbivory in Determining Temperate Forest Stand and Canopy Structural Complexity." *Journal of Applied Ecology* 59, no. 3 (2021): 812–21. https://doi.org/10.1111/1365-2664.14095.

Reed, Sharon E., Sylvia Greifenhagen, Qing Yu, Adam Hoke, David J. Burke, Lynn K. Carta, Zafar A. Handoo, et al. "Foliar Nematode, *Litylenchus crenatae* ssp. *mccannii*, Population Dynamics in Leaves and Buds of

Beech Leaf Disease-Affected Trees in Canada and the US." *Forest Pathology* 50, no. 3 (2020): e12599. https://doi.org/10.1111/efp.12599.

Reed, Sharon E., Daniel Volk, Danielle K. H. Martin, Constance E. Hausman, Tom Macy, Tim Tomon, and Stella Cousins. "The Distribution of Beech Leaf Disease and the Causal Agents of Beech Bark Disease (*Cryptoccocus fagisuga, Neonectria faginata, N. ditissima*) in Forests Surrounding Lake Erie and Future Implications." *Forest Ecology and Management* 503 (2022): 119753. https://doi.org/10.1016/j.foreco.2021.119753.

Reese, April. "Bird Population Plummets in Piñon Forests Pummeled by Climate Change." *Audubon Magazine*, August 14, 2018.

Refsland, Tyler K., and J. Hall Cushman. "Continent-Wide Synthesis of the Long-Term Population Dynamics of Quaking Aspen in the Face of Accelerating Human Impacts." *Oecologia* 197, No. 1 (2021): 25–42. https://doi.org/10.1007/s00442-021-05013-7.

Rehfeldt, Gerald E., James J. Worrall, Suzanne B. Marchetti, and Nicholas L. Crookston. "Adapting Forest Management to Climate Change Using Bioclimate Models with Topographic Drivers." *Forestry* 88, no. 5 (2015): 528–39. https://doi.org/10.1093/forestry/cpv019.

Reich, Peter B., Raimundo Bermudez, Rebecca A. Montgomery, Roy L. Rich, Karen E. Rice, Sarah E. Hobbie, and Artur Stefanski. "Even Modest Climate Change May Lead to Major Transitions in Boreal Forests." *Nature* 608 (2022): 540–45. https://doi.org/10.1038/s41586-022-05076-3.

Reichgelt, Tammo, David R. Greenwood, Sebastian Steinig, John G. Conran, David K. Hutchinson, Daniel J. Lunt, Leonie J. Scriven, and Jiang Zhu. "Plant Proxy Evidence for High Rainfall and Productivity in the Eocene of Australia." *Paleoceanography and Paleoclimatology*, May 9, 2022. https://doi.org/10.1029/2022pa004418.

Reid, John W, and Thomas E. Lovejoy. *Ever Green: Saving Big Forests to Save the Planet.* New York: Norton, 2022.

Reidmiller, D. R., C. W. Avery, D. R. Easterling, K. E. Kunkel, K. L. M. Lewis, T. K. Maycock, and B. C. Stewart, eds. *Impacts, Risks, and Adaptation in the United States: The Fourth National Climate Assessment*, Volume II, 2018. https://doi.org/10.7930/nca4.2018.

"Removal of Emerald Ash Borer Domestic Quarantine Regulations." *Federal Register*, December 15, 2020.

Renault, Marion. "Found: One Oak Tree, Famously Missing." *New Republic*, July 7, 2022.

Renner, Susanne S., and Constantin M. Zohner. "Climate Change and Phenological Mismatch in Trophic Interactions among Plants, Insects, and Vertebrates." *Annual Review of Ecology, Evolution, and Systematics* 4 (2018): 165–82. https://doi.org/10.1146/annurev-ecolsys-110617-062535.

Reo, Nicholas J., and Laura A. Ogden. "Anishnaabe Aki: An Indigenous Perspective on the Global Threat of Invasive Species." *Sustainability Science* 13 (2018): 1443–52. https://doi.org/10.1007/s11625-018-0571-4.

Reo, Nicholas James, and Angela K. Parker. "Re-Thinking Colonialism to Prepare for the Impacts of Rapid Environmental Change." *Climatic Change* 120 (2013): 671–82. https://doi.org/10.1007/s10584-013-0783-7.

"Resisting the Hemlock Woolly Adelgid." *In Defense of Plants*, podcast, April 23, 2023.

Rice, Anna, Petr Šmarda, Maria Novosolov, Michal Drori, Lior Glick, Niv Sabath, Shai Meiri, et al. "The Global Biogeography of Polyploid Plants." *Nature Ecology & Evolution* 3 (2019): 265–73. https://doi.org/10.1038/s41559-018-0787-9.

Riley, Christopher B., Daniel A. Herms, and Mary M. Gardiner. "Exotic Trees Contribute to Urban Forest Diversity and Ecosystem Services in Inner-City Cleveland, OH." *Urban Forestry & Urban Greening* 29 (January 2018): 367–76. https://doi.org/10.1016/j.ufug.2017.01.004.

Rivers, Malin, Adrian C. Newton, and Sara Oldfield. "Scientists' Warning to Humanity on Tree Extinctions." *Plants, People, Planet* 5, no. 4. (August 31, 2022). https://doi.org/10.1002/ppp3.10314.

Robbins, Jim. "Global 'Stilling': Is Climate Change Slowing down the Wind?" *Yale E360.* September 13, 2022.

Robbins, Jim. *The Man Who Planted Trees: A Story of Lost Groves, the Science of Trees, and a Plan to Save the Planet.* New York: Spiegel & Grau, 2015.

Roddick, Christopher, Beth Hanson, and Brooklyn Botanic Garden. *The Tree Care Primer.* Brooklyn, NY: Brooklyn Botanic Garden. 2007.

Rogers, Paul C. *Biodiversity within Aspen Forests.* Western Aspen Alliance, WAA Brief #7, 2019. Logan: Utah State University.

Rogers, Paul C. "Guide to Quaking Aspen Ecology and Management." Western Aspen Alliance, Wildland Resources Department, and Ecology Center, Utah State University. Produced in cooperation with US Department of the Interior Bureau of Land Management, 2017.

Rogers, Paul C. "Pando's Pulse: Vital Signs Signal Need for Course Correction at World-Renowned Aspen Forest." *Conservation Science and Practice* 4, no. 10 (2022). https://doi.org/10.1111/csp2.12804.

Rogers, Paul C., and Jody A. Gale. "Restoration of the Iconic Pando Aspen Clone: Emerging Evidence of Recovery." *Ecosphere* 8, no. 1 (2017): e01661. https://doi.org/10.1002/ecs2.1661.

Rogers, Paul C., Bradley D. Pinno, Jan Šebesta, Benedicte R. Albrectsen, Guoqing Li, Natalya Ivanova, Antonín Kusbach, et al. "A Global View of Aspen: Conservation Science for Widespread Keystone Systems." *Global Ecology and Conservation* 21 (March 2020): e00828. https://doi.org/10.1016/j.gecco.2019.e00828.

Roos, Christopher I., Christopher H. Guiterman, Ellis Q. Margolis, Thomas W. Swetnam, Nicholas C. Laluk, Kerry F. Thompson, Chris Toya, et al. "Indigenous Fire Management and Cross-Scale Fire-Climate Relationships in the Southwest United States from 1500 to 1900 CE." *Science Advances* 8, no. 49 (2022). https://doi.org/10.1126/sciadv.abq3221.

Rosenthal, Zach. "Forest Fires Burn Twice as Many Trees as Two Decades Ago, Report Finds." *Washington Post*, August 24, 2022.

Rotbarth, Ronny, David J. Cooper, Logan Berner, and Roman Dial. "The World's Boreal Forests May Be Shrinking as Climate Change Pushes Them Northward." *The Conversation*, November 3, 2023.

Ruess, Roger W., Loretta M. Winton, and Gerard C. Adams. "Widespread Mortality of Trembling Aspen (*Populus tremuloides*) throughout Interior Alaskan Boreal Forests Resulting from a Novel Canker Disease." *PLOS ONE* 16, no. 4 (2021): e0250078. https://doi.org/10.1371/journal.pone.0250078.

Rush, Elizabeth. *Rising: dispatches from the new American shore.* Minneapolis, Minnesota: Milkweed Editions, 2019.

Rustad, Lindsey, John Campbell, Jeffrey S. Dukes, Thomas Huntington, Kathy Fallon Lambert, Jacqueline Mohan, and Nicholas Rodenhouse. *Changing Climate, Changing Forests: The Impacts of Climate Change on Forests of the Northeastern United States and Eastern Canada.* Gen. Tech. Rep. NRS-99. Newtown Square, PA: US Department of Agriculture, Forest Service, Northern Research Station, 2012.

Rutkow, Eric. *American Canopy: Trees, Forests, and the Making of a Nation.* New York: Scribner, 2012.

Ryan, John C., Patricia Vieira, and Monica Gagliano, eds. *The Mind of Plants: Narratives of Vegetal Intelligence.* Santa Fe, NM: Synergetic Press, 2021.

Sabatini, Alec. "Addressing the Urban Forestry Labor Shortage with Leslie Berckes of the Society of Municipal Arborists." Nadina Galle, blog. May 2023.

Sadok, Walid, and S.V. Krishna Jagadish. "The Hidden Costs of Nighttime Warming on Yields." *Trends in Plant Science*, July 2020. https://doi.org/10.1016/j.tplants.2020.02.003.

Sahagún, Louis. "California Drought, Bark Beetles Killing the Oldest Trees on Earth. Can They Be Saved?" *Los Angeles Times.* June 27, 2022.

Santini, Alberto, Andrew Liebhold, Duccio Migliorini, and Steve Woodward. "Tracing the Role of Human Civilization in the Globalization of Plant Pathogens." *ISME Journal* 12, no. 3 (2018): 647–52. https://doi.org/10.1038/s41396-017-0013-9.

Sapes, Gerard, Cathleen Lapadat, Anna K. Schweiger, Jennifer Juzwik, Rebecca Montgomery, Hamed Gholizadeh, Philip A. Townsend, John A. Gamon, et al. "Canopy Spectral Reflectance Detects Oak Wilt at the Landscape Scale Using Phylogenetic Discrimination." *Remote Sensing of Environment* 273 (May 2022): 112961. https://doi.org/10.1016/j.rse.2022.112961.

Sasnett, Peri, Andrew Smith, and Michael Faist. "Headwaters," podcast.

Scaven, Victoria L., and Nicole E. Rafferty. "Physiological Effects of Climate Warming on Flowering Plants and Insect Pollinators and Potential Consequences for Their Interactions." *Current Zoology* 59, no. 3 (2013): 418–26. https://doi.org/10.1093/czoolo/59.3.418.

Schönbeck, Leonie C., Philipp Schuler, Marco M. Lehmann, Eugénie Mas, Laura Mekarni, Alexandria L. Pivovaroff, Pascal Turberg, et al. "Increasing Temperature and Vapour Pressure Deficit Lead to Hydraulic

Damages in the Absence of Soil Drought." *Plant, Cell & Environment* 45, no. 11 (2022): 3275–89. https://doi.org/10.1111/pce.14425.

Schuster, Richard, Ryan R. Germain, Joseph R. Bennett, Nicholas J. Reo, and Peter Arcese. "Vertebrate Biodiversity on Indigenous-Managed Lands in Australia, Brazil, and Canada Equals That in Protected Areas." *Environmental Science & Policy* 101 (November 2019): 1–6. https://doi.org/10.1016/j.envsci.2019.07.002.

Schuurman, G. W., C. Hawkins Hoffman, D. N. Cole, D. J. Lawrence, J. M. Morton, D. R. Magness, A. E. Cravens, et al. "Resist-Accept-Direct (RAD)—A Framework for the 21st-Century Natural Resource Manager." National Park Service, Fort Collins, Colorado, 2020. https://doi.org/10.36967/nrr-2283597.

Schwalm, Christopher R., Christopher A. Williams, Kevin Schaefer, Dennis Baldocchi, T. Andrew Black, Allen H. Goldstein, Beverly E. Law, Walter C. Oechel, Kyaw Tha Paw U, and Russel L. Scott. "Reduction in Carbon Uptake during Turn of the Century Drought in Western North America." *Nature Geoscience* 5 (2012): 551–56. https://doi.org/10.1038/ngeo1529.

Scott, Michon, and Rebecca Lindsey. "What's the Hottest Earth's Ever Been?" NOAA: *climate.gov*, November 22, 2020.

Seidl, Rupert, Dominik Thom, Markus Kautz, Dario Martin-Benito, Mikko Peltoniemi, Giorgio Vacchiano, Jan Wild, et al. "Forest Disturbances under Climate Change." *Nature Climate Change*, May 31, 2017. https://doi.org/10.1038/nclimate3303.

Seneviratne, Sonia I., Xuebin Zhang, M. Adnan, W. Badi, C. Dereczynski, A. Di Luca, S. Ghosh, et al. "Weather and Climate Extreme Events in a Changing Climate." In *Climate Change 2021: The Physical Science Basis. Contribution of Working Group I to the Sixth Assessment Report of the Intergovernmental Panel on Climate Change*, edited by V. Masson-Delmotte, P. Zhai, A. Pirani, S.L. Connors, C. Péan, S. Berger, Y Chen, et al., 1513–1766. Cambridge: Cambridge University Press, 2021. https://doi.org/10.1017/9781009157896.013.

Shafak, Elif. "In the Battle to Save the World's Forests, Women Are Leading the Resistance." *The Guardian*, August 26, 2023.

Sheldrake, Merlin. *Entangled Life: How Fungi Make Our Worlds, Change Our Minds and Shape Our Futures*. New York: Vintage, 2021.

Shepherd, V. A. "From Semi-Conductors to the Rhythms of Sensitive Plants: The Research of J.C. Bose." *PubMed* 51 (2005): 607–19.

Shriver, Robert K., Charles B. Yackulic, David M. Bell, John B. Bradford, and Arndt Hampe. "Dry Forest Decline Is Driven by Both Declining Recruitment and Increasing Mortality in Response to Warm, Dry Conditions." *Global Ecology and Biogeography* 31, no. 11 (2022): 2259–69. https://doi.org/10.1111/geb.13582.

Sibley, David A. *The Sibley Guide to Trees*. New York: Knopf, 2009.

Simard, Suzanne. *Finding the Mother Tree: Discovering the Wisdom of the Forest*. New York: Knopf, 2021.

Simisky, Tawny, and Zoe Robinson. "Elongate Hemlock Scale." Center for Agriculture, Food, and the Environment, September 29, 2022.

Singer, Jack A., Rob Turnbull, Mark Foster, Charles Bettigole, Brent R. Frey, Michelle C. Downey, Kristofer R. Covey, et al. "Sudden Aspen Decline: A Review of Pattern and Process in a Changing Climate." *Forests* 10, no. 8 (2019): 671. https://doi.org/10.3390/f10080671.

Six, Diana L. "Climate Change and Mutualism." *Nature Reviews Microbiology* 7 (2009): 686. https://doi.org/10.1038/nrmicro2232.

Six, Diana L., Clare Vergobbi, and Mitchell Cutter. "Are Survivors Different? Genetic-Based Selection of Trees by Mountain Pine Beetle during a Climate Change-Driven Outbreak in a High-Elevation Pine Forest." *Frontiers in Plant Science* 9 (July 2018). https://doi.org/10.3389/fpls.2018.00993.

Smith, Bruce, and Allen Padgett. *On Rope.* Vertical Section National Speleological Society, 1996.

Sniezko, Richard A., and Jennifer Koch. "Breeding Trees Resistant to Insects and Diseases: Putting Theory into Application." *Biological Invasions* 19 (2017): 3377–3400. https://doi.org/10.1007/s10530-017-1482-5.

Sniezko, Richard A., and C. Dana Nelson. "Resistance Breeding against Tree Pathogens." *Forest Microbiology* (2022): 159–75. https://doi.org/10.1016/B978-0-323-85042-1.00007-0.

Sniezko, Richard A., Jeremy S. Johnson, Angelia Kegley, and Robert Danchok. "Disease Resistance in Whitebark Pine and Potential for Restoration of a Threatened Species." *Plants, People, Planet* 6, no. 2 (2023): 341–61. https://doi.org/10.1002/ppp3.10443.

"Some Magnolia Flowers Have Built-in Heaters." *In Defense of Plants*, podcast, April 11, 2021.

Sowards, Adam M., and Rebecca Stunz. "Mobile Nature, Cooperative Management, and Institutional Adaptation in Pacific Northwest Blister Rust Control in the 20th Century." *Pacific Northwest Quarterly* 105, no. 4 (2014): 159–74. https://www.jstor.org/stable/24632130.

Spary, Sara. "The Secret Mission to Save Australia's Prehistoric Trees." *CNN.* January 16, 2020.

"'Spongy Moth' Adopted as New Common Name for *Lymantria dispar.*" *Entomological Society of America.*

Stafford, Fiona. *The Long, Long Life of Trees.* New Haven: Yale University Press, 2017.

Stanke, Hunter, Andrew O. Finley, Grant M. Domke, Aaron S. Weed, and David W. MacFarlane. "Over Half of Western United States' Most Abundant Tree Species in Decline." *Nature Communications* 12 (2021). https://doi.org/10.1038/s41467-020-20678-z.

Stein, William E., Christopher M. Berry, Jennifer L. Morris, Linda VanAller Hernick, Frank Mannolini, Charles Ver Straeten, Ed Landing, et al. "Mid-Devonian *Archaeopteris* Roots Signal Revolutionary Change in Earliest Fossil Forests." *Current Biology.* February 3, 2020. https://doi.org/10.1016/j.cub.2019.11.067.

Steiner, Julie E. "Guardians of Municipal Public Trees: Commonwealth of Massachusetts Tree Wardens' Authority and Accountability." *SSRN Electronic Journal*, January, 2016.

Stephens, S. Sky, Sheryl A. Romero, and Frank J. Krist. *Major Forest Insect and Disease Conditions in the United States: 2021*. US Department of Agriculture, Forest Service, Forest Health Protection, 2021.

Stern, Rebecca L., Paul G. Schaberg, Shelly A. Rayback, Paula F. Murakami, Christopher F. Hansen, and Gary J. Hawley. "Growth of Canopy Red Oak near Its Northern Range Limit: Current Trends, Potential Drivers, and Implications for the Future." *Canadian Journal of Forest Research*, April 20, 2020. https://doi.org/10.1139/cjfr-2019-0200.

Stevens-Rumann, Camille S., and Penelope Morgan. "Tree Regeneration Following Wildfires in the Western US: A Review." *Fire Ecology*, no. 15 (2019). https://doi.org/10.1186/s42408-019-0032-1.

Stiers, Joanie. "New Nematode Named after Ohio Plant Pathologist." *Farm Flavor*, October 24, 2020.

Still, C. J., A. Sibley, D. DePinte, P. E. Busby, C. A. Harrington, M. Schulze, D. R. Shaw, et al. "Causes of Widespread Foliar Damage from the June 2021 Pacific Northwest Heat Dome: More Heat than Drought." *Tree Physiology* 43, no. 2 (2023): 203–09. https://doi.org/10.1093/treephys/tpac143.

Stone, Marisa, David Lindenmayer, Kurtis Nisbet, and Sebastian Seibold. "Decaying Forest Wood Releases a Whopping 10.9 Billion Tonnes of Carbon Each Year. This Will Increase under Climate Change." *The Conversation*, September 1, 2021.

Stuart-Smith, Sue. *The Well-Gardened Mind: The Restorative Power of Nature*. New York: Scribner, 2021.

Sunderland Historical Commission. "Sunderland Buttonball Tree." 2008.

"Surprising Genetic Diversity in Old Growth Trees." *In Defense of Plants*, podcast, July 23, 2019.

Swann, Abigail L. S., Marysa M. Laguë, Elizabeth S. Garcia, Jason P. Field, David D. Breshears, David J. P. Moore, Scott R. Saleska, et al. "Continental-Scale Consequences of Tree Die-Offs in North America: Identifying Where Forest Loss Matters Most." *Environmental Research Letters*, May 16, 2018. https://doi.org/10.1088/1748-9326/aabaof.

Sweeney, Jim. "Birding the Cumberland Farms Fields in Middleboro/Halifax." *Bird Observer* 36, no. 5 (2023): 1.

Taft, Dave. "London Plane: A Tree with Gritty Roots." *New York Times*, December 22, 2016.

Tallamy, Douglas W. *The Nature of Oaks: The Rich Ecology of Our Most Essential Native Trees*. Portland, OR: Timber Press, 2021.

Thomas, P. I. "*Araucaria heterophylla*." *Threatened Conifers of the World*, 2018.

Thomas, Peter. *Trees*. Glasgow, Scotland: William Collins, 2022.

Thomas, Peter A. *Trees: Their Natural History*, 2nd edition. New York: Cambridge University Press, 2014.

Thompson, R. Alexander, Henry D. Adams, David D. Breshears, Adam D.

Collins, L. Turin Dickman, Charlotte Grossiord, Àngela Manrique-Alba, et al. "No Carbon Storage in Growth-Limited Trees in a Semi-Arid Woodland." *Nature Communications* 14, no. 1 (2023). https://doi.org/10.1038/s41467-023-37577-8.

Tibbetts, John H. "In Minnesota, Researchers Are Moving Trees Farther North to Save Forests." *Smithsonian Magazine*, March 15, 2024.

Tomback, Diana, Robert Keane, and Richard A. Sniezko, eds. "Special Issue on Ecology and Restoration of High Elevation Five-Needle White Pines." *Forest Ecology and Management*, Vol, 521, October 2022. https://doi.org/10.1016/j.foreco.2022.120425.

Tomimoto, Sou, and Akiko Satake. "Modelling Somatic Mutation Accumulation and Expansion in a Long-Lived Tree with Hierarchical Modular Architecture." *Journal of Theoretical Biology* 565 (May 2023): 111465. https://doi.org/10.1016/j.jtbi.2023.111465.

Tonet, Vanessa, Madeline Cairns-Murphy, Ross Deans, and Timothy J. Brodribb. "Deadly Acceleration in Dehydration of *Eucalyptus viminalis* Leaves Coincides with High-Order Vein Cavitation." *Plant Physiology*, January 2023. https://doi.org/10.1093/plphys/kiad016.

Traverse, Alfred. "Plant Evolution Dances to a Different Beat." *Historical Biology*. Volume I, 1988. https://doi.org/10.1080/08912968809386480.

Tribal Adaptation Menu Team. "Dibaginjigaadeg Anishinaabe Ezhitwaad: A Tribal Climate Adaptation Menu." Odanah, Wisconsin: Great Lakes Indian Fish and Wildlife Commission, 2019.

Trouet, Valerie. *Tree Story: The History of the World Written in Rings.* Baltimore: Johns Hopkins University Press, 2022.

Trowbridge, Amy. "Evolutionary Ecology of Chemically Mediated Plant–Insect Interactions." In *Ecology and the Environment,* edited by Russell K. Monson, 143–76. Berlin: Springer, 2014.

Trowbridge, Amy M., et al. "Drought Supersedes Warming in Determining Volatile and Tissue Defenses of Piñon Pine (*Pinus edulis*)." *Environmental Research Letters* (2019) 14 065006.

Tucker, Clay S., and Jessie K. Pearl. "Coastal Tree-Ring Records for Paleoclimate and Paleoenvironmental Applications in North America." *Quaternary Science Reviews* 265 (August 2021): 107044. https://doi.org/10.1016/j.quascirev.2021.107044.

Tudge, Colin. *The Secret Life of Trees: How They Live and Why They Matter.* London: Folio Society, 2008.

Tulowiecki, Stephen J., David Robertson, and Chris P. S. Larsen. "Oak Savannas in Western New York State, circa 1795: Synthesizing Predictive Spatial Models and Historical Accounts to Understand Environmental and Native American Influences." *Annals of the American Association of Geographers* 110, no. 1 (2019): 184–204. https://doi.org/10.1080/24694452.2019.1629871.

Turner, Monica G. "Here's How Forests Rebounded from Yellowstone's Epic 1988 Fires—and Why That Could Be Harder in the Future." *The Conversation.* August 28, 2018.

Tyukavina, Alexandra, Peter Potapov, Matthew C. Hansen, Amy H. Pickens, Stephen V. Stehman, Svetlana Turubanova, Diana Parker, et al. "Global Trends of Forest Loss Due to Fire from 2001 to 2019." *Frontiers in Remote Sensing* 3 (March 2022). https://doi.org/10.3389/frsen.2022.825190.

United States v. Cumberland Farms of Connecticut, 647 F. Supp. 1166 (D. Mass. 1986).

USDA Forest Service Eastern Region Oak Wilt Suppression Program Participation Guidelines. Compiled by Eastern Region Forest Health Protection Forest Pathology Staff. September 2020.

US Department of Agriculture, Forest Service. "*Tsuga canadensis* (L.) Carr.: Eastern Hemlock." Southern Research Station.

US Global Change Research Program. "Fifth National Climate Assessment," 2023.

Van der Heijden, Marcel G. A., Francis M. Martin, Marc-André Selosse, and Ian R. Sanders. "Mycorrhizal Ecology and Evolution: The Past, the Present, and the Future." *New Phytologist*, February 2, 2015. https://doi.org/10.1111/nph.13288.

Van Nuland, Michael E., S. Caroline Daws, Joseph K. Bailey, Jennifer A. Schweitzer, Posy E. Busby, and Kabir G. Peay. "Above- and Belowground Fungal Biodiversity of Populus Trees on a Continental Scale." *Nature Microbiology* 8 (2023): 2406–19. https://doi.org/10.1038/s41564-023-01514-8.

Veryard, Ryan, Jinhui Wu, Michael J. O'Brien, Rosila Anthony, Sabine Both, David F.R.P. Burslem, et al. "Positive Effects of Tree Diversity on Tropical Forest Restoration in a Field-Scale Experiment." *Science Advances* 9, no. 37 (2023). https://doi.org/10.1126/sciadv.adf0938.

Vincent C.T. Hanlon, Sarah P. Otto, and Sally N. Aitken. "Somatic Mutations Substantially Increase the Per-Generation Mutation Rate in the Conifer *Picea sitchensis*." *Evolution Letters* 3, no. 4 (2019): 348–58. https://doi.org/10.1002/evl3.121.

Vis, Matt. "Ontario Forest Fires Burned Record Area of Land This Summer as They Displaced First Nations in Northwest." *CBC*, November 10, 2021.

Vries, Jan de, and John M. Archibald. 2018. "Plant Evolution: Landmarks on the Path to Terrestrial Life." *New Phytologist*. January 10, 2018. https://doi.org/10.1111/nph.14975.

Voggesser, Garrit, Kathy Lynn, John Daigle, Frank K. Lake, and Darren Ranco. "Cultural Impacts to Tribes from Climate Change Influences on Forests." *Climatic Change* 120 (2013): 615–26. https://doi.org/10.1007/s10584-013-0733-4.

Vovides, Alejandra G., Marie-Christin Wimmler, Falk Schrewe, et al. "Cooperative Root Graft Networks Benefit Mangrove Trees under Stress." *Communications Biology* 4 (2021): 513. https://doi.org/10.1038/s42003-021-02044-x.

Walsh, Megan. "A Consolidated History of Women's Climbing Achievements." *Climbing*, November 17, 2022.

"Warm Summer Nights." *Climate Central*, July 20, 2022.

Warren, Karen J. "Feminist Environmental Philosophy." *Stanford Encyclopedia of Philosophy Archive*, 2015.

Warwell, Marcus V., and Ruth G. Shaw. "Climate-Related Genetic Variation in a Threatened Tree Species, *Pinus albicaulis*." *American Journal of Botany* 104, no. 8 (2017): 1205–18. https://doi.org/10.3732/ajb.1700139.

"We Must Get a Grip on Forest Science—before It's Too Late." *Nature*, August 16, 2022. https://doi.org/10.1038/d41586-022-02182-0.

Weiss, Abby. "Fading Winters, Hotter Summers Make the Northeast America's Fastest Warming Region." *Inside Climate News*, June 27, 2020.

Westerhold, Thomas, Norbert Marwan, Anna Joy Drury, Diederik Liebrand, Claudia Agnini, Eleni Anagnostou, James S. K. Barnet, et al. "An Astronomically Dated Record of Earth's Climate and Its Predictability over the Last 66 Million Years." *Science*, September 11, 2020. https://doi.org/10.1126/science.aba6853.

Weston, Phoebe. "UK Forests Face Catastrophic Ecosystem Collapse within 50 Years, Study Says." *The Guardian*, November 8, 2023.

White, Elliott E., Jr., Emily A. Ury, Emily S. Bernhardt, and Xi Yang. "Climate Change Driving Widespread Loss of Coastal Forested Wetlands throughout the North American Coastal Plain." *Ecosystems*, August 2021. https://doi.org/10.1007/s10021-021-00686-w.

Whitebark Pine Ecosystem Foundation.

Whyte, Kyle. "Settler Colonialism, Ecology, and Environmental Injustice." *Environment and Society* 9, no. 1 (2018): 125–44.

Williams, A. Park, Benjamin I. Cook, and Jason E. Smerdon. "Rapid Intensification of the Emerging Southwestern North American Megadrought in 2020–2021." *Nature Climate Change* 12 (February 2022). https://doi.org/10.1038/s41558-022-01290-z.

Willis, K. J., and J. C. McElwain. *The Evolution of Plants*, 2nd edition. Oxford: Oxford University Press, 2014.

Winn, Marie. *Red-Tails in Love: A True Wildlife Drama in Central Park*. New York: Vintage, 1999.

Wohlleben, Peter. *The Hidden Life of Trees: What They Feel, How They Communicate—Discoveries from a Secret World*. Glasgow, Scotland: William Collins, 2017.

Wolf, Kathleen L., Sharon T. Lam, Jennifer K. McKeen, Gregory R. A. Richardson, Matilda van den Bosch, and Adrina C. Bardekjian. "Urban Trees and Human Health: A Scoping Review." *International Journal of Environmental Research and Public Health* 17, no. 12 (2020): 4371. https://doi.org/10.3390/ijerph17124371.

Wolkovich, E. M., B. I. Cook, J. M. Allen, T. M. Crimmins, J. L. Betancourt, S. E. Travers, S. Pau, et al. "Warming Experiments Underpredict Plant Phenological Responses to Climate Change." *Nature* 485 (2012): 494–97. https://doi.org/10.1038/nature11014.

"Women in Arb: Boel Hammarstrand." *Forestry Journal*, March 2, 2020.

Woolf, Virginia. *To the Lighthouse*. London: Hogarth Press, 1927.

Worrall, James J., Gerald E. Rehfeldt, Andreas Hamann, Edward H. Hogg, Suzanne B. Marchetti, Michael Michaelian, and Laura K. Gray. "Recent Declines of *Populus tremuloides* in North America Linked to Climate." *Forest Ecology and Management* 299, July 2023: 35–51. https://doi.org/10.1016/j.foreco.2012.12.033.

Woudstra, Jan, and Camilla Allen. *Politics of Street Trees*. New York: Routledge, 2022.

Wright, C.D. *Casting Deep Shadeo*. Port Townsend, WA: Copper Canyon Press, 2019.

Wyka, Stephen A., Isabel A. Munck, Nicholas J. Brazee, and Kirk D. Broders. "Response of Eastern White Pine and Associated Foliar, Blister Rust, Canker and Root Rot Pathogens to Climate Change." *Forest Ecology and Management* 423 (September 2018): 18–26. https://doi.org/10.1016/j.foreco.2018.03.011.

Wyka, Stephen A., Cheryl Smith, Isabel A. Munck, Barrett N. Rock, Beth L. Ziniti, and Kirk Broders. "Emergence of White Pine Needle Damage in the Northeastern United States Is Associated with Changes in Pathogen Pressure in Response to Climate Change." *Global Change Biology* 23, no. 1 (2016): 394–405. https://doi.org/10.1111/gcb.13359.

Xu, Xiyan, Anqi Huang, Elise Belle, Pieter De Frenne, and Gensuo Jia. "Protected Areas Provide Thermal Buffer against Climate Change." *Science Advances* 8, no. 44 (2022). https://doi.org/10.1126/sciadv.abo0119.

Yirka, Bob. "China Releases 600 Million Wasps to Combat Moths." *Phys Org,* August 10, 2011.

Young, Stephen S., and Joshua S. Young. "Overall Warming with Reduced Seasonality: Temperature Change in New England, USA, 1900–2020." *Climate* 9, no. 12 (2021): 176. https://doi.org/10.3390/cli9120176.

Yuan, Wenping, Yi Zheng, Shilong Piao, Philippe Ciais, Danica Lombardozzi, Yingping Wang, Youngryel Ryu, et al. "Increased Atmospheric Vapor Pressure Deficit Reduces Global Vegetation Growth." *Science Advances* 5, no. 8 (2019): eaax1396. https://doi.org/10.1126/sciadv.aax1396.

Zhang, Cici. "Citrus Greening Is Killing the World's Orange Trees. Scientists Are Racing to Help." *Chemical & Engineering News*, June 9, 2019.

Zhao, Bo Guang, Kazuyoshi Futai, Jack R. Sutherland, and Yuko Takeuchi. *Pine Wilt Disease*. Tokyo: Springer, 2008.

Zhuang, Yizhou, Rong Fu, Benjamin D. Santer, Robert E. Dickinson, and Alex Hall. "Quantifying Contributions of Natural Variability and Anthropogenic Forcings on Increased Fire Weather Risk over the Western United States." *Proceedings of the National Academy of Sciences* 118, no. 45 (2021). https://doi.org/10.1073/pnas.2111875118.

Zlinszky, András, Bence Molnár, and Anders S. Barfod. "Not All Trees Sleep the Same—High Temporal Resolution Terrestrial Laser Scanning

Shows Differences in Nocturnal Plant Movement." *Frontiers in Plant Science* 8 (2017). https://doi.org/10.3389/fpls.2017.01814.

Zweifel, Roman, Frank Sterck, Sabine Braun, Nina Buchmann, Werner Eugster, Arthur Gessler, Matthias Häni, et al. 2021. "Why Trees Grow at Night." *New Phytologist*, June 12, 2021. https://doi.org/10.1111/nph.17552.

Index

Page numbers in *italics* indicate illustrations.